FUNDAMENTAL PRINCIPLES OF LAW

The Law of Trusts

by

D. J. Hayton, M.A., LL.B., LL.D.
*of the Inner Temple and Lincoln's Inn, Barrister and sometime Recorder
and Acting Justice of The Bahamas' Supreme Court,
Professor of Law, London University, King's College*

Fourth Edition

LONDON
SWEET & MAXWELL
2003

Published in 2003 by
Sweet & Maxwell Ltd
100 Avenue Road,
London NW3 3PF
Typeset by YHT Ltd, London W13 8NT
Prtinted in Great Britain by Creative Print and Design Group, Wales, Ebbw Vale

No natural forests were destroyed to make this product;
only farmed timber was used and replanted.

A CIP catalogue record for this book is available from
the British Library.

ISBN 0 421 857609

FUNDAMENTAL PRINCIPLES OF LAW

The Law of Trusts

AUSTRALIA
Law Book Co.
Sydney

CANADA and USA
Carswell
Toronto

HONG KONG
Sweet & Maxwell Asia

NEW ZEALAND
Brookers
Wellington

SINGAPORE and MALAYSIA
Sweet & Maxwell Asia
Singapore and Kuala Lumper

PREFACE

The purpose of this book is to introduce readers to the nature of the trust as a flexible living organism responsive to changing circumstances. It should help them to develop an understanding of the operation of the trust and trusteeship. It is designed for three types of readers.

Obviously, it may be used as a basic text by students studying trust law (with further reference via a library or the internet to cases in the footnotes). They will benefit from quickly reading the book a couple of times as they commence their study, slowly reading a relevant chapter before commencing detailed study of its subject-matter, and finally reading the book as a whole shortly before their examination, so as to help them view the trust in three-dimensional perspective. For detailed study of points raised in the book they—and other readers—may find it useful to refer to the student text-book, Hayton and Marshall *Commentary and Cases on the Law of Trusts and Equitable Remedies* (11th ed., 2001) or even the practitioners' textbook, Underhill and Hayton, *Law of Trusts and Trustees* (16th ed., 2003).

Intelligent laymen interested in the trust, perhaps because involved or about to be involved in trust matters as settlors or trustees or beneficiaries, should also find the book helpful. As the chapter headings reveal, the book has a pragmatic approach: it does not analyse the trust into the usual academic topics.

Foreign lawyers should obtain illumination, especially from Chapter One, if trust issues arise within their jurisdiction, particularly if their State has implemented The Hague Trust Convention on The Recognition of Trusts (*e.g.* Italy, Malta and the Netherlands) in which I was involved as Head of the UK delegation to The

Hague Conference. Even if their State does not recognise the trust as such under its system of private international law, it is still necessary to appreciate the true nature of a trust if an appropriate civil law analogue is to be found to give effect so far as practicable to the trust in question. Foreign lawyers may find it useful to refer further to Hayton (ed) *Extending the Boundaries of Trusts and Similar Ring-Fenced Funds* (2002, Kluwer).

As an incidental feature of writing on fundamental principles some fundamental issues emerge which are easy to overlook when involved with detailed complexities of the law. Thus, there should be some food for thought even for knowledgeable trust lawyers: some of the most elemental issues are not the most straightforward. A short book cannot fudge issues the way a longer book can.

The book is concerned with the law of trusts in England and Wales, primarily expounding the law as it is, but indicating possible developments where such seem likely. The survey is not uncritical, and reference is made to trust law in other jurisdictions where this may highlight the nature of English trust law or indicate the flexible scope for developments in trust law.

The new edition brings out the dynamic role of equity and trusts (*e.g.* in considering the law on a cohabitee's informal acquisition of an interest in the home). It also emphasises equity's reliance on the conscience of the defendant being affected before intervening against the defendant and equity's insistence on treating wrong-doing trustees as good men (disentitled from taking advantage of any wrongdoing) so as to safeguard the interests of beneficiaries as fully as possible.

The book has benefited much from discussions with generations of undergraduates and postgraduates, and with foreign lawyers at meetings of The Hague Conference on Private International Law and of the international working group that prepared "Principles of European Trust Law": See Hayton, Kortmann & Verhagen (eds) *Principles of European Trust Law* (1999, Kluwer). It is based on sources available up to May 2003.

David Hayton
May 10, 2003

CONTENTS

TABLE OF CASES

TABLE OF STATUTES

CHAPTER ONE

The Heart of the Matter

"THE GUARDIAN ANGEL OF THE ANGLO-SAXON"

Trusts play a vital role as protected pools of ring-fenced assets in British society and in countries governed by the British in earlier eras, for example USA, Canada, Australia, New Zealand and India. Even European and other countries which do not have the British concept of the trust in their domestic law are becoming prepared to recognise many aspects of foreign trusts as a matter of private international law when matters involving such trusts arise in their jurisdictions. Indeed, their legislation has provided protection for pools of ring-fenced assets in limited areas, *e.g.* those involving financial services.

One cannot even hazard a guess at the amount of trust funds world-wide. In the United Kingdom charitable trust funds and funds of charitable corporations have income of over £26,000 million a year, with assets exceeding £70,000 million, and the value of their tax and related benefits is over £3,000 million a year. Huge amounts are held on private trusts established by will or by deed for benevolent or paternalistic or dynastic reasons. Inland Revenue figures indicate that in the United Kingdom there are over 65,000 discretionary (and accumulation and maintenance) trusts with an aggregate value over £8,000 million. Most such trusts are of relatively small value, the really large trusts normally being off-shore trusts in places like Jersey, Bahamas and the Cayman Islands. It is commonplace for persons of ordinary means to take out a life policy to be held on trust for spouses and children. All land in England and Wales that is owned by more than one person is held on trust for the co-owners with power to sell. Assets of unincorporated clubs are held on trust for club members. Over £200,000 million is invested in United Kingdom unit trusts by nearly three million persons. Trade union funds of vast amounts are held on trusts. Over eight million employees are members of occupational pension schemes and pension fund trusts in the United Kingdom are worth over £700,000 million. Much property of companies is charged in favour of trustees as security to be held on trust for debenture holders who have lent money to the company in return for debenture stock. Eurobonds are issued under a "trust deed" and when the trustee intervenes in case of default to collect money due to the bondholders he holds such money on trust for the bond-holders. Nations even combine to set up trusts. Thus, the United Kingdom, Australia and New Zealand in 1987 set up the Tuvalu Trust Fund (of £12 million) to help the inhabitants of Tuvalu, formerly the Ellice Islands, south east of Nauru, after winding up the British Phosphate Commissioners. The winning nations of the First World War, in implementing the Young Plan for German Reparations, arranged in 1929 for the creation of the Bank of International Settlements to act as trustee to whom payments should be made by Germany and by whom the distribution to the appropriate recipients should be managed.

This latter arrangement led Pierre Lepaulle, a renowned French lawyer, colourfully to write:

"Thus from settlement of the greatest of wars down to the simplest inheritance on death, from the most audacious Wall Street scheme down to the protection of grandchildren, the trust can see marching before it the motley procession of the whole of human endeavour: dreams of peace, commercial imperialism, attempts to strangle competition or to reach paradise, hatred or philanthropy, love of one's family or the desire to strip it of everything after one's death, all those in the procession being dressed either in robes or in rags, and either crowned with a halo or walking with a grin. The trust is the guardian angel of the Anglo-Saxon, accompanying him everywhere, impassively, from the cradle to the grave."[1]

Earlier, the great legal historian and Equity lawyer, Maitland had written:

"If we were asked what is the greatest and most distinctive achievement performed by Englishmen in the field of jurisprudence I cannot think that we should have any better answer

---

[1] *Traité théorique et pratique des trusts en droit interne, en droit fiscal et en droit international*, Paris 1932, p. 113.

to give than this, namely the development from century to century of the trust idea."[2]

ANTI-TRUST LAW

Lepaulle's reference to Wall Street and attempts to strangle competition enables us to deal with the red-herring of anti-trust law which takes its nomenclature from the nineteenth century American Sherman Antitrust Act concerned to prevent monopolies developing. In those distant days laws in the USA prohibited the ownership by one company of shares in another company, but there was nothing to stop the trust being used as a device to avoid this restraint on the consolidation of economic power. A trust, or rather trustees since a trust is not a legal person, could own controlling shareholdings in several companies and perform the function now carried out by a "holding company". It was against this use of the trust in the development of monopolistic empires that the Antitrust Act was directed. The pejorative expression "anti-trust" is still used in America to denote "anti-monopoly" and is often thus used on this side of the Atlantic, for example to describe European Union anti-monopoly law as EU anti-trust law.

Of course, trusts, like companies or guns, can be used for good or bad purposes. Thus, for example, dispositions on trust intended to defeat the claims of the settlor's creditors or wife or dependants may be set aside.[3] Also, if a particular type of trust is regarded as unfairly avoiding or minimising tax liabilities, then fiscal legislation may be enacted to rectify this situation.[4] Furthermore, to prevent the dead ruling the living for too long, trusts (other than charitable trusts) cannot last for longer than a particular perpetuity period, nor can income be accumulated and rolled over into capital for longer than a particular shorter accumulation period.

WHAT IS A TRUST?

A trust is not a legal person, like an individual or a company, capable of owning property. For there to be a trust, property must be subject to a trust, so the property will be owned by a trustee or trustees (who may be individuals or companies) or by a nominee on behalf of the trustee (though here the trustee's rights against the nominee may be regarded as property held by the trustee). Trustees hold property as joint tenants, so on a trustee's death the property

---

[2] In *Selected Essays* (1936), p. 129.
[3] See Insolvency Act 1986, ss.339, 341, 342, 423, 424, 425, Inheritance (Provision for Family and Dependants) Act 1975, s.10, Matrimonial Causes Act 1973 s.37.
[4] As in Income and Corporation Taxes Act 1988, ss.663, 689, 739–745.

passes automatically by the right of survivorship (*ius accrescendi*) to the surviving trustees: if the last surviving trustee does not appoint more trustees, then on his death the property will be held by his personal representative who should appoint new trustees.

Unless otherwise authorised by the terms of the trust or by a statute, the trustees are under altruistic fiduciary obligations imposed by the law, so that they cannot exploit their position for their own benefit or where it is possible that harm may be caused to their beneficiaries. They also have equitable obligations to use reasonable care to manage the trust property for the benefit of beneficiaries or for charitable or other permitted purposes: this will involve the trustees in personal liabilities for taxes or in contract and in tort when dealing with outsiders. The trust property cannot be used as part of the trustee's property whether on death, since his interest ceases then, or on divorce or bankruptcy: the trust property constitutes an independent fund available only for the beneficiaries or the charitable or other permitted purposes. If trust property, whether in its original form or transmuted into some new form is wrongfully held out by the trustee as belonging personally to the trustee (for example where proceeds of the sale of trust property are paid into his private bank account and then out to purchase a painting) or wrongfully comes into the hand of a third party (as where the trustee donates the asset to his wife or brother) who is not a purchaser of it without notice of the trust, then it can be traced and recovered if not previously dissipated: compare subrogation rights in civil law jurisdictions to ascertain what property is commercial partnership property or property subject to a matrimonial regime.

Traditionally, it is as the result of a gratuitous disposition from the settlor to the trustees for the beneficiaries that the trust of property is constituted, so just as a donor's rights cease after making a gift so do the settlor's rights cease. Once a valid trust is created a bi-partite relationship arises: it is only the beneficiaries—and not the settlor—who can enforce it, so the trustees' duty is to keep the beneficiaries—and not the settlor—happy. A gift on trust is much more flexible than an outright gift, especially when one considers the possible range of beneficiaries under a discretionary trust (for example for such of the settlor's descendants as the trustees may decide to benefit with income or capital in their absolute discretion) over a lengthy period and the opportunities for the settlor to reserve certain powers. These might include powers to revoke the trust, or to remove the trustees and replace them with others, or to delete certain beneficiaries, or to add new beneficiaries, or to determine which members of a class of discretionary beneficiaries, such as grandchildren, will receive capital after expiry of a 21-year accumulation period or after the death of the beneficiary entitled to income. If he wishes, the settlor may confer such powers on his widow or brother or on whoever happen to be the trustees from time to time, especially where the powers may be exercisable throughout the perpetuity period that is the duration of the trust, for example 80 years from the creation of the trust (see p.106 below).

The settlor in his trust instrument will set out how the trustees are to distribute at the end of the trust perpetuity period whatever capital then remains. The trust may terminate earlier, however, if the trustees have earlier exercised their discretionary powers to distribute capital so as to exhaust the trust fund, or if no beneficiaries or potential beneficiaries exist any longer, or if the trustees or other person with any express power to advance the closing date for the trust exercise such power.

The continuous trustee-beneficiary relationship is the foundation of the trust. The arrangement between the settlor and the trustees under the trust instrument (which will expressly give the trustees, as an incident of their holding and managing the trust fund, the power to pay themselves out of the fund for their services and expenses) confers extensive enforceable rights on the beneficiaries, though they neither provide consideration for the arrangement nor are parties to the arrangement. The trust concept thus overcame the weakness of the contract concept because until the Contracts (Rights of Third Parties) Act 1999, in English law to enforce a contract a person had to be a party to it and provide consideration for the other party's promise. Moreover, persons as yet unborn or unascertained may come to have rights under a trust for their benefit. The trust thus has tremendous utility, especially since it is so flexible and so simple to create and operate and terminate, or, perhaps, even to relocate abroad without any termination, unlike a company.

This flexibility led in the twentieth century to many trusts arising out of a contract arranging for collective investment of the payers' moneys, for example in a unit trust or debenture trust or a pensions fund trust where a payer may be not only a settlor but a beneficiary or even a trustee. However, because it is a nonsense to talk about a person having a relationship with himself or rights against himself, a settlor, S, cannot hold property on trust for himself alone but, otherwise, he may be interested in a trust in any capacity and so be a beneficiary and a trustee even if he himself created the trust. Thus, S can vest property in the names of X and Y or of S and Y on trust for S for life, with remainder to S's children in equal shares unless S by deed or will appoints the capital to his children in some different shares.

Although a settlor normally constitutes a trust by transferring specific property to a trust corporation or two or more trustees and declaring trusts, it is possible for a settlor to retain his property and declare that he himself is now to be trustee of a certain specific item appropriated by him to be held on certain declared trusts. Thus, he might designate his personal deposit account with the Woolwich Building Society "Nephew Norman Nelson Trust Account", having written to his brother telling him that the money already in such account and such other money as he may add to it is being held by him on trust for one-year-old Norman, contingent upon Norman attaining 25 years of age, the income till then to be used for the maintenance, education or benefit of Norman. The subject-matter of such trust is a chose in action, S's legal right to whatever sum of money is credited from time to time to the account.

DEFINITION OF A TRUST

The fundamental features of the English trust have just been described. There is no statutory definition of the trust which can be used as a major premise from which rules relating to the trust can be deduced./ It has been the courts that, over the years, have developed the rules relating to the trust, so all one can do is provide a description of the trust, which reflects those rules and which enables people in a general way to know what is meant when talking about a trust.

To this end, when the Hague Recognition of Trusts Convention was prepared Art.2 stated:

"For the purposes of this Convention, the term 'trust' refers to the legal relationship created—*inter vivos* [in lifetime] or on death—by a person, the settlor, when assets have been placed under the control of a trustee for the benefit of a beneficiary or for a specified purpose.

A trust has the following characteristics:

(a)   the assets constitute a separate fund and are not a part of the trustee's own estate;

(b)   title to the trust assets stands in the name of the trustee or in the name of another person on behalf of the trustee:

(c)   the trustee has the power and the duty, in respect of which he is accountable, to manage, employ or dispose of the assets in accordance with the terms of the trust and the special duties imposed upon him by law.

The reservation by the settlor of certain rights and powers, and the fact that the trustee may himself have rights as a beneficiary, are not necessarily inconsistent with the existence of a trust."

Article 11 then expressly provides that a trust created in accordance with the applicable law governing creation of the trust "shall be recognised as a trust". It then states in a second and third paragraph:

"Such recognition shall imply, as a minimum, that the trust property constitutes a separate fund, that the trustee may sue and be sued in his capacity as trustee, and that he may appear or act in this capacity before a notary or any person acting in an official capacity.

In so far as the law applicable to the trust requires or provides, such recognition shall imply, in particular:

(a) that personal creditors of the trustee shall have no recourse against the trust assets:

(b) that the trust assets shall not form part of the trustee's estate upon his insolvency or bankruptcy;

(c) that the trust assets shall not form part of the matrimonial property of the trustee or his spouse nor part of the trustee's estate upon his death;

(d) that the trust assets may be recovered when the trustee, in breach of trust, has mingled trust assets with his own property or has alienated trust assets. However, the rights and obligations of any third party holder of the assets shall remain subject to the law determined by the choice of law rules of the forum."

In addition to the last sentence, Article 15 requires the court of the forum to apply the mandatory provisions of the law determined by the choice of law rules of the forum to:

(e) the transfer of title to property and to security interests in property

(f) the protection of third parties acting in good faith."

Article 15 and the last sentence of Article 11 thus properly restrict a beneficiary's right to trace, and so recover, trust property in the hands of donees or bankers or custodians (having title to intangible assets like shares) or purchasers from the trustee with notice of the trust. Under standard private international law principles the *lex situs* (the law of the place where property is situated) normally determines questions of transfer of title to property and whether or not a donee or a purchaser has obtained good title free from other claims. If the *lex situs* is the law of a state which has the trust in its domestic law and so has traditional tracing rules this will not matter very much, except to the extent that such state may have registration of title statutes which may confer a good title irrespective of notice. If the *lex situs* is the law of a state which does not have the trust in its domestic law and so has no equitable tracing rules, this will make the right to trace meaningless, except to the extent that a receipient's actual knowledge of a breach of trust may make it possible to take advantage of rules of the *lex situs* concerning fraud. Such rules may make the fraudster personally liable for damages or, if he is solvent and still has the property, may require him to return it.

As just seen, Article 11 requires civil law states to recognise the trust as such rather than to try to transpose it into some analogous civil law concept. An understanding of the civil law's problems here is a means of understanding the essential characteristics of the common law trust. After all, in civil law states there often arises the same need for property to be entrusted to T for the benefit of B.

Civil Law States

In the civil law, which is derived from Roman law, ownership is an abstract concept in absolute terms: it is axiomatic that ownership of property requires the owner to have all ownership rights, namely rights of disposition, management and enjoyment. Two or more persons cannot be owners of an asset except as co-owners when each co-owner is the absolute owner of his undivided fraction of the whole (*i.e.* is a tenant in common, and not a joint tenant, viewed from the perspective of a common lawyer).

Persons other than the owner of the asset can either have proprietary rights over that owner's asset or personal rights merely against the owner himself. The former rights against the thing itself are regarded as *in rem* or "real" rights and the number of such rights is regarded as definitive and closed (the so-called *numerus clauses*), and many such rights require to be registered. These rights cover servitudes (like easements and restrictive covenants over land), mortgages and usufructs (where the usufructuary is entitled to the enjoyment of property or its income for life or a lesser period).

Without breaking the absolute ownership principle or extending the list of "real" rights, a well-developed law of agency exists by virtue of the special contracts of deposit (bailment) and mandate (agency). Indeed, in many civil law jurisdictions, if an agent has used money of his undisclosed principal to buy an asset, such principal can recover such asset as his asset if the agent becomes insolvent. Moreover, bailment in those jurisdictions, as opposed to common law jurisdictions (see p.77) extends beyond tangibles to intangibles, so there can be a bailment of stocks and shares (impossible in English law where the custodian has to have the legal title). The concept of administration of another's property is also present in that part of the law of persons dealing with tutorship and curatorship and in the law relating to matrimonial property régimes. In the law of succession on the death of the deceased his heir becomes owner of the deceased's estate, standing in the deceased's shoes, subject to certain personal obligations (for example to pay debts and give effect to legacies), though it is possible for a testator to appoint a testamentary executor (with more limited powers than an English executor), for example *exécuteur testamentaire* or *Testamentsvollstrecker*.

Civil law has developed certain concepts from the Roman law concepts of *fiducia* and *fideicommissum*. The gist of *fiducia* is that the owner transfers ownership to the fiduciary, who undertakes to use the ownership in a particular way only and then to retransfer it back to the original owner or to transfer it to a third party. Only a personal remedy lies against the fiduciary, so the position is unsatisfactory if the fiduciary wrongly sells the property or goes bankrupt. In the Netherlands, however, a special application of the *fiducia cum amico* has developed so that if a lawyer maintains a nominee account with a bank for the benefit of his clients, such account is a separate fund for the clients and is not available for creditors of the lawyer if he becomes bankrupt. In Germany the *Treuhand* has developed from the *fiducia*: the beneficiaries of a *Treuhandkonto* or a *fiduziarische Treuhand* are protected against creditors of the fiduciary (*Treuhander*).

Civil law has developed fideicommissary substitutions from the Roman *fideicommissum*: by *inter vivos* or testamentary disposition S may transfer ownership to O (the institute) to take as owner but subject to ownership passing to P (the substitute) on O's death or a specified earlier event. Unlike the case of transferring ownership to P subject to a usufruct in O, it is not necessary for P to be alive or ascertainable at the date of S's disposition. It will be necessary for O to preserve the property intact for P, but if P predeceases O (or the specified event) then O's interest really is absolute. There are restrictions on substitutions, for example consanguinity limits or generation limits.

Indeed, one has to remember that there are also restrictions on dispositions as a result of matrimonial property régimes, while by virtue of forced heirship rights (reserve hereditaire, *Pflichtteil*) under which, for example, children have rights on a parent's death to indefeasible fixed shares in the parent's estate, taking into account earlier donations, such forced heirs can sue earlier donees to obtain sufficient money to make up the full amount of their forced shares as a fraction of the parent's actual estate plus the notionally added-back earlier gifts.

The civil law concept of contract is much broader than the common law concept with its doctrine of consideration and, until the Contracts (Rights of Third Parties) Act 1999, of privity of contract. In civil law, "cause" or "causa" is required for a valid "contract", so that a contract may be gratuitous or for value and there can be a contractual *stipulatio per alterum*, *i.e.* for the benefit of a third party which the third party may enforce. Thus, "contract" is extensive enough to cover the trust arrangement whereby a settlor gratuitously transfers property to trustees who accept that they are to hold the property for beneficiaries, who may then enforce their beneficial rights against the trustees. However, these rights under a "contract" will merely be personal, as opposed to proprietary, rights, so they will be unenforceable against the trustees' creditors or wrongful transferees from the trustees.

Alternatively, the trust (or at least a charitable purpose trust) may be regarded as a *fondation* or *Stiftung* which consists of the dedication of a fund to a specified object with an appropriate organisation for its administration so that it has legal personality. An alternative to legal personality is the concept of a *patrimoine affecté, une masse de biens affectés à un but*, an assembly of assets and liabilities earmarked for a specific function, for example for paying off an insolvent person's creditors so far as possible.

Common Law States

The common law never concerned itself with ownership of land since all land was—and still is—owned by the Crown! In the feudal hierarchy the King granted an *estate* in land, for example a life estate or fee simple estate, to his major supporters in certain types of *tenure* from him which involved various burdensome incidents. In turn, they granted part of this land in certain types of tenure from them (with burdensome incidents) to their supporters for particular estates and this process of subinfeudation repeated itself down the line until it was prohibited by statute in 1290. The incidents of tenure gradually came to have little economic significance so that the type of tenure, the quality of a man's holding of his land, lost its significance. It was the estate or quantum of a man's rights that became significant.

A man might have rights to dispose, manage and enjoy the land for the duration of his life (the estate for life), for so long as he had lineal descendants (the estate in fee tail), or for so long as he had heirs which become for ever when estates could be devised by will and when feudal escheat of the estate to his feudal lord for lack of heirs disappeared (the estate in fee simple). These were the three common law estates that became known as legal estates to distinguish them from equitable estates.

Equitable estates arose when it became the practice for a knight going off to the Crusades to vest his estate in land in a friend to hold "to the use of" the knight, and, until his return, the knight's lady and children, or if he died abroad to the use of the knight's eldest son. This was done because legal actions had to be brought by an adult male claiming a better right to possession of the land than some interloper. The land would be defenceless against such interloper if the knight were abroad for 10 years without having earlier transferred his estate in the land to his friend. If the friend refused to retransfer the estate in the land on the knight's return there was no remedy in the common law courts because the friend was the estate owner in their eyes. The knight could only petition the King to remedy the wrong because in equity the "friend" should be forced to recognise the knight's interest and retransfer the estate. It was vital to the position of the knight in the feudal hierarchy that the King order the knight's friend to transfer the land back to the knight. Similarly, if vows of poverty prevented land being conveyed directly to an Order of Franciscan Friars so that it was conveyed to a knight to hold to the use of the Franciscan Order, and the knight retained the benefits for himself, the Order would petition the King to force the knight to disgorge the benefits and convey the land to a more sympathetic knight or bishop to hold to the use of the Order.

In equity, the King, as the *fons et origo justitiae* (fountain and source of justice), was also petitioned about the injustices resulting from defects in the common law or its courts whether due to intimidation or the absence of an appropriate procedure or writ (there being no remedy without a writ). The King and his Council referred these petitions to the Chancellor as the King's closest adviser. He was an ecclesiastic usually learned in Roman law and canon law, and so well qualified to advise on these matters of conscience and equity: it is likely that he was influenced by the Roman *fiducia* and *fidei commissum*. The Chancellor then began to make decrees on his own authority and failure to obey the decrees resulted in the offender being committed to prison till the decree was obeyed. The Chancellor came to sit in what became known as the Court of Chancery where he began systematically to develop rules of equity, so that the court was also known as a Court of Equity. By 1615, in the *Earl of Oxford's Case*, it was established that orders of the Court of Chancery prevailed over orders of common law courts and that rules of equity prevailed over common law rules if there was any conflict between them, a position preserved by statute now that since 1875 all courts administer equity and common law rules. In 1818 the Chancellor, Lord Eldon, remarked, "Nothing would inflict on me greater pain than the recollection that I had done anything to justify the reproach that the equity of this Court varies like the [size of the] Chancellor's foot." As Bagnall J. said in 1972, "In the field of equity the length of the Chancellor's foot has been measured or is capable of measurement. This does not mean that equity is past child-bearing; simply that its progeny must be legitimate—by precedent out of principle."

The Chancellor in the Court of Chancery recognised legal estates in land just like the common law courts, but went further by compelling the legal estate owner to use his legal ownership for the benefit of the beneficiaries, who in equity were supposed to benefit exclusively from the land vested in the legal estate owner. The beneficiaries could thus have equitable estates corresponding to the types of legal estate.

What began life as the "use" came to be known as the "trust" as the result of the Statute of Uses 1535. Uses of land were then very common. The prohibition against devising land by will could be evaded by conveying land (by feoffment with livery of seisin) to feoffees to the use of the settlor for life, remainder to the uses declared by his last will. Furthermore, burdensome feudal incidents arising as the result of death, especially if there was an infant heir, could be avoided if land was conveyed to a number of feoffees (who would ensure that the land was never left vested in a sole surviving feoffee to uses since only on his death would feudal burdens arise). To prevent avoidance of the valuable feudal incidents, Henry VIII had the Statute of Uses enacted. Under this 1535 statute the use was "executed" so that where A, B and C (the feoffees to uses) held land to the use of X (the *cestui que* use) the legal estate was taken out of A, B and C and vested in X, so that on his death the feudal incidents would be leviable. In 1540 the Statute of Wills was enacted as a result of a rebellion against Henry VIII so that it became possible to devise land by will at common law.

What if land were conveyed to A and B to hold to the use of A and B to hold to the use X? At first, the first use was executed and the second use was treated as void as repugnant to the first use: thus A and B were legal owners for their own benefit. Later, the second use came to be enforced, first as an exceptional matter to prevent fraud perpetrated by A and B or to remedy a mistake and, then, as a matter of standard practice, the feudal incidents having by then lost all economic significance. The enforced use came to be known as the trust to distinguish it from the "executed" use and the drafting formula became "Unto and to the use of A and B and their heirs in trust for", for example, X for life, remainder to his eldest son and the heirs of his body.

Over the years X's equitable interest came to be enforced in the Court of Chancery not just against the trustee or a donee from the trustee, but as a proprietary interest against anyone having the legal estate other than a bona fide purchaser of it for value without notice. Such person is traditionally referred to as "Equity's darling" as if equity specially looks after him but, in reality, "Equity" in the form of the Court of Chancery simply had no jurisdiction to deal with such bona fide purchaser and prevent him from exercising his straightforward legal rights in the common law courts. Equity can only intervene[5] if there is a special equitable ground to compel the legal owner to hold the benefits of ownership for another since to retain the benefits for himself would be unconscionable, for example because the legal owner had innocently received trust property as a gift from a wrongdoing trustee or had purchased trust property with notice of the trust or had taken it upon himself to act as trustee of property known by him to be trust property.

A person has notice of an equitable interest if he has actual knowledge of it ("actual" notice) or would, as a person of reasonable intelligence, have had such knowledge if he had made such inquiries and inspections as ought reasonably to have been made ("constructive" notice): actual or constructive notice of a person's agent is imputed to him ("imputed" notice). In the case of purchases of land there are many standard inquiries and inspections that must reasonably be made, but for movables a purchaser may take things at their face value unless there are suspicious circumstances and yet he deliberately or recklessly fails to make the further investigations that an honest and reasonable man should make (so he exhibits a lack of honesty).

To simplify matters for purchasers of land, so long as a purchaser pays the purchase moneys to two trustees or a trust corporation (as defined in English law: see p.163 below) the interests of the beneficiaries, whether or not the purchaser has notice of them, are "overreached", *i.e.* detached from the land and attached to the proceeds of sale.[6] The beneficiaries then have a right to trace and claim the proceeds or the specific property purchased therewith. Thus, the purchaser obtains a good title free from the equitable interests of the beneficiaries even if he knows of them: the beneficiaries are protected since the value of their interests is unaffected, being reflected in cash (or property purchased therewith) held by the trustees instead of an equivalent land value. This serves to emphasise the concept of the trust *fund* in which the beneficiaries are interested irrespective of what particular investments happen from time to time to be the trust property comprised in the trust fund. Thus, a life tenant has throughout his life an entitlement to the income from the trust fund, while his entitlement to the income from particular property comprised in the trust fund is a temporary one until that property is sold and replaced by other property.

Originally, a trust fund would have consisted solely of land (with some cash) because land was the main source of wealth. The trust concept proved so useful and worthwhile in respect of land that

---

[5] Prevailing over the common law courts in case of conflict since the *Earl of Oxford's Case*, 1615.

[6] See Law of Property Act 1925, ss.2, 27 and *City of London Building Society v Flegg* [1988] A.C. 54.

when other forms of property (like shares in companies, antiques, paintings) became significant sources of wealth, the trust was a well-known convenient receptacle for holding such property without the need to rely on common law concepts like agency, bailment or guardianship that would otherwise have had to be utilised.

Full Transposition of Trust by Analogues Impossible

The systems of law in civil law states were satisfactory without the need for an additional equity jurisdiction so no concept of equitable ownership arose, nor was there any feudal doctrine of estates since there had been a thorough reception of Roman law with its concept of absolute ownership. Major problems therefore arose when civil law courts had to try to fit the trust into civil law systems and consider who should be the absolute owner in the case of foreign trusts: the trustees, the beneficiaries or one of them, the settlor, the personified trust itself? Must it depend on which type of trust is in question? Should the variety of equitable interests possible under trusts all be capable of being real proprietary rights enforceable against the trust property held by the "owner"? What a cuckoo in the nest this might be! Does the trust pertain to the law of property or to the law of obligations (a broad civil law category covering tort, contract, unjust enrichment and alimentary obligations arising by operation of law from family relationships)?

In *Harrison v Crédit Suisse*[7] the Swiss Federal Court held that a trust of Swiss assets held by a Zurich bank as "trustee" related to the law of obligations, being a mixed contract of mandate, of donation, of a fiduciary transfer of property, and of a contract for the benefit of a third party. Since such mixed contract could be given effect to as such in Switzerland, Harrison's "trust" was not void or voidable. This prevented Harrison's wife from having his Zurich "trust" set aside and claiming the property as sole legatee under his will, though it would give no proprietary rights to the beneficiaries under the trust, for example if the trustee became bankrupt or the property wrongfully came into the hands of third parties. Nowadays, reforms to the Swiss Code of Private International Law have led foreign trusts to be treated as if companies.[8]

In France the Tribunal de Grande Instance de Bayonne[9] has held that the trustee is the owner of the trust property, but with powers limited by the trust instrument and rules of equity, and that the

[7] A.T.F. 96, 1970, II, 79.
[8] "The Trust in Switzerland-Revisited" [2000] J.T.C.P. 141, DG Forbes-Jaeger and E Stormann.
[9] 28 April 1975 Rev crit de dr. int.pr. 1976 p.331. On recognition of trusts in civil law States see further my chapter in Glasson: *International Trust Laws* (Jordan Publishing Co Ltd).

beneficiaries have no ownership rights though their interests are "guaranteed" by equity.

The Hague Convention recognises that non-trust jurisdictions, as they adopt the Convention, must recognise the trust as such as a matter of their private international law but without the need to introduce the trust and a division between legal and equitable ownership into their own domestic law for their own citizens. Article 2 of the Convention deliberately does not mention legal and equitable ownership, countries like Scotland, India and South Africa already having the trust concept without such a division of ownership: Italy, Malta and the Netherlands have therefore implemented the Convention.

PRINCIPLES OF EUROPEAN "TRUST" LAW

To encourage the development of a trust-like ring-fenced fund concept in Europe, which is already present to some extent in most jurisdictions and which will be useful for collective security trusts supporting loans for all sorts of valuable purposes, for managing property for the benefit of minors and other persons lacking capacity, for protecting client accounts of solicitors, estate agents and other temporary custodians of client moneys and for creating more harmony in an increasingly federal Europe, an international working group has produced eight articles set out in the Appendix hereto, supported by a general commentary and various national commentaries. It is hoped that such principles,[10] especially if coupled with implementation of the Hague Trusts Convention, will lead to increasing flexibility in the laws of mainland European jurisdictions which will maximise opportunities for wealth preservation and wealth generation.

The key is Article 1, which has as the core of the European "Trust" concept a segregated trust fund owned by the trustee apart from his private patrimony and so immune from the claims of his creditors, spouse or heirs. The idea of a segregated fund is already represented in various civil law systems, for example the segregation of a deceased's assets vested in the heir until he accepts them with the benefit of an inventory of assets and liabilities, the assets of an undisclosed principal in the hands of his agent are protected aganist the agent's insolvency under Swiss and Italian law, the Italian *fondo patrimoniale* under Arts 167–171 of the Civil Code which concerns assets held by the spouse(s) for satisfying the needs of the family, and the Dutch notary's client account. However, it is up to each

---

[10] *Principles of European Trust Law* (eds Hayton, Kortmann & Verhagen; Kluwer Law International, 1999).

jurisdiction how far it develops special personal or even proprietary rights against the trustee or third parties.

Encouragement is given to regarding trusts not as contracts because of the dangers that it might then be thought that a breach of trust could, like breach of contract, provide grounds for treating the trust as at an end, or that the settlor must have rights of enforcement, or that the death or mental incapacity of the settlor or the trustee might affect the existence of the trust, or that all the beneficiaries have to be in existence at the creation of the trust. To categorise the trust as a type of contractual obligation would too much inhibit the scope for its growth over the next century. A trust obligation is an independent type of obligation, normally involving continuous duties for a lengthy period and having a life of its own, although having no legal personality: the trustees are the legal personalities who alone can sue or be sued, but the office of trustee remains to be filled by another person if the current trustee dies or becomes mentally incompetent or commits a breach of trust. Where compensation is sought for a breach of trust a beneficiary is not normally suing for loss to himself but is, in essence, bringing a representative action on behalf of all beneficiaries for the trustees to restore to the trust fund value lost through their breach of trust (see p.28 below).

EXPRESS TRUSTS OF PROPERTY

The vast majority of trusts are expressly created in the sense that a settlor expressly transfers property to trustees to hold on declared trusts or, exceptionally, declares himself trustee of his own property specifically appropriated for satisfying certain declared trusts. The existence of a separate trust fund is the key to a trust: the recipient of property cannot be a trustee if he is free to mix the property with his own property as part of his own assets, so that he is simply a debtor of the transferor. It is a simple matter to create a trust, no formalities being required (above those required for the transfer of property or for making a will) except that trusts of land must be evidenced in writing at some stage. There is no register of trusts to ascertain how many hundreds of thousands of trusts there are, although there is a register of charitable trusts (other than exempt and excepted charities) on which over 170,000 charities are registered so that tax privileges may then be claimed.

Express trusts will be fixed trusts or discretionary trusts. A fixed trust is one where the beneficiary has a fixed entitlement to demand net income or capital from the trustees, for example on trust for A for life (so A can demand to receive net income), remainder to A's children equally (so on A's death the children can demand to receive the capital). A discretionary trust is one where the beneficiaries only obtain income or capital when the trustees exercise their discretion which they must exercise in favour of one or more particular beneficiaries, for example property held on trust for distributing income between such of the issue of A as the trustees shall see fit until the expiry of the perpetuity period whereupon the capital shall be distributed between such of A's issue then alive as the trustees shall select in their discretion.

A trust instrument may create a fixed trust and then a discretionary trust (or vice versa) for example on trust for A for life, remainder for such of A's children as the trustees shall select in their discretion (or as A's widow shall select in her discretion). A similar result may be achieved by a fixed defeasible trust for A for life, remainder to his children equally unless the trustees (or A's widow) by deed appoint the capital amongst the children in such unequal shares as they shall select in their discretion.

RESULTING TRUSTS OF PROPERTY

The orthodox view, expressed by Lord Browne-Wilkinson, is that a resulting trust arises in two sets of circumstances to give effect to presumed intention.[11]

First, where A makes a voluntary transfer to B of money or shares (but not land because it seems[12] s.60(3) of the Law of Property Act 1925 ousts a presumption of resulting trust where gifts of land are concerned) or pays wholly or partly for the purchase of property which is vested in B alone or jointly in A and B, there is a presumption that A did not intend to make a gift or loan. It is thus presumed that the property is held on trust for A absolutely as the sole provider thereof or, in the case of a joint purchase by A and B, for A and B in shares proportionate to their contributions. This is only a presumption which can easily be rebutted either by direct evidence of A's intention to make a gift or loan or by the counter-presumption of advancement (applying where B is A's child or wife or fiancée or probably, in these days of equality, A's husband or fiancé).[13]

Secondly, where A transfers property to B on express trusts but the trusts declared do not exhaust the whole beneficial interest, for example A transfers property to B on trust for C for life or on trusts for present and future members of the C Club for Club purposes

---

[11] *Westdeutsche Landesbank v Islington LBC* [1996] A.C. 669 at 708, and in his Holdsworth Club Lecture 1991 "Constructive Trusts and Unjust Enrichment" (1996) 10 Trust LI 198.

[12] *Lohia v Lohia* [2001] W.T.L.R. 101 at 112, endorsed in *Ali v Khan* [2002] EWCA Civ 974.

[13] *Nelson v Nelson* (1995) 184 C.L.R. 538; Art.5 of Seventh Protocol to European Convention on Human Rights.

only when, after the death of C or the dissolution of the C Club, B will hold on trust for A. This presumption can be ousted or rebutted by evidence that A had abandoned any beneficial interest in the trust property, so that such property will pass to the Crown as *bona vacantia* (ownerless property) unless intended by A to pass to Club members at the time of dissolution of the Club as part of the Club's assets.[14]

Lord Browne-Wilkinson cites *Barclays Bank v Quistclose Investments Ltd*[15] as falling within this second head. The principle established in this case is that if money is loaned by A to B for a specific purpose intended to benefit B which is then carried out, B is simply a debtor of A, but otherwise B holds the money on a resulting trust for A (if, indeed, an express trust for A has not been agreed for such circumstances). From the outset A has the right to prevent the money being used for anything but the specific purpose[16]: A has no right to compel performance of the purpose or terminate the purpose or the loan, unless the purpose was for A's benefit or he reserved such rights.

Lord Browne-Wilkinson[17] usefully made clear that: "A person solely entitled to the full beneficial ownership of money or property, both at law and in equity, does not enjoy an equitable interest in that property. The legal title carries with it all rights. Unless and until there is a separation of the legal and equitable estates, there is no separate title." It follows that if A transfers property to B in circumstances where an express or resulting trust arises in favour of A, while one can say that A remains absolute beneficial owner one cannot say that A retains an equitable interest because he never had any equitable interest before the transfer: the transfer creates a new equitable interest in favour of A,[18] so that A becomes equitable beneficial owner, having been legal beneficial owner.

Lord Browne-Wilkinson in *obiter dicta*[19] firmly rejected extending the law on resulting trusts so as to provide a plaintiff with a proprietary equitable interest as a restitutionary response to the unjust enrichment of a defendant. However, Robert Chambers in his book, *Resulting Trusts*,[20] in which he develops many ideas of

[14] *Westdeutsche Landesbank v Islington LBC* [1996] AC 669 at 708; *Re Bucks Constabulary Fund* [1979] 1 W.L.R. 936.

[15] [1970] A.C. 567.

[16] Further see *Twinsectra Ltd v Yardley* [2002] UKHL, [2002] 2 A.C. 164, paras 77 to 102.

[17] *Westdeutsche Landesbank v Islington LBC* [1996] A.C. 669 at 706.

[18] *ibid*, at 706 and 714, in explaining *Chase Manhattan Bank v Israel-British Bank* [1981] Ch. 105; *DKLR Holding Co. (No. 2) Pty Ltd v Commissioner of Stamp Duties* (1982) 40 A.L.R. 1.

[19] [1996] A.C. 669 at 709, 716. See also Lord Goff at 689; WJ Swadling (1996) 16 Legal Studies 110; C Rickett & R Grantham (2000) 116 L.Q.R. 15 at 19.

[20] Published by Clarendon, Oxford, 1997.

Professor Peter Birks, has put forward a well argued case (but unlikely to be judicially accepted) for so extending resulting trusts.

He contends that the resulting trust arises not out of the presumed intention of A to create a trust but out of A's lack of intention to benefit the recipient, B, so leading to a resulting trust arising by operation of law. If lack of intention to benefit B is at the core of the imposition of a resulting trust, then resulting trusts should be capable of extending to a transfer of A's property where A did not really want to make the transfer because his intent to benefit B was absent or was vitiated by mistake, duress, or undue influence, or was conditional on the happening of certain events which failed to materialise, so long as such property had never been a freely available part of B's general assets before the right to the restitution arose.[21] He also maintains that a resulting trust should arise where A is equitable owner of property vested in T as trustee who wrongfully transfers it to B without A's consent, where B is not a bona fide purchaser of the property without notice of A's equitdhable interest. A's equitable interest affects the property as a matter of the law of priorities affecting interests in property, but most consider that, on appreciating this, B becomes constructive trustee under a duty to transfer the property to A or to A's order so as to vindicate the original express or resulting trust for A.

This is an immensely complicated area, full of difficult case law, particularly when some of such alleged resulting trusts instances would simply take over areas already covered by orthodox property principles or constructive trusts to prevent unconscionable conduct, and when other instances not involving an insolvent defendant[22] might be better covered by the imposition of remedial constructive trusts which can be tailored retrospectively or prospectively to the circumstances of a particular case so as not to prejudice innocent third parties.[23]

CONSTRUCTIVE TRUSTS OF PROPERTY

A constructive trust is imposed by law,[24] although the content of some types of constructive trust depends primarily on the intentions

---

[21] R Chambers, *Resulting Trusts*, p.234; *Westdeutsche Landesbank v Islington LBC* [1996] A.C. 669 at 689–90, 712. However, the better view seems that not only a real, but also a mistaken, intent of A for B to treat A's assets as a freely available part of B's general assets should be inconsistent with any proprietary trust relationship arising: Lord Millett (1998) 114 L.Q.R. 399 at 406-407 and 416, and in *Twinsectra Ltd v Yardley* [2002] UKHL 12, [2002] 2 A.C. 164 at para.91, so that the focus is then on the equitable remedy of rescission for mistaken intent.
[22] *Re Polly Peck International plc (No2)* [1998] 3 All ER 812, CA; *Commonwealth Reserves v Chodar* [2001] 2 N.Z.L.R. 374.
[23] See *Westdeutsche Landesbank v Islington LBC* [1996] A.C. 669 at 716; p.20 below.
[24] Generally, see A J Oakley, *Constructive Trusts* (Sweet & Maxwell, 3rd ed., 1997).

of the parties involved (for example secret trusts, mutual wills, common intention constructive trusts of family homes, constructive trusts of land subject to a specifically enforceable contract of sale); the defendant who reneges on what was intended is forced to give effect to what was intended. Currently, English law only recognises an institutional constructive trust as a response to specific types of circumstances, so as to perfect a relied upon expectation, to deter and remedy wrongful conduct or to respond to unjust enrichment. As Lord Browne-Wilkinson states[25]:

> "[It] arises by operation of law as from the date of the circumstances which give rise to it: the function of the court is merely to declare that such trust has arisen in the past. The consequences that flow from such trust having arisen (including the possibly unfair consequences to third parties who in the interim have received the trust property) are also determined by rules of law, not under a discretion. A remedial constructive trust is different. It is a judicial remedy giving rise to an enforceable equitable obligation: the extent to which it operates retrospectively to the prejudice of third parties is in the discretion of the court ... whether English law should follow the United States and Canada by adopting the remedial constructive trust will have to be decided in some future case when the point is directly in issue.'

It is easy to talk of express, resulting and constructive trusts of property as if they are similar substantive institutions. This is not the case. Where there is an express or a resulting trust the court compels an objecting trustee to give effect to the beneficiaries' rights because he knows that the settlor–transferor did not intend him to be a beneficiary himself so that he is an express or resulting trustee with consequences automatically flowing therefrom. If, for example, the trustee uses trust property or his position as trustee to make a profit for himself (for example by investing trust income in purchasing assets for himself or by obtaining a bribe) then the beneficiaries have a right to the profit or the new assets representing the profit, so such will be held on constructive trust for the beneficiaries. Similarly, if a trustee purchases for himself something which he should have purchased for the trust, he will hold it on constructive trust for the trust beneficiaries. Again, if the trustee wrongfully disposes of the trust property to a stranger, who is not a bona fide purchaser for value without notice, the beneficiaries have the right to this property or its traceable equivalent (for example a painting or shares purchased with the proceeds of sale of trust property) in the hands of the stranger who will be constructive

---

[25] *Westdeutsche Landesbank v Islington LBC* [1996] A.C. 669 at 714. Also see *Abacus (CI) Ltd v Grupo Torras*, Jersey Royal Court, June 13 2003, paras 136–149.

trustee thereof for them once he knows of the claim. He will have to transfer the property to them, if they are of full capacity and between themselves absolutely entitled, or to trustees for them.

Here, the constructive trust is dependent upon and ancillary to a valid express or resulting trust. It arises and exists independently of any order of the court just like the trust to which it is a vital remedial adjunct. In other cases, where someone is not a trustee of a valid express or resulting trust of property, equity (meaning the body of principles developed by the Court of Chancery) in special limited circumstances prevents such person from retaining all or part of the beneficial interest in his property by constructively treating him as if he were a trustee of the property for another. It is because some principle of equity in special limited circumstances compels the defendant to hold property wholly or partly in equity for the plaintiff that the defendant is constructive trustee thereof: it is not because the defendant is a constructive trustee that he is compelled to hold his property in equity for the plaintiff.

The special limited circumstances which give rise to a constructive trust by way of remedy are circumstances where equity considers it unconscionable for the owner of particular property to hold it purely for his own benefit. It is necessary to prove a case which fits the accepted special circumstances directly or by analogy, since the court cannot impose a constructive trust to provide a remedy on grounds of "justice and good conscience".

Examples of the special circumstances which justify the imposition of a constructive trust are as follows. To prevent K from taking advantage of exercising undue influence upon B, K will hold property thereby acquired upon constructive trust for B. If K unlawfully kills B, then K will hold property thereby acquired under B's will or intestacy for those who would be entitled if K had predeceased B (except to the extent that relief may be afforded under the Forfeiture Act 1982 if it was not murder for which K was convicted).

When property is stolen or obtained by fraud, the property and its traceable product can be recovered in equity if common law remedies are inadequate, a constructive trust arising.[26] However, where a loan is obtained by fraud (for example £1 million borrowed by virtue of a fraudulent misrepresentation) because there was an intent only to create a debtor-creditor relationship, the lender cannot be better off than if the loan had been valid (for example he can only recover the £1 million and not specific property purchased with the loan which has increased in value).[27]

---

[26] *Westdeutsche Landesbank v Islington LBC* [1996] A.C. 669 at 715; *Bishopsgate Investment Management Ltd v Maxwell* [1993] Ch. 1 at 70; *Foskett v McKeown* [2001] 1 A.C. 102 at 113 & 128.

[27] *Halifax B.S. v Thomas* [1995] 4 All E.R. 673.

Where B receives money, not as a loan or contractual consideration, from A or A's agent in circumstances where honesty requires B to repay the money forthwith to A, then first instance decisions indicate that an equitable interest in favour of A springs up at the time of receipt of the money and B will become constructive trustee thereof. Examples are where A's agent mistakenly pays B a second payment of £1 million, A having already paid B the money,[28] or where B Ltd receives money from A, to pay for services provided by C to A, at a time when B Ltd has decided to cease trading because of insolvency problems so that if such money became part of B Ltd's assets available generally for creditors the money would be lost, leaving A to find further money of its own to pay C.[29]

Here, however, one sees the overlap with resulting trusts of the *Quistclose* variety. The former example can be regarded as one where the mistaken payer, A, paid the money for a purpose which was incapable of fulfilment because the debt had already been discharged, while the latter can be regarded as one where A paid the money to B Ltd for the purpose of an equivalent sum being paid by B Ltd to C but in circumstances where it was probably unlawful for the directors of B Ltd to pay such sum to C because that would have amounted to unlawful trading.

If H and W make mutual wills which they agree not to revoke, and H leaves his property to W for life remainder to X, and W leaves her property to H for life, remainder to X, then X has an interest under a constructive trust as soon as H dies. As beneficiary under such a trust, X can enforce it against W's personal representatives if she makes a new will purporting to leave the property to someone else: as a third party, due to the doctrine of privity of contract before the Contracts (Rights of Third Parties) Act 1999, X would not have been able to enforce the contract for his benefit.

As will be fully explained in Chapter 9, a constructive trust can also be imposed on a house registered in M's name in order to give effect to the express or inferred common intention of M and W that W is to have a beneficial interest therein, so leading W to act to her detriment in reliance on that intention, which makes it unconscionable to allow M to deny W the beneficial interest by pleading absence of the necessary statutory written formalities. Here, it may

---

[28] *Chase Manhattan Bank v Israel British Bank* [1981] Ch. 105; but its validity is uncertain due to comments of Lord Browne-Wilkinson in *Westdeutsche Landesbank v Islington LBC* [1996] A.C. 669 at 714-715 and to Lord Millett's preference for reliance, instead, on the equitable remedy of rescission subject to the usual equitable bars thereon: (1998) 114 L.Q.R. 399 at 406-407, 416-417. It was applied in *Papamichael v National Westminster Bank plc* [2003] 1 Lloyd's Rep. 341.

[29] *Neste Oy v Lloyds Bank* [1983] 2 Lloyd's Rep. 658 and *Re Japan Leasing (Europe) plc* [2000] W.T.L.R. 301.

be said that the constructive trust represents the remedy by which W seeks to vindicate an informal express trust founded upon a common intention which M later repudiates.

The same may be said of secret trusts where T by will devises Blackacre to S absolutely on S's oral undertaking to hold it on trust for B for life, remainder to her child, C, absolutely. After T's death S cannot take advantage of the absence of the necessary written formalities to keep Blackacre for himself: he must hold it for B and C since "Equity will not allow statute to be used as an instrument of fraud." By the Law of Property Act 1925, s.53(1) trusts of land must be evidenced in writing, but by section 53(2) this does not apply to the creation or operation of resulting or constructive trusts. The better view[30] is that S holds Blackacre on constructive trust under section 53(2) so that section 53(1) is inapplicable: others take the view that S holds Blackacre on express trust within section 53(1) but that the equitable maxim above quoted means that S is not allowed to plead section 53(1) in court, so that the express trust is enforceable despite section 53(1). The same result is reached under either view.

PROPRIETARY LIABILITY AND PERSONAL ACCOUNTABILITY

If a person has an equitable interest under an express, resulting or constructive trust of property, then the owner of that property (or a person claiming under the owner other than as bona fide purchaser of the owner's legal title without notice of the equitable interest) holds such property to give effect to the equitable interest under the trust, just as he would hold such property, if land, subject to equitable easements or restrictive covenants (servitudes) or equitable charges to secure payment of a sum of money.[31] Thus, the owner has an interest in property from which are subtracted equitable interests under trusts (or charges, easements or restrictive covenants) which are proprietary liabilities, affording priority to the equitable owners over the legal owner's general creditors on his bankruptcy.

In most cases the trustee of an express, resulting or constructive trust of property will know he is such. However, in exceptional cases[32] even the trustee of an express trust may not know he is such,

---

[30] *Kasperbauer v Griffith* [2000] W.T.L.R. 333 at 343, *Paragon Finance v Thakerar* [1999] 1 All E.R. 400 at 409.
[31] *Westdeutsche Landesbank v Islington LBC* [1996] A.C. 669 at 706–707.
[32] *Fletcher v Fletcher* (1844) 4 Hare 67; *Childers v Childers* (1857) 1 De. G. & J. 482; *Re Vinogradoff* [1935] W.N. 68. A testator may create testamentary trusts without the trustee's knowledge, while title to some property may be the subject of a lifetime transfer to a trustee without the latter's knowledge.

yet the beneficiaries thereunder will have an equitable interest capable of binding the trustee and his successors (other than bona fide purchasers without notice). While an outright gift from A to X is not complete until X accepts it,[33] a transfer of property from A to X on trust for C is regarded as creating a perfect completed trust for C once A has completed the unilateral action necessary for him to transfer the relevant property to X; even if X disclaims as soon as he discovers the position, equity will not allow a trust to fail for want of a trustee so that A himself will become trustee for C.[34]

Where X knows he is trustee of an express trust, then he is under a personal liability to account to the beneficiaries for the value of the property and for what he has done or failed to do with it, which is at least co-extensive with his proprietary liability to hand the property over to, or hold it for the benefit of, C. However, Lord Browne-Wilkinson states,[35] "Innocent receipt of property by X subject to an existing equitable interest does not by itself make X a trustee, despite severance of the legal and equitable titles" so that, although X is subject to a proprietary liability, no personal liability can arise until X knows he is trustee. Similarly, no personal liability as a resulting or constructive trustee can arise until X knows he is such a trustee, although the personal duties of such a trustee are normally fairly light (like nomineeship duties) compared to those of an express trustee who, by accepting his trusteeship, thereby voluntary accepts fairly extensive continuing duties.

In Lord Browne-Wilkinson's view a beneficiary will have an equitable proprietary interest under an express, resulting or constructive trust of property owned by X, but X will not be a trustee thereof and personally accountable as such until he knows he is a trustee. Previously, it was generally thought that X objectively was a trustee as soon as his property became subject to an express, resulting or constructive trust, although he could not be personally liable as a trustee until he knew he was a trustee. This is a semantic distinction without any practical difference.

EXTENSION OF PERSONAL ACCOUNTABILITY

As just seen, personal accountability of trustees of express, resulting or constructive trusts of property vested in them goes hand in hand with proprietary liability in relation to such property once the trustee knows he is trustee of such property. However,

---

[33] *Hill v Wilson* (1873) 8 Ch. App. 888 at 896.
[34] *Mallott v Wilson* [1903] 2 Ch. 494; *Re Rose* [1949] Ch. 78.
[35] *Westdeutsche Landesbank v Islington LBC* [1996] A.C. 669 at 707.

once the trustee has wrongfully parted with the trust property in circumstances where such property is not replaced with other property, in which the beneficiaries will be treated as having an equitable proprietary interest, the trustee cannot be subject to any proprietary liability. He can, however, be subject to a personal liability to account if he knew he was a trustee when he wrongfully parted with the property, but as Lord Browne-Wilkinson stated: "unless he has the requisite degree of knowledge he is not personally liable to account as trustee." In case it be thought that a person who innocently receives trust money, due to a wrong act of the trustee, and then spends it innocently on paying off his old secured or unsecured debts will escape liability and so be unjustly enriched, the beneficiaries have the equitable restitutionary remedy of being subrogated to the claims of such secured or unsecured creditors: they will then have proprietary or personal claims (as the case may be) against such innocent defendant by standing in the shoes of his creditors.[36] Of course, if the defendant dishonestly dealt with the trust property he received he will be personally liable to the beneficiaries.

Exceptionally, as a fiction to provide an equitable remedy to a claimant against a defendant who would otherwise escape personal liability, a defendant, who never had property vested in him of which he could be a constructive trustee, but who was a dishonest instigator of, or accessory in, a breach of trust or other fiduciary relationship in respect of particular property, can be made personally liable to account to the plaintiff as if he had been a wrongdoing trustee of such property.

For example, a father produced a forged marriage certificate to trustees so that they innocently believed his children were legitimate and so entitled to trust property which was duly distributed to them. When it transpired that the children were non-marital, those really entitled to the trust property sued the trustees, the non-marital children and the father. It was held that the father was personally liable to account (as constructive trustee) for whatever could not be recovered from the children.[37] No trust property had ever been in his hands: the imposition of constructive trusteeship so that he became personally accountable in the same fashion as an express trustee was merely a fictitious formula for equitable relief.

Similarly, if a solicitor, accountant or banker is suspicious that his trustee client may be committing a breach of trust in requesting

---

[36] *Boscawen v Bajwa* [1995] 4 All E.R. 769; *Wenlock v River Dee Co.* (1887) 19 Q.B.D. 155; *McCullough v Marsden* (1919) 45 D.L.R. 645, 646–647; *Banque Financiere de la Cité v Parc (Battersea) Ltd* [1998] 1 All E.R. 737, HL; *Dubai Aluminium Co Ltd v Salaam* [2002] UKHL 48; [2003] 1 All ER 97 para. 87; further see p.174.

[37] See *Eaves v Hickson* (1861) 30 Beav 136.

him to arrange for the transfer of trust assets to a third party, but he deliberately or recklessly fails to make such inquiries as an honest and reasonable man would make in suspicious circumstances, he will be liable for dishonest assistance in a breach of trust if the arrangement turns out to be a breach of trust.[38]

A person like a solicitor, accountant or banker worried about this potential liability can seek directions from the court as to what to do and these directions can override any professional confidentiality.[39]

For a dishonest facilitation of a breach of trust to be dishonest he must not only do something objectively regarded as dishonest by honest people but he must subjectively know that what he is doing would be regarded as dishonest by honest people.[40]

KNOWLEDGE AND NOTICE

It is vital to appreciate the difference between "knowledge", as requisite to establish dishonesty for personal accountability, and the doctrine of "notice", relevant to proprietary liability. Once a defendant's conscience is affected by knowledge that he is about to assist in a breach of trust or has received trust property in breach of trust or is about to deal with trust property in breach of trust, then he must not so assist or he must not deal with the property inconsistently with the terms of the trust: otherwise he will be acting dishonestly and so be personally accountable to the beneficiaries. It suffices that the defendant has actual knowledge or deliberately shut his eyes to the obvious (as Admiral Nelson did when putting his telescope to his blind eye, so as to ignore flag signals at the Battle of Copenhagen, hence the expression "Nelsonian knowledge") or, in the face of suspicious circumstances, deliberately or recklessly failed to make the inquiries an honest and reasonable man would make in such suspicious circumstances (let us call this "naughty knowledge").[41]

In the law of property an equitable proprietary interest will bind everyone except a bona fide purchaser of the property affected by such interest, who did not have notice of such interest when he

---

[38] *Agip (Africa) Ltd v Jackson* [1990] Ch. 265. the director of a company which is a trustee and which, with the assistance of the director, commits a breach of trust can be made personally liable for dishonest assistance: *Royal Brunei Airlines v Tan* [1995] 2 A.C. 378.

[39] *Finers v Miro* [1991] 1 W.L.R. 35.

[40] *Twinsectra Ltd v Yardley* [2002] UKHL 12; [2002] 2 A.C. 164 paras 20 and 32.

[41] *Eagle Trust v SBC* (No. 2) [1996] 1 B.C.L.C. 121 at 152; *Hillsdown plc v Pensions Ombudsman* [1997] 1 All E.R. 862 at 902. *Assets Co Ltd v Mere Roihi* [1905] A.C. 176 at 201; *Manifest Shipping Co Ltd v Uni-Polairs Shipping Co Ltd* [2001] UKHL; [2001] 3 All E.R. 743 paras 23-26 and 112-116; *Armitage v Nurse* [1998] Ch. 241 at 251 (reckless indifference).

purchased the property. This doctrine developed in respect of purchasers of land who are expected to make various inspections of the land and various inquiries as to the documentary title so as to reveal whether any equitable interests subsist in the land. This enables them or their agents whose notice is *imputed* to them, to have *actual* notice of an equitable interest or, if they fail to make such inquiries and inspections as ought reasonably to have been made, *constructive* notice of an equitable interest so as to be bound by such interest. There is no scope for constructive notice in ordinary commercial dealings in property other than land, only in out-of-the-ordinary dealings where the circumstances are such that a defendant can be treated as having actual "Nelsonian" or "naughty" knowledge of a breach of trust or other fiduciary obligation.[42]

If the defendant still has the original trust property or has its traceable product, then he must deliver it up for the benefit of the beneficiaries if he is not a *bona fide* purchaser of it for value without notice (actual, constructive or imputed) of the equitable interest of the beneficiaries, *i.e.* if he is a donee or a purchaser with notice. He is simply returning something to which he is not entitled and "the cold calculus of constructive and imputed notice"[43] is an appropriate artificial instrument to achieve this end. It is self-evidently just that someone who obtained property, belonging in equity to another, by way of gift or with actual or constructive notice, and who still retains such property or its traceable product should deliver it up.

OVERREACHING

To simplify the purchase of land where beneficial co-ownership or successive interests often subsist under trusts, so long as a purchaser pays purchase moneys to two trustees or an EU trust corporation (see p.163 below) it is immaterial that he has notice of any such beneficial interest. Such interests are overreached by statute,[44] so that they are detached from the land and attached to the proceeds of the sale in the hands of the trustees. Overreaching authorised by the trust instrument will occur where the trustees do what they are authorised to do, such as sell X plc shares and buy Y plc shares, so that the beneficiaries' interest are detached from the X plc shares and attached to the Y plc shares.

---

[42] *Polly Peck International plc v Nadir* [1992] 4 All E.R. 769; Lord Browne-Wilkinson in "Equity in a Fast-Changing World", New Zealand Commonwealth Law Conference Papers, p. 177; *Macmillan v Bishopsgate Investment Trust plc* (No. 3) [1995] 1 W.L.R. 978 at 1044.

[43] *Re Montagu's Settlements* [1987] Ch. 264 at 273.

[44] LPA 1925, ss.2, 27, 205(1)(xxi), *City of London BS v Flegg* [1988] A.C. 54.

It is noteworthy that the individual or corporation owning
property as trustee has full power as such individual or corporation
to transfer ownership (legal title) to a purchaser even if such
transfer amounts to a breach of that person's obligations as a
trustee. Beneficiaries would be entitled, if they learnt in time, to
restrain the transfer in breach of trust. If they only discovered the
breach after the transfer, the transferee, if he took with notice (and
the statutory overreaching provisions for sales of land were not
applicable) would be obliged to restore the property to the trust
fund and so to transfer the property back to the original or replacement trustee(s) for the beneficiaries, but the transfer to the
transferee by the original trustee(s) would not have been a nullity.[45]
Otherwise, the transferee obtains a good title[46] and the beneficiaries'
claims are only against the wrongdoing trustees.

MEASURE OF PERSONAL ACCOUNTABILITY TO BENEFICIARIES

While a defendant in a common law action such as in contract or
tort is liable to pay damages, a trustee or other fiduciary liable
under the equitable jurisdiction must produce accounts of his
stewardship of the trust property and is liable to account for any
unauthorised profits made by him or for losses flowing from his
conduct. "The Court of Chancery never entertained a suit for
damages occasioned by fraudulent conduct or for breach of trust.
... It was a suit for the restitution of the money or thing, or value of
the thing, of which the cheated party had been cheated."[47]

The "cheated party" is really the personified trust since a beneficiary (unless a bare trust for him has arisen) is not suing just on his
own behalf but to restore to the trust fund what is properly due to
it. He is seeking to make the trustee account to the trust fund for
money or other assets which the trustee has not received but ought
to have received ("surcharging" the accounts in essence) or for
money or other assets which the trustee has disposed of or dissipated when he ought not ("falsifying" the accounts in essence).

When a beneficiary falsifies the accounts because the trustee has
done what he is not authorised to do, the obligation of the trustee to
restore to the trust fund the assets of which he deprived it or their
value is of a more absolute nature than the common law obligation

[45] *Rolled Steel Products (Holdings) Ltd v British Steel Corporation* [1986] Ch. 246 at
303; *Hammersmith & Fulham LBC v Monk* [1992] 1 A.C. 478 at 493; *Vigier v IRC*
[1964] 2 All E.R. 907 at 914.
[46] An exception exists under Trusts of Land and Appointment of Trustees Act 1996,
ss.8(1), 16(3).
[47] *per* James and Bagallay L.JJ. in *Re Collier, Ex p. Adamson* (1878) 8 Ch.D. 807 at
819.

to pay damages for tort or breach of contract. It suffies that the ultimate loss would not have occurred but for the initial unauthorised conduct of the trustee. As Lord-Browne-Wilkinson states[48]:

"the basic rule is that a trustee in breach of trust must restore or pay to the trust estate either the assets which have been lost to the estate by reason of the breach or compensation for such loss. Courts of Equity did not award damages but, acting in personam, ordered the defaulting trustee to restore the trust estate: see *Nocton v Lord Ashburton* [1914] A.C. 932 at 952, 958, *per* Viscount Haldane L.C. If specific restitution of the trust property is not possible, then the liability of the trustee is to pay sufficient compensation to the trust estate to put it back to what it would have been had the breach not been committed: *Caffrey v Darby* (1801) 6 Ves. 488; *Clough v Bond* (1838) 3 My. and Cr. 490. Even if the immediate cause of the loss is the dishonesty or failure of a third party, the trustee is liable to make good that loss to the trust estate if, but for the breach, such loss would not have occurred: see *Underhill and Hayton, Law of Trusts and Trustees* (14th ed., (1987)) pp.734–736: *Re Dawson decd.; Union Fidelity Trustee Co Ltd v Perpetual Trustee Co Ltd* [1966] 2 N.S.W.R. 211; *Bartlett v Barclays Bank Trust Co Ltd (Nos. 1 and 2)* [1980] Ch. 515. Thus, the common law rules of remoteness of damage and causation do not apply."

Thus, if T wrongfully pays £x to Y or invests £x in unauthorised investments the expenditure and any assets purchased will be disallowed in the accounts. T will be strictly treated as having been a good man and spent his own £x, so that T is treated as retaining the £x in the trust fund and so has to restore £x. Indeed, if he had wrongfully sold an authorised investment worth £x to purchase an unauthorised investment now worth half of £x, when the authorised investment if retained would have been worth £2x, T must restore such investment or its value to the trust by selling the unauthorised investment and making up the balance of £2x (after taking account of the proceeds of sale) out of his own pocket.[49] The beneficiaries have a right to elect whether or not to falsify the accounts and so will not complain if the unauthorised investment has appreciated in value, although they can insist on it being sold and replaced with an authorised investment.

When a beneficiary surcharges the trustee's accounts for doing

---

[48] *Target Holdings Ltd v Redferns* [1996] A.C. 421 at 434; *Hodgkinson v Simms* (1994) 117 D.L.R. (4th) 15; *Re Duckwari plc* [1999] Ch.253 at 262–267.
[49] *Phillipson v Gatty* (1848) 6 Hare 26, 7 Hare 516; *Re Bell's Indenture* [1980] 3 All E.R. 425 at 437–439.

badly what he is authorised to do, he will make T account for what the value of the trust fund ought to have been but for the failure of T to act with due diligence. Thus, T is accountable for losses caused by his lack of skill and care but it is necessary to prove that the loss would not have happened but for his negligence or recklessness.[50] However, the losses have to be restored to the trust estate as a gross sum, not a sum net of tax that the beneficiaries would have had to pay if the breach of trust had not occurred: the beneficiaries' liabilities do not enter into the picture because they arise not at the point of restoration of value of the trust fund but only at the point of distribution of capital or income out of the trust fund.[51] Otherwise, equity applies similar rules to the common law rules on causation and remoteness of damage[52] except that Lord Browne-Wilkinson has suggested, that, to encourage high standards in trustees, losses may be assessed with the benefit of hindsight,[53] even if hindsight cannot be used to determine whether or not conduct amounted to a breach of trust.[54]

Deterring trustees from breaking their fiduciary duty of undivided loyalty to the beneficiaries are strict rules preventing trustees from exploiting their strong position against vulnerable beneficiaries and so making them liable for profits made out of trust property or out of their position.[55] They are under a strict proprietary liability under a constructive trust of the profits made out of trust property or their position as trustee, while also under a strict personal liability to account for such profits. It is immaterial that the beneficiaries suffered no loss and that the trustee acted honestly in the interests of the beneficiaries who also benefited but would not have profited but for the trustee's conduct.[56] Equity makes every presumption against a trustee who breaches his fiduciary duties. Thus, if he improperly takes for himself property for which he is accountable to the beneficiaries he cannot escape liability merely by delivering up the property (with any income received therefrom) where the property has fallen in value. He is, instead, presumed to have sold the property at its highest value between the date of his breach of duty and the date of judgment.[57]

---

[50] *Target Holdings Ltd v Redferns* [1996] A.C. 421.
[51] *Bartlett v Barclays Bank Trust Co. Ltd* (No. 2) [1980] Ch. 515 at 543.
[52] *Bristol & West B.S. v Mothew* [1998] Ch.1; Sir Peter Millett, "Equity's Place in the Law of Commerce" (1998) 114 L.Q.R. 214.
[53] in *Target Holdings v Redferns* [1996] A.C. 421 at 439.
[54] *Re Chapman* [1896] 2 Ch. 763 at 774; *Nestle v National Westminster Bank (No. 2)* [1993] 1 W.L.R. 1260.
[55] *Boardman v Phipps* [1967] 2 A.C. 46; *Att.-Gen. of Hong Kong v Reid* [1994] A.C. 324.
[56] *Warman International Ltd v Dwyer* (1995) 68 A.L.J.R. 362; *Boardman v Phipps* [1967] 2 A.C. 46.
[57] *Nant-y-glo & Blaina Ironworks Ltd v Grave* (1878) 12 Ch.D. 738.

An example of the interaction between falsifying and surcharging the trustee's accounts is provided by *Target Holdings v Redferns*,[58] as explained by Millett L.J.[59] In that case the defendant, a solicitor, held the plaintiff's money on trust for the plaintiff, but with authority to use it to enable the defendant's client to buy premises in exchange for a duly executed mortgage of the premises in favour of the plaintiff and the supporting documents of title. The defendant paid the money over to the client's order without obtaining the documents. This was an unauthorised application of trust money which entitled the plaintiff to falsify the account, so that the money would be treated as retained by the defendant and still available for the authorised application. The subsequent obtaining of the relevant documents three weeks later perfected the authorised task, so that the plaintiff could not falsify the account. There only remained the possibility of surcharging the account if the plaintiff proved that the loss caused to it by the client's mortgage fraud (resulting in the plaintiff lending one and a half million pounds on premises subsequently sold for half a million pounds) would not have happened but for the defendant's failure to obtain the relevant documents before paying over the plaintiff's money. Thus, the plaintiff could not obtain summary judgment for one million pounds but would have to prove at a full trial that its loss was caused by the defendant's failure to obtain the relevant documents before parting with the plaintiff's money.

The rate of interest payable by trustees in respect of capital that they have to replace is the rate payable by the court's special account for funds invested with the court.[60] However, a higher rate will be charged where the trustee actually received a higher rate (for example in respect of misappropriated capital) or should have received a higher rate (for example sold an authorised investment bearing 10 per cent for an unauthorised investment bearing five per cent) or the commercial rate (one per cent above the London clearing banks' base lending rate) is applicable. Such rate applies where he has made, or is presumed to have made as a result of falsifying the account, unauthorised use of trust moneys for his own purposes but the actual return from such use is unascertainable: compound interest is payable.[61]

---

[58] [1996] A.C. 421. Further see *Youyang Pty Ltd v Minter Ellison* [2003] H.C.A. 15.
[59] "Equity's Place in the Law of Commerce" (1998) 114 L.Q.R. 214 at 225–227.
[60] Court Fund Rules 1987, rr.26, 27.
[61] *Wallersteiner v Moir (No. 2)* [1975] Q.B. 373 at 388, 397; *Westdeutsche Landesbank v Islington LBC* [1996] A.C. 669.

TRUSTEE'S PERSONAL LIABILITY TO OUTSIDERS

Trusts have no legal personality so it is the trustees who are personably liable, jointly and severally, to the full extent of their own private property for debts, contracts, torts or taxes arising in respect of their acts or omissions as trustees,[62] unless they specifically contract that they shall not be under personal liability but shall only be liable to the extent that recourse may be had to the trust assets or unless legislation so provides, for example the Inheritance Tax Act 1984, s.204. The beneficiaries are not liable to such creditors since the trustees are not regarded as the beneficiaries' agents (though where the beneficiaries of full capacity are between themselves collectively entitled to the trust property the trustees normally have a personal right of indemnity against them[63] and it seems that this right may be exercised by the creditors by way of subrogation).

Where the trustees' obligations were incurred in the authorised administration of the trust they have a right of indemnity with an equitable lien against the trust assets, so reducing the assets available for the beneficiaries. This right enables a trustee to pay expenses out of the trust assets or to reimburse itself after personally paying the expenses, assuming that the state of accounts between the trustee and the beneficiaries (taking into account any losses flowing from breaches of trust) is such that there is some balance in the trustee's favour to which the right of indemnity may attach.

If the trustee does not pay up then the creditors have a claim by way of subrogation to the trustee's right of indemnity. Since the creditors stand in the shoes of the trustees their right is no better than the trustee's, so they will need to show that their debt was incurred in the authorised administration of the trust and that the state of accounts between the trustee and the beneficiaries leaves a balance for satisfying the debts.

Exceptionally, in the case of charitable or public trusts where members of the organisation or employees in improperly carrying out the charitable or public purposes commit torts the charitable or public corporation or the charitable trustees will be obliged to resort to the charitable or public funds to compensate victims of the torts.[64]

---

[62] *X v A* [2000] 1 All E.R. 490.
[63] *Balkin v Peck* (1998) 1 I.T.E.L.R. 717, (1998) 43 N.S.W.L.R. 766.
[64] *Mersey Docks & Harbour Board Trustees v Gibb* (1866) LR 1 HL 93; *Re Christian Brothers of Ireland in Canada* (2000) 184 D.L.R. (4th) 445, 3 I.T.E.L.R. 34.

BENEFICIARIES' RIGHTS AGAINST OUTSIDERS

It is the trustees who manage the trust property, and rights and duties thereby arising involve only them and not the beneficiaries, unless they have given possession of a trust asset (for example a painting or necklace) to a beneficiary who may then bring a common law action against outsiders to protect his better legal claim to possession. The trustees have full powers under s.15 of the Trustee Act 1925 to compromise claims and compound liabilities.

If the trustees have not exercised or do not properly exercise such powers then it may be that they can be replaced by new trustees who will obtain for the trust, for example, the benefit of a settlor's or borrower's covenant (a promise in a deed) or of a claim in negligence against some adviser. Instead, especially if replacement by the court will be messy and protracted then, exceptionally, the beneficiaries may bring an action as claimants against the outsider but joining the trustees as co-defendants, so that all interested parties will be present and be bound by the judgment.

If outsiders dishonestly assist trustees to commit a breach of trust then, even though trust property no longer is in their possession or never was in their possession, the outsiders will be personally liable to account for resulting losses, though this will be of little value if they are bankrupt.

If outsiders, who are not bona fide purchasers of the trust property without notice or who have not paid the purchase price of land to two trustees or a trust corporation (which has the statutory effect of detaching the beneficiaries' interests from the land and attaching them, instead, to the proceeds of the sale), have trust property or its traceable product in their possession then they hold it on constructive trust for the beneficiaries, who will thus be fully protected even if the outsiders are bankrupt. In reality, however, most persons who become insolvent realise all assets at their disposal to pay off pressing creditors, who will be bona fide purchasers without notice of the beneficiaries' interests, so often there will be no traceable trust property.

PATERNALISTIC FUNCTION OF COURT OF CHANCERY

Under Part 64 of the Civil Procedure Rules it is a straightforward matter for the trustees or beneficiaries to apply to the Chancery Division of the High Court for guidance on any aspect of the trust relationship, the costs to be paid out of trust funds. Trustees can only recover their costs if acting reasonably so, to ensure that the trustees may charge to trust funds any costs of any legal proceedings against outsiders involving them as claimants or defendants, the leave of the Chancery Court will always be sought to take part in such proceedings.[65] The court has power under s.61 of the Trustee Act 1925 to relieve a trustee from what is or may be a breach of trust but only if he acted honestly and reasonably and ought fairly to be excused for the breach *and for omitting to obtain the directions of the court* in the matter in which he committed such a breach or possible breach. It is thus expected that the directions of the court will be sought in all matters of doubt.

SUPREMACY OF THE TRUST INSTRUMENT

The settlor in his trust instrument may modify or exclude the non-mandatory rules otherwise applicable to trusts, so, for example, allowing a trustee to profit from the trust without accounting therefore if an independent co-trustee approves, or exempting a trustee from liability for losses so long as he acted in good faith, or directing the trustee to retain a controlling shareholding in a private company (which comprises 80 per cent of the value of the trust fund) and not to diversify the trust fund, unless advised otherwise by a person specified as a "protector" or the majority of a designated committee. The settlor may give the trustees exclusive power to determine issues of fact and to determine what expenses should be charged to capital and to income, and what receipts should be allocated to capital or to income, irrespective of whether such receipts be characterised as of capital or income nature, but he cannot oust the jurisdiction of the court to determine legal issues concerning the validity and construction of the trust and the extent of rights thereunder or to characterise expenses or receipts as capital or income in nature.

Indeed, if the settlor goes too far in exempting his trustees from duties and liabilities to the beneficiaries so that the beneficiaries really have no rights to enforce, the court will characterise the trustees as trustees only for the settlor or as themselves, full legal and beneficial owners. The essence of the trust is that there are beneficiaries who can enforce their rights against the trustees, the Attorney General exercising these rights on behalf of the Crown as *parens patriae* in the case of charitable purpose trusts. Thus, non-charitable purpose trusts have often been stated to be void for lack of beneficiaries capable of enforcing them.

As Millett L.J. stated in *Armitage v Nurse*[66]: "I accept that there is an irreducible core of obligations owed by the trustees to the beneficiaries and enforceable by them which is fundamental to the concept of a trust. If the beneficiaries have no rights enforceable against the trustees there are no trusts."

---

[65] *Re Beddoe* [1893] 1 Ch. 547; *Alsop Wilkinson v Neary* [1995] 1 All E.R. 431.
[66] [1998] Ch. 241 at 253.

Exceptionally, where there is a trust for beneficiaries and they are all of full capacity and between them absolutely entitled to the trust property, they can take advantage of their proprietary right as collective absolute owner to claim the property for themselves to do with as they wish, despite the terms of the trust instrument or the settlor's current wish that the trust continue.[67]

Otherwise, the settlor's wishes prevail so that he can, in his trust instrument, make the exercise by the trustees of some of their functions subject to the consent of himself and after his death, of a protector (whether an individual or a company, for example owned by the settlor). However, if the real deal between the settlor and the trustee is that during the settlor's lifetime the income and the capital will be held to the order of the settlor despite the terms of the trust instrument, then the trust will be a sham.[68] Powers often reserved to a person normally referred to as a protector are the power to agree the trustees' remuneration, the power to remove a trustee and appoint new or additional trustees, and the power to change the law governing the validity and administration of the trust. It is even possible to structure a trust so that the trustees in managing the trust assets are responsible to a governing board responsible for an overall strategy, which the trustees have discretion to implement as they see best, although they are liable to be replaced by other trustees appointed by the board if the board loses confidence in them. Another possibility is for the trust instrument to require that the discretionary portfolio manager of the trust assets is to be the settlor (though expressly restricted from using that position to benefit himself or his spouse) with provisions to protect the trustee from liability in respect of the settlor's activities.

DYNAMIC ROLE OF EQUITY AND TRUSTS

A renowned equity judge, Sir George Jessel M.R. said of the rules of equity[69]:

> "It is perfectly well-known that they have been established from time to time—altered, improved, and refined from time to time ... We can name the Chancellors who first invented them and state the date when they were first introduced into Equity jurisprudence ... The doctrines are progressive, refined and improved."

He contrasted the rules of equity with the rules of the common law which were "supposed to have been established from time imme-

---

[67] See below pp.51, 101.
[68] *Rahman v Chase Bank (CI) Trust Co* [1991] Jersey LR 103.
[69] *Re Hallett's Estate* (1880) 13 Ch. D. 696 at 710.

morial". As his use of the word "supposed" reveals, this is a fiction to which no-one even pays lip-service nowadays, when it has become very obvious that rules of the common law can and do change and when the House of Lords' Practice Statement of 1966 makes clear that their Lordships can overrule their earlier decisions. However, the courts in their equitable jurisdiction have more scope for developing the law in a conscionable manner than they have in their common law jurisdiction. Thus, relatively recent decisions[70] on common law principles of contract and commercial law reveal the technical nature of the judicial function ignoring morality and conscience, while Chancery judges are increasingly putting less weight on technical rules and more weight on underlying principles of conscionable and unconscionable behaviour,[71] taking advantage of equity's "inherent flexibility and capacity to adjust to new situations by reference to mainsprings of the equitable jurisdiction".[72]

Barristers who specialise in equity generally practise in Lincoln's Inn and it is from their ranks that judges are normally chosen for the Chancery Division of the High Court where cases primarily concerned with equity are heard. However, all lawyers and judges need to be well aware of equitable principles and remedies which reflect in refined fashion as a source of law the notion of equity as the natural sense of discretionary justice inherent in conscience. It is crucial to be able to supplement common law normal vision with equity "spectacles" and also European Community law "spectacles". We all need to have some ability as equity lawyers.

In litigation, claimants are well supported by equitable *in personam* injunction orders[73] compelling disclosure of assets or of evidence, freezing of assets so preserving them till the outcome of litigation, or even compelling a defendant in the jurisdiction to bring assets or evidence outside the jurisdiction into the jurisdiction or to transfer title to an immovable outside the jurisdiction to the plaintiff demanding this as absolutely entitled beneficiary.[74] The equitable remedy of specific performance may well be appropriate

---

[70] *Kleinwort Benson Ltd v Malaysia Mining Corporation* [1989] 1 W.L.R. 379; *Bank of Nova Scotia v Hellenic Mutual War Risks Assoc.* [1989] 2 Ll Rep. 238; *Banque Financiere de la Cité v Westgate Insurance Co Ltd* [1989] 2 All E.R. 952, [1990] 2 All E.R. 947; *Law Debenture Trust Corp v Ural Caspian Oil Corp.* [1995] 1 All E.R. 157.

[71] *Re Montagu's S.T.* [1987] Ch. 264 at 278; *Gillett v Holt* [2001] Ch.210 at 232; *Wayling v Jones* (1993) 69 P. & C.R. 170.

[72] *Lonrho plc v Fayed (No. 2)* [1991] 4 All E.R. 961 at 969.

[73] *Mareva* "freezing" injunctions, *Anton Piller* "search" orders and ancillary orders.

[74] *Webb v Webb* [1994] Q.B. 696 (the father's action against his son, who owned a French house, related to the internal trustee-beneficiary in *personam* relationship, so the French court of the *lex situs* did not have exclusive jurisdiction under Art. 16 of the Brussels Convention).

or the remedy of personal liability to account as a fictitious or constructive trustee to impose secondary liability on a person involved in the primary liability of a fiduciary in breach of his fiduciary obligations. "Fiduciary" is an expanding accordion term: one can say that equity will regard a person as a fiduciary in his relationship with another when and in so far as that other is entitled to expect that he will loyally act in that other's interest (or in their joint interest to the exclusion of his own separate interest).

The archetypal fiduciary is a trustee of whom the highest standards of probity are expected: you ought to be able to trust a trustee! Indeed, notions of trust, embodied in the law relating to trustees, provide a key contribution to the commercial and social cement of society. A model of behaviour (for example in avoiding a conflict between one's fiduciary duty and one's private self-interest) is provided for fiduciaries like agents, employees, partners, company directors and some financial intermediaries, who, depending on the circumstances, will need to a greater or lesser extent to live up to the standards prescribed for trustees.

The fiduciary obligation is proscriptive, not prescriptive, and requires the fiduciary, unless otherwise authorised,[75] not to profit from his position and not to place himself in a position where there is a sensible possibility of a conflict between his self-interest and his altruistic duty or, if he is in such a position, he must prefer his duty over his self-interest. Nor must he put himself, unless authorised, into a position where his duty to one person or group of persons may sensibly conflict with his duty to another person or group of persons; while, if he is in such a position, he cannot prefer one over the other but must cease acting for both normally.[76] Breach of his fiduciary obligation of individual loyalty is strictly treated by the courts, with the fiduciary held responsible for all losses directly flowing from the breach, including losses increased by a general fall in land values or stock market values,[77] but breaches of a fiduciary's non-fiduciary obligations, like the duty to take care, are, however, treated in the ordinary way.[78]

There is more scope for lawyers and judges to use equity rather than common law to move with the times. The trust has been a very powerful instrument of social experimentation. In effect, it enabled a landowner to devise his land by will until Parliament made this directly possible at law. In effect, through deed of settlement companies, it enabled entrepreneurs to form joint-stock companies

---

[75] *Kelly v Cooper* [1993] A.C. 205.
[76] *Bristol & West B.S. v Mothew* [1998] Ch 1.
[77] *Hodgkinson v Simms* (1994) 117 DLR (4th) 151; (2003) 119 L.Q.R. 246, 267–268.
[78] *Smith New Court Securities Ltd v Scrimgeour Vickers* [1997] A.C. 254; *Bristol & West BS* (above).

within a limited liability framework[79] until Parliament made this directly possible at law. In effect, in enabled a married woman (whose property was wholly controlled by her husband at law) to have property for her own use until Parliament made this directly possible at law (so that there was then no longer one law for women with rich fathers and another for women without rich fathers). Currently, as Chapter 9 will show, constructive trusts and equitable proprietary estoppel are being utilised to provide a cohabitee (married or unmarried) with an equitable interest in a home belonging at law to the other cohabitee where to allow the legal owner full beneficial ownership would be unconscionable.

However, equity is man-made and so cannot be perfect; more-over, social and economic change requires the law to change. The procedures in the Court of Chancery were notoriously imperfect in the nineteenth century as Charles Dickens so vividly brought out in *Bleak House*. The courts, also, were too ready to find that precatory words created a trust, such officious kindness amounting to a cruel kindness indeed in some cases (for example where a widow was held not to have the capital for the benefit of herself and her children, but only to be life tenant interested in income, the capital passing to her children on her death), till the court's approach changed towards the end of that century. Equity's intervention to allow a mortgagor to redeem his mortgage (and so recover his property belonging at law to the mortgagee) even though the date for redemption had passed at law, was obviously just and conscionable, but it went too far in striking down all collateral advantages (for example, the mortgagor of an inn buying beer for an agreed period from the mortgagee) negotiated between the parties once the mortgage had been redeemed. In the twentieth century it had to adapt to commercial realities and allow the advantages to continue unless this would be unconscionable in the circumstances or in restraint of trade.

After the Second World War Lord (later Viscount) Simonds led the House of Lords to be very strict on what could rank as a valid charitable purpose trust. However, if the trust could be char-acterised not as a purpose trust (and so void if not charitable) but as a discretionary trust for a large class of people, it faced the problem that the test for certainty of objects of a trust was based on the formal distinction between a *trust* (imposing a mandatory duty on the trustees in favour of *beneficiaries*) and a *power* (giving trustees the option if they wished to benefit *objects* of the power). For a

---

[79] See F.W. Maitland, "The Unincorporate Body," *Collected Papers*, iii, 278, though nowadays the courts have become more sophisticate in preventing the exploitation of trading trusts: see my Chapter "Trading Trusts" in Glasson (ed.) *The International Trust* (Jordan Publishing, 2002).

power of appointment to be valid it simply sufficed if the trustees could say of any person who might be presented to them, that he was or was not within the class of objects of the power, but for a trust to be valid it was necessary to be able to draw up a definite comprehensive list of everyone within the class of beneficiaries of the trust. This meant that a discretionary trust for a large class of people, not amounting to a section of the public so as to make the trust charitable, would often be void because of the impossibility of drawing up a comprehensive list of each and every member of the discretionary class. Thus, many socially desirable trusts were void.

Lord Wilberforce therefore led the House of Lords by a 3:2 majority in 1970 to make the certainty test for discretionary fiduciary powers apply also to discretionary trusts, leaving fixed trusts (*i.e.* for distribution of property equally between a class of beneficiaries) alone subject to the comprehensive fixed list test. He was fortified in moving the goalposts by some very old case law and by the reality that the weak position of B, a member of a large discretionary class of *beneficiaries* of a trust or of *objects* of a fiduciary power, is actually in practice almost the same whether interested under a trust or a power.

Where the "conscience" of the Court of Equity has developed beyond a "crystallised" living conscience and, most exceptionally, become a "fossilised" conscience with no scope for regeneration, then the legislature has to intervene, as it did in 1964 in lengthy complex fashion in respect of the Rule against Remoteness (or Perpetuities) which in many cases had become a capricious snare for the unwary, though there was some need to prevent the dead ruling the living for too long through the medium of trusts. Some consider that the effect of the beneficiary principle as a rule against pure purpose trusts, unless they are charitable, needs to be changed because it prevents the implementation of desirable social, professional or commercial purposes. However, any change will need to take into account, through consultation and research, of wide-ranging policy issues and the problems of enforcement. It may be that legislation will be necessary, as for example in Bermuda, Jersey, the Isle of Man and the Cayman Islands, where legislation requires appointment of an "enforcer" before non-charitable purpose trusts can become enforceable if the English courts are to go beyond construing some apparent pure purpose trusts as in substance trusts for the benefit of beneficiaries with a right to enforce the trust.[80]

On the other hand, such foreign non-charitable purpose trusts

[80] *e.g. Re Denley's Trust Deed* [1969] 1 Ch. 373; *Re Lipkin's W.T.* [1976] Ch. 235. On the amazingly flexible Cayman "STAR" trusts for purposes or for people or both, see D.J. Hayton (1998) 8 Offshore T.R. 43.

with expressly appointed enforcers have to be recognised as such under the Recognition of Trusts Act 1987 unless this would be manifestly incompatible with English public policy.[81] It is hard to see the manifest incompatibility of a non-charitable purpose trust enforceable by an expressly appointed enforcer with a charitable trust enforceable by the Attorney General or the Charity commissioners or an "interested person",[82] or with a private trust for beneficiaries enforceable by the beneficiaries or, if they are minors, unborn or otherwise unascertained, enforceable against third parties by the trustees or by replacement trustees if the original trustees had been acting in breach of trust. In each case there is an enforceable obligation as required at the core of the trust concept: just as a car needs an engine so a trust needs an enforcer, one could say.[83]

Once an otherwise English trust is valid as a non-charitable purpose trust because, say, Jersey law has been made the governing law and an enforcer has been appointed, one wonders why such a trust should not be allowed to develop as a valid English trust if limited to a valid perpetuity period and the purposes are certain and workable: the old cases rejecting non-charitable purpose trusts can be explained as really void for perpetuity or for unworkability.

Similarly, under the trust laws of some jurisdictions the settlor retains rights to enforce the trust, although not under English domestic law, but it would seem English private international law would afford the settlor locus standi. Indeed, since a person holding the office of protector appears to have locus standi before the courts in matters affecting that office,[84] there seems no reason why the settlor should not be expressly appointed protector with the right to see trust accounts (with supporting information) and to make the trustees account for their stewardship of the trust property so long as there are any unborn or unascertained beneficiaries: adult beneficiaries must have the right to decide for themselves what they do.

The Court of Equity in dealing with trusts has a liberal facilitative approach within limits set by the formalities requirements; by the 1964 Perpetuities and Accumulations Act; by the practical need for the enforceability by someone of certain and administratively workable trusts; and by the collective property right of a group of beneficiaries, between them absolutely entitled in equity to

[81] Art.18 of The Hague Trusts Convention incorporated into English law by Recognition of Trusts Act 1987. A non-assignable life interest valid in Scots, but not English, domestic law was upheld by the Court of Appeal in *Re Fitzgerald* [1904] 1 Ch. 573.

[82] Charities Act 1993, s.33 (1).

[83] D J Hayton (2001) 117 L.Q.R. 97 reprinted and updated in D J Hayton (ed.) *Extending the Boundaries of Trusts and Similar Ring-Fenced Funds* (Kluwer, 2002).

[84] Pt 64 Civil Procedure Rules; *Re Hare Trust* (2001) 4 I.T.E.L.R. 288.

the property, to divide the property between themselves (or otherwise dispose of it as they unanimously agree), regardless of the settlor's wish that a trustee should administer their property for purposes benefiting them. Once a valid trust has been created the court generally allows the trustees plenty of autonomy in their distributive functions to pay or apply capital and income for the benefit of the beneficiaries. The court will not interfere with the exercise of distributive discretions unless, in essence, bad faith is proved, which is very difficult. In commercial trusts like pension fund trusts where members of the trust scheme to secure[85] their benefits have earned their interests, there is a little more scope for intervention by the court taking into account the purpose of the trust in the employer-employee contractual relationship. However, the flexibility that allows the duties of trustees to be dramatically cut down from the 100 per cent imposed by equity in the absence of contrary intention in the trust instrument, to an irreducible core of, say, 25 per cent has led to statutory intervention insisting on a greater irreducible percentage for pension trusts. Indeed, pension trustees and any discretionary portfolio managers employed by them cannot be exempted from liability for negligent investment.[86] There are also statutory restrictions[87] preventing trustees of unit trusts or debenture trusts from exempting themselves from liability for negligence. Because trust law is so facilitative, statute has to intervene from time to time to set limits in the public interest. The Law Commission, indeed, is currently considering whether professional trustees should be prohibited from exempting themselves from liability for breach of trust.[88]

---

[85] *Wrightson Ltd v Fletcher* [2001] UKPC 23, para.28.
[86] Pensions Act 1995, s.33.
[87] Companies Act 1985, s.192, Financial Services and Markets Act 2000, s.253.
[88] Consultation Paper No.171 required responses by May 1, 2003.

CHAPTER TWO

Different Types of Express Trusts

PROLOGUE

Some obvious points merit mention. In his lifetime, a settlor may set up an *inter vivos* trust and he may by will provide on his death for the creation of a *testamentary* trust. It is possible for the *inter vivos* trust to be something of a "will substitute", for example S transfers virtually all his property to S and T on trust for S for life, remainder to S's children in equal shares, but with powers for S to revoke the trust, for S to appoint the capital by deed or by will in unequal shares to his children, and for S and T to appoint capital to S from time to time if they see fit. On S's death T may then administer S's estate without the need for taking out a grant of probate to S's estate which will reveal S's wealth to the world (including prospective writers of begging letters or even kidnappers). It is crucial that T exercises an independent discretion (and does not, under an arrangement with S, simply do whatever S tells him) because otherwise the trust will be regarded as a sham and the trust property will remain part of S's estate passing under his will or intestacy.[1]

A settlor can create a *capital* settlement by transferring certain assets outright to the trustees or can create an *income* settlement by covenanting with the trustees to transfer to them each year over a specified period a specified amount or a specified fraction of annual income to be used for the benefit of granchildren or employees. In the case of an asset, like a life assurance policy, transferred to the trustees there will be a capital settlement, though the settlor will

---

[1] *Rahman v Chase Bank (CI) Ltd* [1991] J.L.R. 103.

keep up payments of the assurance premiums as part of his regular expenditure out of income when such payments will be ignored for inheritance tax purposes.

INTERPLAY OF TRUSTS AND POWERS

A trust instrument will normally create not only fixed trusts or discretionary trusts but also *distributive* powers of appointment of income or capital (as opposed to *administrative* or *managerial* powers over the trust fund). The settlor can make a person that he intends to benefit or to be capable of benefiting if the trustee positively so decides fall into one of the following four categories.

(1) A beneficiary with a *fixed entitlement*, e.g. for A for life, then for B absolutely, so that A *must* be paid income and, on his death, B must receive the capital.

(2) A beneficiary with a *discretionary entitlement*, e.g. for such of my children and grandchildren as my trustee shall select in its discretion, so that the trustee *must* distribute to one or more of them income or capital as the case may be, but has power in its discretion to decide if a beneficiary receives nothing or such small or large amount as it chooses.

(3) An object of a *fiduciary power of appointment*, e.g. where there is the above fixed trust or discretionary trust, but the trustee has power, instead, in its discretion to appoint income or capital, as the case may be, to or for the benefit of the settlor's nephews and nieces if it so chooses: the trustee *may* if it wishes benefit some nephews and nieces to the extent it see fit, but, otherwise, it *must* benefit A and B or children and grandchildren as the case may be.

(4) An object of a *non-fiduciary personal power of appointment*, e.g. where there is a discretionary trust for a class of beneficiaries or a discretionary fiduciary power of appointment in respect of a class of objects, but the settlor or the settlor's widow or a designated protector or even the trustee has a power to add anyone in the world (other than himself and his spouse or issue or an associated company) to such class or a power directly to appoint income or capital to anyone (other than as above), and it is expressly stated - or necessarily implicit - that the holder of such power is under no duty from time to time to consider whether or not to exercise the power, that the holder is only subject to the duty not to exercise the power fraudulently outside its scope (e.g. by appointing assets to X in return for a share thereof or a bribe), and that this

duty is owed exclusively to the beneficiaries entitled to the trust property in default of any exercise of the power. The key is that the object of such a personal power is relegated to having merely the right to retain whatever property may happen to be appointed to him in due course.

It is important to appreciate that for a permitted accumulation period (see p.107 below) the settlor can confer on the trustee either a *power* to accumulate income so that income becomes part of the capital of the trust fund to the extent the power is exercised and income is therefore not paid to beneficiaries, or a *trust* to accumulate income, so that it must be added to the capital unless the trustee has a power-which the trustee exercises - to pay income instead to beneficiaries.

A final noteworthy feature is that most family discretionary trusts are drafted so that the trust instrument first sets out a power or trust to accumulate income and fiduciary powers of appointment of income or capital in favour of a class, before providing for a discretionary trust of capital for such members of that class as are alive at the date the trust terminates.

STATUTORY TRUSTS

Parliament has created statutory trusts for policy reasons to cover certain common situations.

Bankruptcy

Under the Insolvency Act 1986 a bankrupt's estate (which excludes property held on trust by the bankrupt) automatically vests in the trustee in bankruptcy, who is the official receiver or other person appointed under the Act. The trustee in bankruptcy's duties are to administer and realise the bankrupt's estate for the benefit of the creditors so as to satisfy their claims to as great an extent as is possible.

Intestacy

Under the Administration of Estates Act 1925 on a person's death intestate, those who take out letters of administration to his estate hold the estate on trust with power to sell it, to use the proceeds for paying his debts, expenses and other liabilities and, then, to distribute the estate amongst those entitled under the intestacy rules.

Co-ownership of Land

Whenever land in England and Wales is beneficially co-owned the Law of Property Act 1925, as affected by the Trusts of Land and Appointment of Trustees Act 1996, treats the land as held on trust for the co-owners with power to sell the land. Thus, if P and Q purchase a house in the name of P alone or of P and Q, then P or P and Q will hold the house on trust for P and Q with power to sell it. If a purchaser knows or ought to know (for example has constructive notice through actual co-occupation of the premises) that there is a trust he must pay his purchase money to two trustees or a trust corporation to obtain a good title free from any co-owner's equitable interest.[2]

Solicitors or licensed conveyancers acting for two co-owners will thus vest the legal title in the co-owners as joint tenants. Where land was unregistered land the trust for the co-owners, either as joint tenants or as tenants in common in equal or unequal but undivided shares, will have been set out in the conveyance. Where there are two registered proprietors of registered land the Land Registrar will enter a "restriction" on the register of title preventing dispositions from taking effect unless moneys are paid to two trustees or a trust corporation: he will only allow payment to one proprietor if satisfied that the survivor of the two registered proprietors will be entitled to give a valid capital receipt as sole beneficial owner under the *ius accrescendi* of a joint tenancy.

It was to simplify conveyancing and to make co-owned land more easily marketable that the Law of Property Act 1925 decreed that the legal estate must be held by the co-owners not as tenants in common but as joint tenants, of whom there can never be more than four. On a death the legal estate remains in the survivors, by virtue of the *ius accrescendi* that is fundamental to a joint tenancy, and they can appoint others to be joint tenants with themselves of the legal estate, though in default the personal representatives of the last surviving joint tenant will appoint new trustees. The legal estate is held by the joint tenants on trust, with power to sell it, for any number of co-owners, who may be minors or mental patients or resident in remote inaccessible places and who will have equitable interests, whether as joint tenants or as tenants in common. The latter have undivided shares which may be freely disposed of *inter vivos* or by will. When a purchaser pays his purchase moneys to the two or more trustees (or a trust corporation solely acting as trustee) he obtains full legal title free from the beneficiaries' interests which are overreached (namely detached from the land and attached to

---

[2] *Williams & Glyn's Bank v Boland* [1981] A.C. 487; *Kingsnorth Trust Ltd v Tizard* [1986] 2 All E.R. 54.

the proceeds of sale to which the beneficiaries' right to trace now relates). Thus, purchasers and beneficiaries live happily ever after, and the requirement for the legal estate to be held only by joint tenants ensures that no co-owned property is left to stagnate because owned by 41 legal tenants in common, some of whom are minors, mental patients, difficult to reach, or plain pig-headed.

If problems arise ss.14 and 15 of the Trusts of Land and Appointment of Trustees Act 1996 enable the court to resolve the position, for example if the trustees refuse to sell or to allow the beneficiary to occupy the land, or they cannot obtain the consent of an equitable co-owner whose consent has been made requisite before sale or leasing can occur. The court may make such order as it thinks fit: it acts on the principle that if the purpose of holding the land for the benefit of the equitable co-owners has broken down, then the property should be sold so as not to lock up the value of one co-owner's interest in the property.[3] More flexible jurisdiction is available under ss.23 and 24 of the Matrimonial Causes Act 1973 in the case of married couples and, wherever possible, applications should be made thereunder to the Family Division, not under the 1996 Trusts of Land and Appointment of Trustees Act to the Chancery Division.[4]

Where a husband's trustee in bankruptcy is entitled to the husband's half (or whatever) share he may apply for an order for sale against the wife with the other share. Under s.335A of the Insolvency Act 1986 the bankruptcy court will make such order as it thinks just and reasonable having regard to the interests of the bankrupt's creditors, the conduct of his spouse so far as contributing to the bankruptcy, to the needs and financial resources of such spouse, to the needs of any children and to all the circumstances of the case other than the needs of the bankrupt. Where application is made one year from the bankrupt's estate vesting in the trustee in bankruptcy, the court must assume, unless the circumstances are exceptional,[5] that the interests of the creditors outweigh all other considerations.

Settled Land Act Settlements and Trust for Sale Settlements

Before the Trusts of Land and Appointment of Trustees Act 1996 made it impossible to create new Settled Land Act settlements, where land was settled on trust—but *not* on trust for sale—for persons by way of succession (for example where a farm or manor-

---

[3] *Re Citro* [1991] Ch. 142; *Mortgage Crpn v Shaire* [2001] Ch.743; *Bank of Ireland Home Mortgages Ltd v Bell* [2001] 2 F.L.R. 809.
[4] *Tee v Tee* [1999] 2 F.L.R. 613.
[5] See *Re Halliday* [1981] Ch. 405; *Re Citro* [1991] Ch. 142.

house was left by will to W for life, remainder to R for life, remainder to S absolutely) a Settled Land Act ("S.L.A.") settlement arose. Under this 1925 Act the legal estate in the land must be vested in the tenant for life who has full powers of sale and limited powers of leasing and mortgaging, and whose powers cannot be ousted, curtailed or hampered in any way. The tenant for life is "king of the castle", but purchase money must be paid to the Settled Land Act trustees (of whom there must be two unless a trust corporation is trustee) if the purchaser is to obtain a good title and the beneficiaries' interests are to be overreached. As time goes by there will be fewer and fewer S.L.A. settlements as their trust periods expire.

The standard practice on creating a settlement for persons beneficially interested successively where the trustees, and not the life tenant, were to be in control, was to vest the property in trustees on trust for sale with power to postpone sale. The trustees for sale then control matters, though it is possible to prevent them selling or leasing without the consent of the life tenant or of X if such consents are expressly made requisite by the trust instrument. Capital moneys must be paid to two trustees for sale or a trust corporation if the purchaser is to obtain a good title and the beneficiaries' interests are to be overreached.

After the 1996 Trusts of Land and Appointment of Trustees Act, co-owning trustees do not have to be trustees for sale with power to postpone sale, so that it is common to vest property in trustees to hold the property with power to sell it or otherwise deal with it. Beneficiaries under trusts for sale of land, like beneficiaries under trusts of land, are now regarded as having interests in land; the doctrine of conversion, based on "Equity looks on that as done which ought to be done", whereby land held under a duty to sell it was regarded notionally as an interest in money (personalty as opposed to realty), was largely abolished by s.3 of the 1996 Act.

CHARITABLE (OR PUBLIC) PURPOSE TRUSTS

Gifts for charity are usually made to charitable trustees, but they may be made to charitable corporations (for example incorporated colleges, hospitals). In the latter case the corporation is vested with full beneficial ownership of the gifted property but it must use the property for the exclusively charitable objects specified in its memorandum of association or constitution, which cannot be changed so as to make the corporation's objects no longer charitable.

Philanthropy is encouraged since gifts for charity are exempt from capital gains and inheritance taxes whilst income tax relief is also available. Charities (whether charitable trusts or corporations) are exempt from income, capital gains, corporation and inheritance taxes, except that they have to pay income or corporation tax on trading income. A charity can indirectly avoid this by forming a trading company and have the company covenant to pay its net profits to the charity for a period exceeding three years or transfer profits back via the Gift Aid Scheme. The Cabinet Office Strategy Unit has proposed removing such need for a separate trading company.

Charitable trusts receive favoured treatment when contrasted with private trusts. They can last indefinitely. They need not have objects which are certain, so long as the settlor revealed a general charitable intention so that a *cy-près* scheme may be formulated by the court (or the Charity Commissioners) so as to lay down certain objects consistent with the general intention. The objects may amount to pure abstract purposes, rather than comprise persons benefiting directly or indirectly and having *locus standi* to sue to enforce the trust, since the Attorney General (acting for the Crown as *parens patriae*) has *locus standi* to enforce the charitable purpose trust. With charitable purpose trusts there is obviously no question of equitable property vested in beneficiaries. The trustees are full owners of the property but must as fiduciaries use it for the charitable purposes. The Attorney General can trace improperly transferred trust assets into the hands of anyone except a bona fide purchaser without notice of the trusts: the trust assets are unavailable for creditors if the trustee becomes bankrupt because the assets are not part of his patrimony. When property has been effectively dedicated to a charitable organisation or purpose which subsequently fails, the property is applied *cy-près* by the court or by the Charity Commissioners for some closely allied organisation or purpose. Thus the property does not revert by way of resulting trust to the settlor or his legatees or devisees.

As will be shown in Chapter 4, for trusts to receive favoured treatment as charitable they must be for the relief of poverty, or satisfy the test of being for the public benefit (rather than for the benefit of a private class of persons) and be for the advancement of religion or for the advancement of education or for other purposes beneficial to the community which have been held charitable or which are analogous to such purposes. Political propaganda masquerading as education is not charitable; neither is a trust with a main object to change the law with new public legislation or to influence foreign policy of the government.

A settlor seeking to set up a new charitable trust, as opposed to adding assets to existing charitable trusts, needs to negotiate the terms with the Charity Commissioners, who will consult with the Inland Revenue before deciding whether to register the trust as a charity. It is possible to appeal to the courts against the Commissioners' decisions but the cost is a major deterrent: it is easier to comply with the Commissioners' requirements. Thus the Strategy Unit has recommended that a new independent tribunal be established to enable decisions to be challenged at a reasonable cost.

In the case of disaster funds charitable status may well be less satisfactory than that of a private discretionary trust for the affected class of people. A charitable trust will have to be for the relief of those in need as a result of a disaster, with the result that those individuals cannot receive benefits over and above those appropriate to their needs, though many of them may consider that the funds should be wholly divided amongst them, no enrichment really being sufficient compensation for the distress. Surplus funds must instead be applied for other allied specified charitable purposes or under the *cy-près* jurisdiction of the court or of the Charity Commissioners. This can cause much bitterness and recrimination as happened in respect of the millions of pounds subscribed following the Aberfan disaster in 1966 when a coal tip avalanche killed 116 children and 29 adults.

Since the 1980's private discretionary trusts, instead of charitable trusts, have been set up and the trustees have produced schemes for allocation of benefits so that the whole fund can be distributed amongst the affected class within a year or so, for example Penlee Lifeboat Disaster Ferry Fund (1981), Bradford City Football Stadium Fire Fund (1985), Herald of Free Enterprise Fund (1987). Though such trusts are subject to income tax at 34 per cent, recipients with lower tax rates can make a tax repayment claim.

PRIVATE FAMILY TRUSTS

Births, marriages, divorces, or intimations of mortality often lead to the creation of trusts. Tax considerations will play a major role in encouraging a settlor to divest himself of his property and in determining the type of trust to be created to preserve the family wealth from the clutches of the taxman and of improvident spendthrift beneficiaries.

The settlor's tax environment is one where income tax is payable on income (including trading profits from disposals of assets by way of trade), capital gains tax is payable on gains made from disposals of assets other than by way of trade (*i.e.* disposals of capital assets and not trading assets), and inheritance tax is payable on the amount by which a person's estate is diminished by a chargeable transfer of value on death, or *inter vivos* to discretionary trustees or by any *inter vivos* gift, if the transferor does not survive his gift (a potentially exempt transfer) by seven years. For 2003–2004 income tax at 10 per cent ("starting-rate") is charged on an individual's taxable income up to £1,960 per annum, 22 per cent from £1,960 to

£30,500 ("basic-rate"), and 40 per cent thereafter ("higher-rate"). Basic- and starting-rate taxpayers pay only 20 per cent on most savings and investment income (the tax normally being deducted at source, so affording a tax credit to the taxpayer), although higher-rate taxpayers have a further 20 per cent to pay. Dividends are taxed at 10 per cent up to the basic limit and at 32.5 per cent above that limit. For net capital gains over £7,900 an individual pays capital gains tax at his highest income tax rate. For inheritance tax on death the rate is 40 per cent once the nil-rate-band of £255,000 is exceeded, while chargeable lifetime transfers to discretionary trustees suffer half that rate once the £255,000 cumulative total of chargeable transfers in the preceding seven years has been exceeded.

The settlor has scope for saving inheritance tax if he survives a potentially exempt transfer by seven years or in the case of transfers on discretionary trusts (other than favoured accumulation and maintenance trusts) takes advantage of the £255,000 nil rate band or of limited exemptions. He may "hold over" his capital gains on assets transferred to the discretionary trustees so that they take over the assets at his original acquisition cost. He will avoid high income tax rates (currently 40 per cent but up to 98 per cent, including the 15 per cent investment income surcharge, in 1978–79) on income from the capital he has irrevocably settled if he and his wife are excluded from all possible benefit and his unmarried infant children are not beneficiaries or otherwise do not receive any benefits till attaining majority or earlier marrying. Income may be accumulated under a valid power in that behalf and thereby capitalised, since by being added to the capital it acquires the nature of capital. Income will bear tax at an additional rate above basic rate tax so taking the rate up to 34 per cent. Accumulated income may usefully be paid out as capital to a beneficiary liable to income tax at higher rates than 34 per cent. If a beneficiary is liable to lower rates than 34 per cent, then unaccumulated income should be paid to him so that he can obtain a tax credit for the tax suffered by the trust and make a tax repayment claim.

Trusts receive different tax treatment depending on whether they are bare trusts, interest in possession trusts, discretionary trusts or specially favoured trusts, for example accumulation and maintenance trusts, protective trusts. The general position is now outlined without going into detailed anti-avoidance principles or exemption ramifications which may be discovered in specialist works.

Bare Trusts

A bare trust is one where the trustee holds property merely as a repository or nominee, with no active duties to keep a fair balance between beneficiaries with successive interests, so that he must transfer the property to or to the order of the absolutely entitled beneficiary or beneficiaries of full age and capacity. Such beneficiary or beneficiaries are regarded as the absolute owner(s). The trustees may have some powers and discretions which the beneficiaries collectively may override as in *Booth v Ellard*[6] where 12 family shareholders transferred their shares to trustees on trust to exercise the voting rights and certain other rights for the settlors' benefit.

One should note under the rule in *Saunders v Vautier*[7] that if property is settled on 10 year old B contingent upon him attaining 25 years of age but for the income to be accumulated for 21 years, so long as not needed for B's education or maintenance, then B once he is 25 years old has an absolute vested interest and can claim the property, so stopping further accumulations. Once he attains 25 the property ceases to be subject to active trusts. There is a bare trust with capital gains tax at 34 per cent becoming payable on B becoming absolutely entitled to the trust property unless B can claims holdover relief and takes over the property at its original base value when acquired by the trustees. Whether B obtains the trust property himself or leaves it outstanding in the names of the trustees he is treated as absolute owner of it for all subsequent tax purposes.

Interest in Possession Trusts (Fixed Interest Trusts)

A beneficiary has an interest in possession in a trust fund where he has a current fixed entitlement to an ascertainable part of the net income, if any, of the fund after deduction of sums paid by the trustees in the exercise of their *administrative* powers of management, for example where property is settled on trust for B for life or for B if he attains 30 years of age where B is an adult (since if he is a minor the effect of s.31 of the Trustee Act, discussed in Chapter 6, is to prevent B having any *right* to income till attaining majority or earlier marrying). If trustees have *distributive* powers giving them a discretion to distribute income to someone else or to accumulate income which may subsequently pass to someone else then, even though B may otherwise be a life tenant entitled to income not so disposed of, there will be no interest in possession.[8] So long as B has a current entitlement to net income, if any (since non-income producing property, like a life policy, may be settled), he has an interest in possession, even if the trustees may at any time terminate such interest by exercising an express power to appoint the capital to be

[6] [1980] 1 W.L.R. 1443.
[7] (1841) Cr. & Ph. 240.
[8] *Pearson v IRC* [1981] A.C. 753.

held on trust for others: until any such appointment B continues to have an interest in possession.

The income arising from an interest in possession trust is taxed as the beneficiary's at his highest marginal rate. The capital supporting the beneficiary's interest is treated for inheritance tax as if owned by the beneficiary, so if B for his life has the right to the income from one-third of a fund worth £900,000 he will be treated as if £300,000 were part of his estate. Thus, if his own estate is worth £150,000 at his death he will be treated as then making a chargeable transfer of £450,000, so inheritance tax at 40 per cent will be charged, the trustees paying the proportion of the tax in respect of the trust property. If he gifted the right to income to his son this would be a potentially exempt transfer of £300,000 with tax payable by the trustees if he died within seven years, but after seven years no tax would then be charged if he died leaving a £255,000 estate within the nil rate band of inheritance tax.

For capital gains tax purposes no tax is payable on the death of the beneficiary with an interest in possession: the base values of the assets are uplifted to the inheritance tax value at death so there is no double charge to both capital taxes. If an interest in possession ends by someone becoming absolutely entitled to the property or part thereof other than on death, then capital gains tax at the marginal income tax rate for that person is payable on such property no longer subject to the trust taxation régime (unless, in the case of business assets only, hold-over relief is claimed, so deferring liability to tax) for example where A remarries when a fund is settled on A for life or until remarriage, remainder to B absolutely, or where C attains 30 years when a fund is settled on C if he attains 30. A disposal by a beneficiary of his equitable interest is not chargeable (unless it is an interest under a non-resident trust or he purchased it) since it is disposals by the trustees of the actual assets within the trust fund that alone are chargeable to capital gains tax, but there is an annual index-linked exempt allowance for gains, currently, of £3,950 (half an individual's allowance) in respect of trustees' disposals which may be spread across other trusts created by the settlor but subject to a minimum exemption of £790 per trust. Disposals by the trustees in managing the trust assets are liable to capital gains tax at 34 per cent. However, if the settlor or his spouse retains an interest in the settled property the chargeable gains are treated as accruing to the settlor and taxed at his marginal income tax rate which will normally be 40 per cent.

Discretionary Trusts (and other No-Fixed Interest Trusts)

The flexibility of discretionary trusts makes them a very attractive vehicle for family money. The settlor can transfer assets to trustees to distribute the income amongst such of the settlor's lawful issue or spouses or persons named in writing by such issue (for example to cover mistresses, illegitimate children, co-habitees of the same sex, poor friends of a beneficiary at boarding school) as the trustees may see fit, from time to time, until 21 years from the death of the last survivor of all the legitimate descendants of Queen Elizabeth II living at the date of the settlement, when the capital has to be distributed amongst such of the above class of beneficiaries then living in such amounts as the trustees shall see fit. The trustees can be given power to accumulate as much of the income as they see fit for up to 21 years from the date of the settlement, power to make interest-free loans (repayable on demand) to the beneficiaries, power to purchase land for rent-free occupation by beneficiaries under a licence (or opposed to a lease diminishing the value of the trust property), and power to appoint capital to any beneficiary or beneficiaries at any time and even power to terminate the trusts well before expiry of the specified perpetuity period. The trustees may, indeed, be given power to appoint non-resident trustees and to transfer all assets to such trustees and to replace English law as the governing applicable law by the law of the state of residence of the new trustees, so long as such state has the trust concept as part of its domestic law.

There is such flexibility so as to deal with fiscal, social or economic change in England as well as to cope with foreseeable or unforeseeable developments affecting a family over 110 years or so. However, discretionary trusts expressed to last no more than two years may often be found in wills where a testator cannot be sure what the needs of his relatives and dependants will be after his death and what will be the most tax-efficient way of dealing with such needs. It is advantageous for inheritance tax purposes that the trustees' dispositions in the two-year period are treated as if effected by the testator.

Every seven years a settlor can transfer the amount of the nil rate band (currently £255,000) into a discretionary settlement without having to pay inheritance tax. He can avoid capital gains tax by taking advantage of hold-over relief so that the trustees can take over his original base value of the asset. So long as the settlor or his spouse cannot benefit under the trust and their unmarried children do not receive benefits thereunder, the trust's income (whether accumulated or distributed) will be taxed at 34 per cent but a beneficiary paying a lower rate of tax can reclaim the tax difference in respect of income received, while higher rate taxpayers may receive capital (including accumulated income) tax-free. Interest-free loans or rent-free occupation of houses or flats will be income tax-efficient but the latter may be treated as the creation of an interest in possession so as to occasion an inheritance tax charge.

The maximum liability to inheritance tax is 6 per cent of the fund levied every 10 years as a periodic charge, but this rate is reduced by 100 per cent or 50 per cent to the extent that the trust fund comprises property qualifying for business or agricultural relief of either 100 per cent or 50 per cent. Death of a discretionary beneficiary or cesser of his interest occasions no inheritance tax charge. If during a 10-year period capital ceases to be subject to discretionary trusts (for example because it is distributed absolutely to a beneficiary or is settled on interest in possession trusts or on favoured trusts like accumulation and maintenance trusts) there will be an exit charge in respect of such capital. Essentially, the exit charge represents a proportion of the periodic charge payable on the next 10-year anniversary and depends on the time elapsed since the last such anniversary (since the full periodic charge is only levied on property subject to discretionary trusts for the whole 10-year period) and on the tax rate charged at the last anniversary. The exit charge rate before the first 10-year anniversary is calculated by reference to the amounts settled, so if shares in a private company worth an amount within the nil rate band are settled and the whole fund is distributed nine years later when worth £1 million (including capitalised income) no inheritance tax will be payable.

When a person (whether a beneficiary or a trustee of another trust) becomes absolutely entitled to part of the settled property as against the trustees, the assets comprised in that part are deemed to have been disposed of by the trustees for market value and capital gains tax at 34 per cent is payable unless inheritance tax is payable or the accumulation and maintenance trust exemption applies so that the gain will be "held-over" (with the person(s) taking over the trustees' original base cost of the assets). Disposals of trust assets by the trustees are liable to capital gains tax at 34 per cent when they sell trust assets in the course of their investments policy and exceed the small £3,950 annual allowance for gains. However, if the settlor or his spouse retains an interest in the settled property the chargeable gains are treated as accruing to the settlor and taxed at his marginal income tax rate which will normally be 40 per cent.

Accumulation and Maintenance Trusts

Settlors often wish to benefit minors but make absolute entitlement contingent on attaining 25 years of age rather than a mere 18 or 21, and this involves the use of trusts. A gift to a person of 25 years or more does not involve that person in inheritance tax charges while he retains the property: it was considered that gifts, having to take the form of trusts, to persons under such age should similarly not involve such persons in inheritance tax charges. Thus, accumulation and maintenance trusts for the benefit of persons under 25 years of age, though being trusts where no one has an interest in possession, are not subject to the periodic or exit charges applicable to discretionary trusts. If a beneficiary with an interest in capital contingent on attaining 25 years obtains an absolute right to income at the age of 18 (as will happen unless s.31 of the Trustee Act 1925 is excluded) so as to have an interest in possession, no inheritance tax charge arises then or when such person on attaining 25 becomes absolutely entitled to the capital, and there will be no capital gains tax charge if advantage is taken of hold-over relief.

For favoured treatment to be accorded to the settled property:

(1) one or more persons ("beneficiaries") must under the terms of the trust, on or before attaining an age not exceeding 25 years, become beneficially entitled to the capital or to the income;

(2) no interest in possession must subsist in it, and the income must have to be accumulated so far as not applied for the maintenance, education or benefit of a beneficiary;

(3) either all the beneficiaries must be grandchildren of a common grandparent or not more than 25 years must have elapsed since the trust was created or conditions (1) and (2) first became satisfied.

Under (1) it suffices that a beneficiary becomes entitled to income on or before attaining 25 years so that entitlement to capital may be postponed to the attainment of a greater age such as 35 or 50 years. These trusts for grandchildren are very useful, especially since the intervening generation's liability to inheritance tax, if, instead its members had an interest in the property passing to the grandchildren, will be "skipped over". There is the further advantage that no inheritance tax will be payable on creation of the settlement (a potentially exempt transfer) if the settlor survives for seven years.

Trusts for Mentally or Physically Disabled

It makes sense to create a trust for disabled persons for whom one is responsible and for whom one fears after one's death, especially if one survives for seven years after creating the trust so that no inheritance tax charge arises. Discretionary trusts for the benefit of those mentally disordered within the Mental Health Act 1983 or those in receipt of an attendance allowance under the Social Security Act 1986 are treated as interest in possession trusts for inheritance tax purposes, so that capital sums applied for their benefit are not taxable. The annual exemption from capital gains tax is the same amount as is available for individuals, *i.e.* £7,900.

Protective Trusts

To protect the spendthrift or the gullible from themselves or from exploitation a settlor may settle property on trust for B for life *until* bankruptcy or voluntary alienation or other event, whereby a third party would become entitled to the income. Thereupon, the trustees are to hold the property on discretionary trust to distribute the income during B's life amongst B, his spouse and issue or, if there is no spouse or issue, amongst B and the persons who would be entitled to the capital or income if B were dead. The expectation is that B will receive only so much as will satisfy his maintenance needs, while his spouse and issue will receive the surplus which may be spent so as indirectly to benefit B. This device became so popular that s.33 of the Trustee Act 1925 enables creation of this form of trust merely by directing that property is to be held for B for life "on protective trusts". It is possible to provide for the discretionary trust, arising after the event terminating the life interest, itself to cease, say, 10 years thereafter if B is then bankrupt no longer and for the property then to be held for B for life on new protective trusts.

In English law it is not possible to make property inalienable by directing that a beneficiary's equitable interest shall not be assigned, whether voluntarily or involuntarily, nor is it possible to flout a course of devolution prescribed by law by giving B an interest in property *on condition that* if he becomes bankrupt it shall pass to C instead of to B's trustee in bankruptcy. In the case of B's conditional interest the settlor gives B the whole interest with one hand but then takes the interest away from B with the other hand on the condition being satisfied: this is not allowed where the condition is bankruptcy, so B's interest is free of the condition and passes to his trustee in bankruptcy.

What is so different if B is given an interest *until* bankruptcy? Here the settlor with the one hand gives B an interest that automatically comes to its natural end on bankruptcy, so no question arises of the settlor wrongly taking away any interest with the other hand.

America does things differently with the "spendthrift trust" developed by case law in some States and by statute in others. A settlor can thereby provide that the beneficiary's equitable interest, giving him future entitlement to income or capital, cannot be assigned voluntarily or involuntarily: assets actually received by virtue of such interest are, however, available for alienation to creditors or others.

The special tax feature of protective trusts or trusts "to the like effect" (as where trustees have power to appoint capital to the beneficiary) is that for inheritance tax purposes the life tenant is

deemed to continue to have an interest in possession despite discretionary trusts having arisen on expiry of his determinable life
interest. Thus no tax is payable when capital is appointed to him.

Secret Trusts and Floating "Trusts"

A man with a mistress and illegitimate child can secretly look after
them while alive. After his death he can provide for them expressly
in his will, but a will is a public document. However, by will T may
leave, say, £150,000 to B absolutely, having obtained B's agreement
secretly:

(1) to hold £100,000 on trust for Joy Rider for life, then for
     her son, Sebastian absolutely; and
(2) to bequeath to Sebastian whatever of the £50,000 and
     interest thereon remains left in a deposit account (which B
     must open) after B has bona fide used as much of the
     account moneys as he requires to satisfy his own personal
     needs in his lifetime.

The former is a valid secret trust[9] enforceable by Joy and Sebastian,
whilst the latter is a floating "trust"[10] where B is absolute owner,
though subject to some fiduciary obligations, and the trust will only
crystallise to bind what is left in the account on B's death.

   Secret trusts may be fully secret, as in the above example where B
takes absolutely beneficially on the face of T's will, or half-secret, as
where B takes as trustee on the face of the will, though the terms of
the trust are not directly revealed, for example "to B to hold as I
have directed him". If this clause continued "by my letter of 21st of
last month" then such letter would be treated as incorporated as
part and parcel of the will. The grant of probate to T's personal
representatives would extend to the will *and* the letter, which would
both become public documents, and if a beneficiary named in the
letter happened to have been one of the two witnesses of the will,
then s.15 of the Wills Act 1837 would prevent him from receiving
any benefit under the letter treated as part of T's will. In contrast, a
beneficiary taking under a fully secret or half-secret trust is regarded
as taking a benefit outside the will (which first operates according to
its terms) so that it does not matter if he witnessed the will. It does
not seem satisfactory that the policy of the Wills Act can be so
easily avoided.

   Re Keen[11] currently creates a major distinction between fully

---

[9] *e.g. Ottaway v Norman* [1972] Ch.698; *Kasperbauer v Griffith* [2000] 1 WTLR 333.
[10] *Ottaway* (above); *Healey v Brown* [2002] W.T.L.R. 849 subject to criticism in
Underhill & Hayton on Trusts (16th ed) pp. 429–430.
[11] [1937] Ch. 236.

secret and half-secret trusts. For the former, it suffices that T's communication of his plan to B and B's acceptance thereof occurs at any time prior to T's death. For the latter, if communication is *after* the date of the will, the half-secret trust is void by virtue of a mistaken analogy with the doctrine of incorporation of documents by reference where it is impossible for a will to incorporate a future document. Once "the pass has been sold" and T can give the "go-by" to Wills Act requirements by creating a fully secret trust and thereafter orally communicating his changes of mind to B right up to his death, there seems no logical reason for prohibiting such communication after the creation of a half-secret trust, though one may sympathise with the court's instinct. Perhaps, legislation should bring fully secret trusts into line with half-secret trusts and extend section 15 of the Wills Act to cover beneficiaries under secret trusts.

Such legislation might also make it clear that *Re Gardner (No. 2)*[12] is hopelessly wrong in deciding that the interest of a beneficiary under a secret trust does not lapse if he predeceases the testator. The High Court judge mistakenly believed that the secret beneficiary obtained an equitable interest under a trust as soon as the secret trustee agreed with the testator to act as trustee of the testator's gratuitous promise for the beneficiary. However, at such stage, there is only a "spes" (a "hope") available for the beneficiary, for whom a completely constituted trust of particular property can only arise at the death of the testator if the beneficiary is then alive. There cannot be a trust of a "spes" (like the hope of inheriting property from T if he does not make a new different will or die insolvent) since such is not property and so cannot be held on trust or otherwise disposed of except pursuant to a contract.[13] You cannot make a *gift* of property which does not yet exist (*i.e.* a *spes*) though you can *contract* to sell or buy property which does not yet exist.

For obvious practical reasons a testator, as a safeguard, should put into the hands of the secret beneficiary some document evidencing the trust and signed by the secret trustee.

Trusts as Will-Substitutes

To avoid the need for a grant of probate and publicity, a settlor, S, can keep his cash and a share portfolio[14] in a joint bank account with W, so that W will take the balance on his death, and can create an immediate *inter vivos* trust of his other property by transferring it

---

[12] [1923] 2 Ch. 230.
[13] *Re Ellenborough* [1903] 1 Ch. 697.
[14] *Aroso v Coutts & Co* [2001] W.T.L.R. 797.

to trustees (of whom he could be one) to hold for S for life, remainder to W or such other persons as S might in his life notify in writing to the trustees, with S reserving in his lifetime either a power to revoke the trust in whole or in part or a power to appoint capital to anyone including himself, so that W only has a defeasible vested interest in remainder. Such a position where the trustees in effect hold the property to S's order *if* he orders it, is crucially different from the case where the trustees simply hold to S's order as where they hold on trust as to capital and income for S absolutely, with whatever remains on S's death passing to W, when there is a bare trust for S combined with a testamentary disposition in favour of W requiring compliance with the Wills Act 1837. However, the former situation would be treated as a sham if S controlled the trustees, and, in any event, the property would be available to satisfy a claim under the Inheritance (Provision for Family and Dependants) Act 1975 as part of S's "net estate". To avoid this the power of appointment should be vested in independent trustees instead of S.

PRIVATE PURPOSE TRUSTS

Anomalous Testamentary Trusts

Except for charitable purpose trusts, a trust must satisfy the beneficiary principle which requires there to be beneficiaries with *locus standi* to enforce the trust if there is to be a valid trust. However, as a concession to human sentiment the Court of Appeal[15] has accepted that there are some anomalous cases, not to be extended, where testamentary trusts have been upheld though the beneficiary principle was not satisfied.

These anomalous cases are trusts for the maintenance of particular animals, trusts for the erection or maintenance of graves and sepulchral monuments, trusts for the saying of masses in private (if this purpose does not rank as charitable), trusts for the promotion and furtherance of fox-hunting. To be valid these trusts must not require the income to be used for the particular purposes for longer than the common law perpetuity period of 21 years (or 21 years from the death of the last survivor of any specified lives in being at the testator's death). These trusts are sometimes referred to as trusts of imperfect obligation since the trustees are not forced to carry out the trust: they have *power* to carry out the trust, but if they do not use this power then the person entitled under the trust in default of exercise of such power will claim the property.

Sympathetic trustees of *inter vivos* or testamentary trusts may also be given *powers* to carry out purposes other than those in the

[15] *Re Endacott* [1960] Ch. 232.

anomalous list in the hope that they will carry them out even if they are not obliged to do so. *Trusts* for such other purposes are void (subject to possible developments if there is an expressly appointed enforcer as discussed p.40 above) and cannot be construed as if they were powers so as to have some validity.

Trusts for Purposes Directly or Indirectly Benefiting Persons

In *Leahy v Attorney General for New South Wales*[16] Viscount Simonds states: "A trust may be created for the benefit of persons but not for a purpose or object unless the purpose or object be charitable. For a purpose or object cannot sue, but if it be charitable the Attorney General can sue and enforce it." The case concerned a testator who left Elmslea and its contents (a 730 acre grazing property with a large 20 room house and various outbuildings) to a contemplative (and thus non-charitable) order of nuns by way of endowment for the religious purposes of the order. This trust offended the beneficiary principle as well as tying up the use of the settled property for longer than the perpetuity period.

Goff J. in *Re Denley*[17] regarded that trust as a type of "purpose or object trust the carrying out of which would benefit individuals, where that benefit is so indirect or intangible or which is otherwise so framed as not to give those persons any *locus standi* to apply to enforce the trust, in which case the beneficiary principle would apply. ... Where, then, the trust though expressed as a purpose is directly or indirectly for the benefit of an individual or individuals, it seems to me that it is in general outside the mischief of the beneficiary principle. ... The beneficiary principle is confined to purpose or object trusts which are abstract or impersonal," like trusts to further the interests of the Labour Party or to abolish vivisection.

He upheld an *inter vivos* trust of land to be maintained and used for a specified perpetuity period for the purpose of a recreation or sports ground for the benefit of employees from time to time of a specified company. These employees had *locus standi* to apply to the court for an order positively directing the trustees to give the employees the use of the land or negatively restraining any improper use or disposition of the land. This would also be the case if the employees were simply regarded as beneficiaries of a discretionary trust as Vinelott J. has pointed out.[18]

From *Barclays Bank Ltd v Quistclose Investments Ltd*,[19] has

[16] [1959] A.C. 457 at 478.
[17] [1969] 1 Ch. 373.
[18] *Re Grant's W.T.* [1980] 1 W.L.R. 360.
[19] [1970] A.C. 567; *Re EVTR* [1987] B.C.L.C. 646.

developed the principle that if A and B agree that A will lend B money for some specific purpose only, then if B effects the purpose there is simply a debtor-creditor relationship between A and B. Otherwise, the money is held on a resulting trust for A if indeed, no express trust for A can be found.[20]

Private purpose trusts have also been regarded as valid for the maintenance and support of two distressed ladies defrauded of their deceased father's estate and for paying funeral expenses of those killed in an horrific accident and caring for those disabled in the accident. In each case after the deaths of all the beneficiaries there was a resulting trust of surplus moneys for those who had subscribed the moneys. Sinking fund trusts of moneys paid to a landlord by tenants in order to build up a capital fund to replace plant and machinery in the building which may need replacement in many years time can also be valid as purpose trusts for the benefit of tenants. Indeed favourable fiscal legislation for maintenance funds for historic buildings underlines the validity of a trust for the purpose of maintaining an historic building for the benefit of the settlor's family in occupation. Also, trusts for providing education[21] for, or holidays for, employees, their spouses and dependants will be valid under *Re Denley* if restricted to the perpetuity period or otherwise saved under the Perpetuities and Accumulations Act 1964 as a discretionary trust for persons (as discussed in Ch.3).

If it happens that the persons benefited by the purposes are all sane adults, ascertained and between them the only persons entitled to benefit from the trust property, they may as the collective absolute owner terminate the trust purposes and divide the property between themselves under the *Saunders v Vautier* principle (fully discussed in Ch.3).

Employee Trusts

Employee Share Ownership Trusts (known as ESOPs for "employee share ownership plans") in conjunction with approved profit-sharing schemes are attractive for companies and employees. The company sets up the trust fund with sums deductible for corporation tax and the trustees then acquire shares in the company which are subsequently distributed to an approved profit-sharing scheme for appointment to individual employees without ranking as their income as perquisites obtained by reason of their employment nexus. Dividends on such shares will thereafter be taxable as the employees' income but if the shares are sold after three years

---

[20] *Twinsectra Ltd v Yardley* [2002] UKHL 12 [2002] 2 A.C. 164; C. Rickett [2002] Rest. LR 112.
[21] *e.g. Wicks v Firth* [1983] 2 A.C. 214.

there will only be a capital gains tax liability, against which each employee may set his annual exemption and any capital losses.

Employee trusts have the practical advantage for companies without a stock exchange quotation of creating a market in their shares, since the trust will have funds to purchase shares from a shareholder or his personal representatives. A company may also look to its employee trust for assistance, for example in fighting off a take-over, but the trustees have to be careful not to infringe their fiduciary duties to the beneficiaries.

Pension Funds (Superannuation Schemes)

It is in the interests of both the state and the individual for proper arrangements to be made for an individual's needs once he retires from paid employment. Private occupational pension schemes approved by the Revenue's Pension Schemes Office (formerly the Superannuation Funds Office) have many attractions. The employer's contributions will not be taxed as the employee's income and they will be deductible from the employer's taxable profits. The employee receives income tax relief on his own contributions through the Pay As You Earn provisions administered by the employer as unpaid collecting agent for the Revenue—trustees perform a similar function for the Revenue where the capital taxes are concerned. The pension fund though no longer exempt from income tax on dividend income is still exempt from capital gains tax on disposal of investments. It is not subjected to the inheritance tax régime for discretionary trusts involving periodic and exit charges, so no charge will arise on that part of an employee's entitlement that he may take as a capital lump sum. Any payment made on the employee's death before retirement to his dependants will not be charged to inheritance tax provided they are made at the trustee's discretion and not as of right. The trustees will almost invariably follow any written declaration of the deceased employee's wishes as to whom he would like to benefit unless those wishes have become out-dated.

If he survives to retirement the employee will either obtain a fixed percentage of his final salary (a maximum of one-sixtieth for each year worked not exceeding 40) under a final salary scheme, other-wise known as a "defined *benefit* scheme", or by virtue of a money purchase scheme, otherwise known as a "defined *contribution* scheme", he will be able to obtain a pension or annuity based on the sum accrued in his favour, taking account of all the defined contributions made over the years. Nowadays, to avoid risk, employers much favour defined contribution schemes with payments being made to a life assurance company.

A defined benefits pension fund is administered by trustees who make investments and pay out on retirement (for example an annual pension and, normally, also a lump sum, for example equivalent to one year's salary) or on death. Alternatively, the employer/employee contributions can be paid as premiums to an insurance company, which takes over the responsibility of providing for payments on retirement or death. Small self-administered schemes with no more than 12 members, who, must all be trustees, are particularly attractive for controlling shareholders of private companies, though there has to be an independent external trustee. The trustees can invest the pension fund money in purchasing shares in the company, lending money to the company, or purchasing premises for leasing to the company. However, for larger schemes the proportion of resources that may be invested in employer-related investments must not exceed five per cent while employer-related loans are prohibited. The trustees have to produce audited accounts and an annual return disclosing employer-related investments and any investment comprising at least 5 per cent of the scheme's assets.

The Pensions Act 1995 was enacted to give effect to most of the recommendations of the Goode Committee,[22] set up by the government in the light of worries as to disposal of surplus trust funds (the funds providing more than enough security for payment of members' entitlements and being capable of satisfying further expectations of members or of the employer) and, especially, as to the security and solvency of pension funds after Robert Maxwell's plundering of his companies' pension funds before his death at sea. It redresses the balance between the interests of employers and employees in favour of employees, so that employers cannot exploit the leeway afforded by use of the trust concept against the employees' interests.

Because of the difficulties for members of pension schemes seeking to challenge maladministration or breaches of trust by their trustees a Pensions Ombudsman has wide power to intervene against trustees on their behalf.[23]

Professional Compensation Funds

Members of certain professions subscribe to funds like the Law Society's Compensation Funds, Lloyd's Central Fund and the Investors' Compensation Scheme, the object of which is to provide compensation for losses or hardship incurred or likely to be incurred through the default or alleged default of persons carrying

---

[22] "Pension Law Reform", 1993 Cm 2342
[23] Pension Schemes Act 1993 ss.145–151 as amended by Pensions Act 1995 ss.157–160 and Child Support, Pensions and Social Security Act 2000 ss.53–54.

on a trade or profession or of their agents or servants. Such discretionary purpose trusts incur no inheritance tax charges.

Assets of Unincorporated Associations

Associations, clubs or societies which are not corporations cannot, as such, hold property since they do not have legal personality. Cash will be kept in a designated club bank account or building society account controlled by the treasurer as sole signatory or joint signatory with, say, the chairman, while other property will be vested in trustees on a bare trust to deal with it as directed by the committee on behalf of the members. This will generally be the result of the club rules (by which all members are contractually bound). Unless such rules prescribe otherwise, the trustees will have a right of indemnity out of the club's property but not against the club members personally. Subscriptions and outright gifts to the club will be regarded as accruing to the club's property held on a bare trust for the benefit of the members according to the club rules. On winding-up the club the property will be divided between the then members, except to the extent that third parties have claims against the club as a result of transactions entered into by the club committee or other managing organisation.[24]

Exceptionally, if a settlor expressly gives property to the club on trust to set it aside as a capital endowment and to use only the income for a prescribed charitable purpose (being one of the club's purposes), then such property will not belong to the club members but will be held separately by the club trustees for the prescribed purpose. If on dissolution of the club these trustees or new trustees appointed by them cannot carry out the prescribed purpose the trust property will be applied *cy-près* to similar purposes under an order made by the Charity Commissioners.

Trade Unions

Trade unions are unincorporated associations if not incorporated as a special registered body, but by ss.10 and 12 of the Trade Union and Labour Relations (Consolidation) Act 1992 they can make contracts in their own names, may sue or be sued in their own names, judgment can be ordered against them as if they were companies, and property will be vested in trustees on trust "for the union". The union is the primary beneficiary but this does not prevent the union members having an enforceable indirect interest in the trust fund which may be protected (for example by injunction and the appointment of a receiver) if the fund is being misused. To

---

[24] *Re Bucks Constabulary Fund Friendly Society* [1979] 1 W.L.R. 936.

counter the possibility that the majority of members may have contractual rights to change the rules retrospectively and excuse the union trustees from liability, s.16 of the 1992 Act provides that a member has *locus standi* to seek an order against the trustees in respect of currently unlawful applications of the union's property and this may lead to appointment of a receiver of the trust property and removal of the trustees.

Unit Trusts and Investment Trusts

In one broad sense the expression "investment trusts" covers pension fund trusts, where contributions of employers and employees are invested by trustees to maximise benefits for the beneficiaries, and unit trusts, where funds are invested (by the managers subject to general supervision by the trustees) to produce as high returns as possible for the unit holders, whether it is income or capital growth that the unit trust is concerned with. In the case of the latter trusts which solicit funds from the public, subscribers have unit certificates representing their interest in the fund: hence the term "unit trust".

In the United Kingdom, as opposed to the North American continent, the practice is to use the expression "investment trust" to mean "investment company", a *company* quoted on the Stock Exchange with the sole activity of making investments, generally in the shares of other companies. These investment trusts are not trusts at all. Indeed, unit trusts were ruled by the court to be illegal as associations of more than 20 persons not registered under the Companies Act 1862, so that they had to convert themselves into investment trust companies registered under the Act. Later the ruling was overruled by *Smith v Anderson*[25] but hardly anyone bothered to change back to unit trusts or to create new unit trusts until the 1930s.

A shareholder in an investment trust company has no legal or equitable interest in the shares and other assets owned by the company. His shareholding in the company will have a value depending not only on the value of the shares and other assets owned by the company but also on the investment and dividend policy of its directors, who are subject to many fewer controls than the managers of most unit trusts. For example, they will have much wider powers of investment, they will have extensive power to borrow money to buy investments so providing a valuable "gearing" effect, they will have extensive "hedging" powers against

---

[25] (1880) 15 Ch.D. 247; overruling *Sykes v Beadon* (1879) 11 Ch.D. 170. On unit trusts generally see K.F. Sin, *The Legal Nature of Unit Trusts* (Clarendon, Oxford, 1997).

currency fluctuations by way of currency options and forward contracts. All these powers may be exercised profitably or unprofitably.

The capital held by the investment trust is fixed (so that the fund is "close-ended" unlike the "open-ended" unit trust where the investment "kitty" fluctuates depending on numbers of new subscribers and numbers of unit holders requiring the managers to redeem their units) and the price of shares of the investment trust company reflects demand (whereas the price of units directly reflects the underlying value of the unit trust's portfolio). Shares in an investment trust, being shares in a company, are bought and sold through a stockbroker or an intermediary, which makes the process more expensive and cumbersome than for units in a unit trust where sales and purchases are directly transacted with the managers.

The share price of investment trusts normally stands at a discount to the net asset value. Discounts can alter quite sharply, especially in a bear market (where sellers outnumber buyers). Take an investment trust with assets of £10 million and 10 million shares priced at 80p each, giving a market value of £8 million and a discount of 20 per cent. Then the trust assets fall in value by 10 per cent to £9 million. Many shareholders sell out so the share price falls to 67p. A shareholder who keeps his shares will have seen them fall by 16 per cent (though assets fall only by 10 per cent). The discount will now have widened to 25 per cent.

The major advantages of investment trusts are that the management costs are low (say, a quarter of one per cent compared with five per cent at the "front end" on purchase, and an annual charge of half a per cent compared with one or one and a half per cent), they can "gear up" purchases by using loans, and they do not need to sell their underlying shares at a time of stock market panic whereas a unit trust may have no option other than to sell.

Authorised Unit Trusts

Authorised unit trusts are trusts created by deed and authorised by the Financial Services Authority under the Financial Services and Markets Act 2000 if satisfying the Regulations for Collective Investment Schemes, for example as to calculation of management charges, redemption of units at prices related to net asset value, supervisory control of the manager (which must be a company) by a trustee (which must be an independent company). Units will be created and issued against cash paid to the manager and deposited with the trustee. The cash will forthwith be applied to purchase investments or be put on deposit pending investment. The manager is responsible for the nature and proportion of the investments within defined types of investment and within defined percentage limits. He also promotes sale of the units to the public. He is bound to purchase units back from unit holders when requested.

Authorised unit trusts pay corporation tax at the rate of 20 per cent but pay no tax in respect of capital gains, though individual unit holders are liable to capital gains tax if their chargeable gains exceed their annual allowance. Income received by unit holders is treated as received with 20 per cent tax deducted from payments to the unit holders: for income and capital gains tax purposes, authorised unit trusts are treated as if they were companies and the units were shares, though payments to unit holders are no longer treated as dividends (entitling company unit holders to use them as deductible franked investment income) but simply as annual payments from which 20 per cent lower rate income tax has been deducted at source which discharges basic rate liability.

Unauthorised Unit Trusts

Unauthorised unit trusts, which may not be publicly promoted, are likely to be fewer than in the past since the Financial Services Authority has taken a more flexible view on authorised unit trusts (for example as to types of asset that may be purchased as investments by authorised unit trusts) than formerly. Most unauthorised unit trusts (for example freehold or leasehold property unit trusts) are confined to bodies exempt from charge to tax on capital gains (for example, pension fund trusts and charities) since otherwise the trustees will be liable for chargeable gains and the unit holders will further be liable on disposing of their units. It is possible to operate time-sharing of holiday homes through unit trusts with varying rights attached to each unit.

Open-ended Investment Companies: "Oeics"

Since 1997 it has been possible to create an open-ended investment company (an "oeic") having the open-ended advantages of unit trusts, with the further advantage of operating on a single price as opposed to one price for buyers and a lower one for settlors (though unit trusts may now also operate on a single price), and having a company structure more acceptable to foreign investors than the alien trust structure. It seems likely that many unit trusts will convert themselves into "oeics" which are taxed in broadly the same way as unit trusts.

Trading Trusts

A trading trust is one where the trustees carry on a trade for the benefit of beneficiaries under the trust. Where the trustees have power to accumulate, and thus capitalise, income the top rate of tax on profits will be 34 per cent (assuming anti-avoidance provisions do not deem the income to be the settlor's) whilst a sole trader or an individual partner has a top rate of 40 per cent (but as high as 83 per cent in 1978–79). However, the small companies' corporation tax rate is only 19 per cent and the full corporation tax rate only 30 per cent, so trading trusts have lost the attraction they had when corporation tax was 50 per cent. Companies pay corporation tax in respect of their chargeable gains (so calculated that the same amount of tax is paid as if the corporation were an individual) and, then, their shareholders pay capital gains tax on disposal of shares: property may get "locked in" a company due to problems caused by company law and income tax problems caused to shareholders by section 703 of the Income and Corporation Taxes Act 1988. Trustees pay capital gains tax on their disposals but beneficiaries do not pay such tax on disposals of their equitable interests: on a beneficiary becoming absolutely entitled to trust property a capital gains tax charge arises, though hold-over relief may sometimes be available.

Trustees are personally liable to creditors of the business, though the trustees, and the creditors by way of subrogation, may normally obtain an indemnity out of the trust assets for liabilities properly incurred, no indemnity being available if the business transaction was *ultra vires* (beyond the powers of the trustees) or the trustees are indebted to the trust.[26] It also seems that an indemnity may be claimed against concurrently entitled beneficiaries of full capacity for liabilities properly incurred, for example where the trustee is a limited liability company and there are insufficient trust assets to satisfy creditors. A trading trustee company will have limited liability, but in practice those closely concerned will often need to give personal security or guarantees so as to be bankrupted if the company fails.

The trading trust may still have tax attractions where income is accumulated and paid out as capital especially where a grandparent creates an accumulation and maintenance settlement for young grandchildren.

The Trust as a Security Device

To guard against the possibility of bankruptcy of the recipient of property who is not intended to benefit outright, it makes sense to require him to hold the property on trust and in the case of cash to hold it in a designated account separate from his own money.

---

[26] Further see my Ch.8 "Trading Trusts" in Glasson's *The International Trust* (Jordan Publishing, 2002).

Hence solicitors, estate agents, stockbrokers etc. have client accounts where money is held on trust for clients. Similarly, tenants' damage deposits or contributions to a sinking fund should be kept by the landlord in a separate designated account.

Money may be loaned to a company for a specific purpose only which, if carried out, will establish a mere debtor/creditor relationship, but where there will be an express term or a necessary implication that to the extent the purpose wholly or partly fails then the money will be held on trust for the payer. Thus, he recovers his money if the company goes into liquidation before being able to use the money for the specified purpose: *Barclays Bank Ltd v Quistclose Investments Ltd.*[27]

Suppliers of materials to companies have tried to safeguard their interests in the event of the company going into liquidation without having paid for the materials. If the supplier has reserved legal title to the materials until paid for, and such unpaid for materials remain unsold in the company's possession, then the supplier can repossess them.[28] If the legal title has passed but the company is supposed by virtue of the supplier's terms to hold the materials on trust for the supplier till payment, this is regarded as an equitable charge over the materials, which will be void if not registered under the Companies Act 1985, s.395, and is not regarded as a proper trust outside s.395. The position will be the same where the company is to use the materials to manufacture goods and the contract provides for the company to hold such goods on trust for the supplier till payment for the materials or until the goods are sold to customers. If the supplier's contract further provides that proceeds of sale of his materials or of goods manufactured using his materials are to be paid into a separate account and held on trust for him until he receives payment of all moneys due to him, again there is a charge registrable under s.395 and not a true trust since the fund is being set aside as security for payment of a debt.[29] However, there will be no charge within s.395 if the company purchaser contracted that it will be trustee of a specified percentage or fraction of the proceeds of sale received by it once such proceeds are received, even in the company's own general bank account. The company having received the materials as full consideration for its contractual promise, "Equity looks on as done that which ought to be done".[30]

---

[27] [1970] A.C. 567 as explained by Lord Millett in *Twinsectra Ltd v Yardley* [2002] 2 A.C. 164.

[28] *Clough Mill Ltd v Martin* [1985] 1 W.L.R. 111; *Armour v Thyssen Edelstahlwerke AG* [1991] 2 A.C. 339.

[29] *Re Bond Worth Ltd* [1980] Ch.228; *Compaq Computer Ltd v Abercorn Group Ltd* [1991] B.C.C. 484; *Re Highway Foods International Ltd* [1995] 1 B.C.L.C. 209.

[30] *Re Lind* [1915] 2 Ch.345 *Barclays Bank v Willowbrook International Ltd* [1987] B.C.L.C. 717.

The supplier, via the equitable tracing process, has a proprietary charge over the bank account: because this arises by way of operation of law under equitable principles this falls outside s.395. To strengthen the supplier's position the purchaser should also be contractually obliged to transfer the relevant amount of money out of its general account within seven working days directly to the supplier or to a trust account for the supplier and meanwhile not permit the amount credited in the general account to fall below the relevant amount held on trust for the supplier.[31]

Because it is not normally practical to fix in advance the precise fraction of the proceeds to be held on trust for the supplier it is the practice expressly to provide that the purchaser will be trustee for the supplier of such percentage of the proceeds of sale received by the supplier as is equivalent to the amount then owing to the supplier.[32]

Where a buyer raises finance on the security of imported goods so that he can pay for, obtain and sell the goods and repay the loan, he will pledge the bill of lading and other shipping documents to the lender. This requires delivery of the bill of lading and other documents to the lender, indorsed to the lender or in blank. The buyer, however, needs those very documents to obtain the goods from the shipping company, but if the lender were to part with possession unconditionally the pledge will be extinguished since it requires continuance of possession. To circumvent these problems the buyer will provide a "trust letter" or "trust receipt", in which he undertakes that, in consideration of the release of the documents to him, he will hold them on trust for the lender, will use them to sell the goods as the lender's agent and will hold the goods themselves until sale, and the proceeds after sale, on trust for the lender. This establishes that delivery of the document to the buyer is for the lender's purposes and not the buyer's purposes, so that the lender is deemed to continue in constructive possession and so continues to have a valid pledge.

As an independent security device there is, of course, the trust for debenture holders where a company charges property to trustees and confers rights on them as security to be held on trust for debenture holders, who lend money to the company in return for debenture stock. The trustee has the exclusive right to sue on the covenant to repay, to waive defaults or agree to amendments of the trust deed, and to enforce the security by sale or by appointing

---

[31] If the supplier from the outset does not insist on fulfilment of the contractual terms but permits the purchaser to use all general account moneys as if beneficially the purchaser's, the arrangement will be regarded not as a true trust but as really a debtor-creditor relationship. The right to trace will also be lost if the purchaser actually dissipates the proceeds.

[32] *Associated Alloys Pty Ltd v ACN 001 452 106 Pty Ltd* (2001) 74 A.L.J.R. 862.

administrative receivers or managers to carry on the business of the company, although the trust deed will normally confer some powers on the majority of the debenture stockholders in general meeting. Section 192 of the Companies Act 1985 negatives any clause purporting to exclude a debenture trustee from liability for negligent breaches of trust but allows the debenture holders to give a subsequent release to a trustee relating to specific acts or omissions. With Eurobonds, in case the trustee might have difficulty in a non-trust jurisdiction in suing to recover money not provided from its own resources but from a large variety of lender-bondholders, the debtor normally gives parallel payment undertakings to the trustee and to the beneficiary bondholders. Payment under one undertaking will *pro tanto* discharge liability under the other. Implementation of the Hague Trust Convention in a non-trust jurisdiction (as has happened in Italy and the Netherlands) should avoid the need for such parallel undertakings because the trustee should be able to sue and recover on behalf of all the lenders.

Another security device is the subordination trust. Subordination is a transaction whereby one creditor, the "subordinated" or "junior" creditor, agrees not to be paid by a debtor until another creditor of that debtor, the "senior" creditor has been paid. This is the price to be paid if the senior creditor is to provide money to assist the debtor. It is important to protect the senior creditor as much as is practicable against the insolvency not just of the debtor but also of the junior creditor. To this end, a trust deed is used under which the junior debt is payable by the debtor to the trustee, who holds the money on trust first to pay the senior creditor an amount equivalent to the senior debt and, then, to pay anything remaining to the junior creditor. Thus, the senior creditor has a prior claim to the junior creditor and its creditors on the debtor's insolvency and on the insolvency of the junior creditor.

The maxim "Equity looks on that as done which ought to have been done" can be exploited where X Ltd wants money now to thrive better and so is prepared to sell to Y Ltd the right to cash that X Ltd expects to receive in respect of debts due to it, or of royalties that will become payable to it, or even of earnings it expects to receive from projected car park business. Once Y Ltd has paid X Ltd the sale price, then any receipts of the relevant moneys by X Ltd will forthwith be held on trust for Y Ltd so as not to be available to the creditors of X Ltd if X Ltd goes into liquidation before paying the moneys over to Y Ltd.[33]

It may be that the purchasing company, Y Ltd, itself needs to borrow the purchase money. Y Ltd will often be a corporate special

---

[33] *Re Lind* [1915] 2 Ch. 345; *Palette Shoes Pty Ltd v Krohn* (1937) 58 C.L.R. 27; *Associated Alhoys Pty Ltd v A CN 001 452 106 Pty Ltd* (2001) A.L.T.R. 862.

purpose vehicle ("SPV") created to receive the relevant moneys directly, or indirectly via appointing X Ltd to be its servicing agent initially receiving the moneys in a separate trust account for the SPV before transferring the moneys promptly to the SPV, for it to use to pay the bondholders who provided the original purchase moneys for the SPV via the issue of trustee debenture bonds.

The SPV can be set up by X Ltd or by a third party. So long as the SPV is not a subsidiary of X Ltd, X Ltd's contractual claims can be taken off its balance sheet. To this end, the shares in the SPV are often held on charitable trusts, although little is available for charity after receipts have been used to pay off bondholders. There are about £60 billion of such securitisation arrangements in the United Kingdom each year.

In the building construction industry retention trust funds are created to provide security for the employer of the building contractor against bad workmanship or the insolvency of the contractor, and to provide security for the contractor and subcontractors if the employer becomes insolvent. Typically, the employer may be entitled under the contract to retain five per cent of moneys certified payable by the architect for work done, which have to be put into a separate trust account, albeit the employer retains the interest thereon and is under no obligation to invest the money. Half the fund becomes payable once the architect provides the certificate of practical completion and the other half becomes payable when the architect provides the certificate of making good defects, but the employer can set off against fund money due the costs incurred by the employer in remedial work to complete the work properly.

ENORMOUS BREADTH OF TRUST PURPOSES

The main sorts of trusts have been outlined above but other sorts of trust exist since one cannot draw up a comprehensive list.[34] A settlor can tailor a trust for any purpose which is not against public policy, illegal or in contravention of the beneficiary principle or the perpetuity and accumulation rules. The duties and powers of the trustees are such as the settlor may choose. The interests of the beneficiaries, so long as specified with sufficient certainty, are such as he may choose: the nature of those interests ranges downwards from the claims of a beneficiary under a bare trust, to the claims of a beneficiary with a life interest, to the claims of a beneficiary under a discretionary trust where all the beneficiaries are ascertainable and to the claims of a beneficiary indirectly benefiting under a

---

[34] For further examples, see Hayton & Marshall, *Commentary and Cases on the Law of Trusts and Equitable Remedies* (11th ed.), pp. 9.

purpose trust where all the discretionary beneficiaries are not currently ascertainable. Moreover, persons may be capable of benefiting as objects of a fidiciary or of a personal power of appointment
(or explained at p.43 above).

Within these limits the purposes for which trusts can be used are
"as unlimited as the imagination of lawyers" as A. W. Scott wrote
in *Trusts*.[35]

---

[35] Volume 1, 4th Edition (Boston (1987)), p.18–24.

CHAPTER THREE

The Validity of Non-Charitable Trusts

INTRODUCTION

The settlor has to comply with the requisite formalities for subjecting property to valid trusts, for example using a deed to transfer unregistered land or a transfer form to transfer registered land, using signed writing to dispose of an equitable interest, producing signed written evidence of trusts relating to land. This will be dealt with in Chapter 5 when looking at matters from the settlor's viewpoint.

A trust is an enforceable, feasible, practicable set of obligations burdening a trustee of property so there must be certainty of intention to create a trust (as opposed to some other legal relationship or some moral obligation), certainty of subject-matter of the trust and certainty of the objects of the trust, so that the trust is administratively workable and capable of being "policed" by the court. The trust must directly or indirectly be for the benefit of persons, so that some beneficiary has *locus standi* to apply to the court to enforce the trust, unless the trust is a testamentary trust for a limited number of anomalous purposes (like maintaining animals or tombs or saying masses) or is a charitable trust. Charitable trusts are a special privileged category and are dealt with in Chapter 4.

The settlor cannot insist on income being accumulated, and so accruing to capital, beyond an accumulation period, nor can he insist on persons becoming entitled to interests outside the perpetuity period or purposes being carried on beyond the perpetuity period. Even within the perpetuity period he cannot insist on the continuation of the trust if all the beneficiaries are sane adults and between them absolutely entitled to the trust property. If unan-

imous, these beneficiaries can terminate the trust under t!
Saunders v Vautier[1] and require the trust property to be
themselves or their nominees. In the great majority of Aᴍᴇ.ᴄᴀ.
jurisdictions this rule does not apply, which seems odd to English
lawyers accustomed to the invalidity of restraints on absolute
ownership, the beneficiaries within the rule being collectively the
absolute equitable owner. In Alberta and Manitoba legislation
makes termination of the trust subject to judicial consent.

Trusts, of course, will be void if for an illegal purpose or contrary
to public policy, for example trusts to pay fines for persons convicted of particular criminal offences, to provide a school for
pickpockets, to encourage a woman to separate from and divorce
her husband, to block up a house for 20 years. Trusts may also be
liable to be set aside in special statutory circumstances by creditors
or by spouses or dependants, for example where created to defeat
claims under the Matrimonial Causes Act 1973 (see s.37) or the
Inheritance (Provision for Family and Dependants) Act 1975 (see
s.10) or the claims of existing or future creditors protected by s.423
of the Insolvency Act 1986.

INTENTION TO CREATE A TRUST

At one extreme, clear technical language may be used in a contract
in an attempt to create a trust so that one party's interests are
safeguarded as much as possible. However, equity looks at the
substance and not at the form, so that if the court considers that the
real nature of the relationship is that of an equitable charge, for
example, since, essentially, property is to be set aside as security for
payment of a debt due to one party, it makes no difference that an
intention to create a trust is expressed in clear form. Conversely, if a
settlor, who knows nothing about trusts, uses informal language in
circumstances where unwittingly he is revealing an intention to
create a trust by indicating his wishes for trust-like consequences,
then a trust will be created. "If he enters into arrangements that
have the effect of creating a trust, it is not necessary that he should
appreciate that they do so; it is sufficient that he intends to enter
into them."[2]

Trust and Equitable Charge

Suppliers of raw materials to companies have tried to safeguard
their interests in the case of liquidation of the purchasing companies

---

[1] (1841) Cr. & Ph. 240.
[2] Per Lord Millett in *Twinsectra Ltd v Yardley* [2002] UKHL 12; [2002] 2 A.C. 164,
para.71.

by creating trusts, so as to avoid the practical problems caused if the companies create charges to secure the debts due to the suppliers. A supplier may supply materials under a particular contract, which provides that the proceeds of sale of his materials or of goods manufactured using, *inter alia*, his materials are to be paid by the supplied company into a separate bank account, to be held on trust for the supplier until full payment is received for materials supplied under any contract between the supplier and the company. The substance of this is the setting aside of a fund as security for payment of debts so there is an equitable charge registrable under s.395 of the Companies Act 1985 and void against the company's creditors if not registered. After all, the supplier is surely supposed only to recover the moneys owed and not to obtain as a windfall the remainder of the moneys in the account representing the company's profit margin on sales and also moneys due to other suppliers of materials used in the manufacturing process.[3]

A person, X, who pays money to a company, whether for goods he wishes to purchase or by way of a tenant's damage deposit paid to his landlord, may try to safeguard his interests in the event of liquidation of the company. In his covering letter he can require the company to pay the money into a separate trust account to hold the money on trust for him until title to the goods has passed to him or on trust to use the money to carry out any necessary repairs or renewals and pay the balance over to him. Here, X retains the beneficial interest, so there is no question of the company as owner by way of security conferring an interest on him which would be a registrable equitable charge.

Incidentally, X cannot fully protect himself. The company might not open a trust account: it might pay the money into its own account and dissipate the money, using it to pay off creditors with no notice of X's trust, so that X's proprietary right will have disappeared and X will be an unsecured personal creditor in the liquidation of the company. Even if a trust account were opened there is a possibility that the bank might honour cheques drawn thereon without knowing that such payments are a breach of trust, in which case no claim could be made against the bank. Furthermore, the payees might be bona fide purchasers without notice or they might have disappeared or be insolvent.

Where Y is a spendthrift pressed by substantial creditors, B, C and D, he may transfer whatever stocks and shares he still owns to trustees and covenant to pay to them one-half of his net earnings each month on trust to pay off B, C and D over a five-year period and then to transfer any balance remaining to himself. This is a

---

[3] *Clough Mill Ltd v Martin* [1985] 1 W.L.R. 111; *Compaq Computer Ltd v Abercorn Group Ltd* [1991] B.C.C. 484. See p.69 above.

valid trust with B, C and D having enforceable equitable interests. If Y merely gives a recently received legacy of £15,000 to T on trust to apply it in paying off Y's creditors generally, then the substance of this arrangement is that it is set up for Y's convenience with T acting as Y's nominee or agent. There is a simple bare trust for Y, who may of course revoke T's instructions, since whoever happen to be Y's creditors have no enforceable equitable interests.

Trust and Agency

The agency relationship was developed by the common law courts where one person, the agent, has express or implied authority to act on behalf of another, the principal. Sometimes an agent will have control of his principal's property, sometimes not: a trustee will have property vested in him. The principal (unlike the settlor or the beneficiaries) can direct the agent and can terminate the agency which will automatically determine on the death of either party. The agent has power to subject the principal to liability in contract or in tort: a trustee is himself personally liable. In the vast majority of cases agency arises as a result of a contract: trusts normally arise from a gratuitous transfer of property. A person cannot be an agent for unborn or unascertained persons nor, except in very limited circumstances, for minors: a person can be a trustee for such persons. The common law relationship between principal and agent is that of debtor and creditor, so that the principal only has a personal claim which will abate with the claims of other unsecured creditors on the insolvency of the agent.

In some circumstances, however, equity supplements the common law position: if the agent is under a contractual duty to keep rents collected on the principal's behalf separate from his own money, the agent will be regarded as holding the rents in a fiduciary capacity so that the principal has an equitable right to trace the rents. If the principal instructs the agent to purchase Blackacre for the principal but the agent purchases it for himself, equity treats the agent as holding Blackacre on trust to transfer it to the principal, subject to the agent being reimbursed the purchase price.

Trust and Bailment

Bailment is another long-recognised common law institution that applies to tangibles but not to intangibles, so that a custodian of stocks and shares has to have title to them and so hold as trustee. If an owner delivers his goods to another on condition that they will be re-delivered to the owner, or according to the owner's directions, when the purpose of delivering the goods has been carried out (for example safe custody, cleaning, repair, hire) this will be a bailment.

The bailee is said to receive a special property in the goods, while the general property remains in the bailor: thus the bailee, unlike a trustee, cannot transfer title to the chattels (subject to certain exceptions that are mainly statutory). The bailor, unlike a settlor *vis-à-vis* trust property, can enforce or vary the bailment which will often result from a contract. The bailor will be unaffected by the bailee's insolvency.

Equity may intervene to supplement the common law position. Thus, if an unauthorised sale is made to a purchaser, who obtains a good title under some statutory exception to the general principle *nemo dat quod non habet*, the bailor will have an equitable right to trace the proceeds of sale. Where the contract of bailment authorises the bailee to sell the goods and the bailee only has to account as debtor to the bailor then the bailor's claim is merely a personal claim and so of little use if the bailee is insolvent. If, exceptionally, the bailee is under a duty to pay the proceeds of sale into a separate designated account the bailor will have an equitable right to trace the proceeds.

Trust and Contract

As mentioned in Chapter 1, a contract is a creature of the common law and creates mere personal claims enforceable only by and against the parties to the contract—or by a third party under the Contracts (Rights of Third Parties) Act 1999–and it is a bargain requiring valuable consideration (or incorporation in a signed, witnessed and delivered deed). A trust is an obligation creating an equitable proprietary interest in the beneficiaries, capable of binding third parties and enforceable by the beneficiaries though not party to the settlor-trustee arrangement. A trust arises from a settlor disposing of his legal or equitable title to property, usually gratuitously, such that the settlor straightaway drops out of the picture and has no rights unless he expressly reserves them in the trust instrument.

Any type of asset may be trust property, for example a life interest in trust X may be assigned to the trustees of trust Y or the benefit of a contract or any other chose in action may be assigned to the trustees of trust Z. Indeed, when A and B are negotiating a contract, A can contract expressly or impliedly as trustee of the benefit of the contract for C, so that A is at once settlor and trustee. If A as trustee does not take appropriate action against B then C, as beneficiary under a trust, can directly enforce his interest against B, though having to join A as a party to the proceedings so that all parties are bound by the outcome. The intention of A to create a trust will need to be positively proved, since the courts were ready to find that the claim to a trust relationship was a transparent device to evade the privity of contract doctrine, while after the Contracts (Rights of Third Parties) Act 1999 a third party may well have personal rights but no proprietary rights unless a trust was established for his benefit.

The trust concept and the contract concept may operate in tandem where loans are concerned. The loan arrangement may commence as a temporary trust to carry out a purpose (for example paying dividends to shareholders in the borrowing company or purchasing particular property) resulting if the purpose is performed in a pure contractual loan relationship, necessarily excluding any trust, but, otherwise, there is a trust of the money in favour of the provider of the money.[4]

Except in this last "successive" situation, loans and trusts are mutually exclusive. If A provides B with £20,000 towards the purchase of property for them in B's name, then B holds the property on resulting trust for A and B in proportion to their contributions to the purchase price. In the event of B's bankruptcy A's proportionate interest (appreciating or depreciating with the value of the property) is not available for B's creditors. If A had merely lent B £20,000 at 10 per cent per annum repayable over 10 years, for B alone to purchase the property, then A would merely have a personal claim to recover the principal with interest. If B had charged (*i.e.* mortgaged) the property to A to secure the loan, then A would be a secured creditor able to sell the property to recover principal, interest and costs, if B became bankrupt, but if the property had doubled in value A would not be able to claim double the amount of his loan.

The following differences between trust and contract are also worth noting. A settlor can declare himself trustee of particular assets that he owns but he cannot contract with himself. A major breach of trust unlike a major breach of contract confers no right on anyone to terminate the trust: the wrongdoing trustee can be replaced by the court (if not voluntarily resigning in favour of a new trustee), while the beneficiaries do not sue for any particular loss suffered by the beneficiary in question but sue for there to be restored to the trust fund the amount due after falsifying or surcharging the trustee's accounts. As an incident attached to the office of trustee under the trust instrument, the trustee can take its expenses and remuneration out of the trust fund. Because trusts are concerned with the management of property, usually for a very long period during which circumstances can change in unforeseeable ways, the court has not just a punitive "policing" role but also a paternalistic role; this enables it to advise trustees on the proper

---

[4] *Barclays Bank Ltd v Quistclose Investments Ltd* [1970] A.C. 567; *Twinsectra Ltd v Yardley* [2002] 2 A.C. 164.

scope of their powers and whether or not a proposed action will be a proper exercise of those powers and to enlarge the trustees' powers if expedient in the interests of the trust as a whole.

Trusts and Powers

When a settlor is creating a *trust* he is imposing mandatory duties on the trustees to deal with the income and capital in particular ways. If property is settled on trust for A for life, remainder to B absolutely, then the trustees must pay the income to A and, after his death, the capital to B. If the property is settled on discretionary trusts to distribute the *income* between such of A, B, C and D, their spouses and issue and in such shares as the trustees may select from time to time until the expiry of 80 years, when the *capital* is to be appointed amongst such of the surviving issue of A, B, C, and D and in such shares as the trustees shall then select, the trustees *must* distribute income and *must* appoint capital, though having *power* to select which of a limited class of beneficiaries actually do benefit. As a result, discretionary trusts are sometimes referred to as trust powers: the trustees *must* pay out, though they have a choice of payees.

Trustees will have *administrative* or management *powers*, for example to invest the trust fund in a range of investments, to employ agents, to recoup their expenses properly incurred on the trust's behalf, to pay themselves remuneration, to compound liabilities. Trustees will often also have *distributive powers*, for example power to appoint income or capital to specific persons who are not any of the beneficiaries under the fixed or discretionary trust, or power to accumulate income for 21 years, so that the income is capitalised and passes to the beneficiaries entitled to capital rather than to those who would have been entitled to the income if the power of accumulation had not been exercised. The trustees *may or may not* choose to pay out (or accumulate) under *distributive powers*: only if they choose to pay out is there a further choice as to who should be the payees if the power is exercisable in favour of two or more persons.

Although a trustee need not exercise his *fiduciary* distributive powers, he is under a duty responsibly to consider from time to time whether or not to exercise such powers, and, to this end, to take reasonable steps to ascertain persons within the scope of the power and to consider their needs.[5] Sometimes, distributive powers are conferred on someone who is not a trustee, for example where E and F are trustees of a testator's will trusts for his widow for life,

---

[5] *Re Hay's S.T.* [1982] 1 W.L.R. 202; *Schmidt v Rosewood Trust Ltd* [2003] UKPC 26 [2003] 2 W.L.R. 1442.

remainder to such of his grandchildren as his widow may by deed or will appoint, but in default of appointment for his grandchildren in equal shares unless the trustees within six months of the widow's death see fit to appoint capital between the grandchildren in unequal shares. Here, the widow has a *personal* power, so that she does not even have to consider whether or not to exercise it and she may exercise it capriciously, though, of course, the courts can restrict her to benefiting grandchildren and no-one else. If she fails to exercise her personal powers then the trustees have a *fiduciary* power exercisable within six months of her death: they must investigate the circumstances of the grandchildren and bona fide consider whether or not to exercise the power so as to give deserving grandchildren large shares and undeserving grandchildren small shares. Their exercise of the power will be justiciable (*i.e.* capable of challenge by application of judicial workable criteria) in the courts if they act capriciously or irrationally or perversely to any sensible expectation of the settlor.[6] Unless authorised by the trust instrument, trustees cannot release fiduciary powers (vested *ex officio* in whoever are the trustees from time to time), while a personal power can be released at any time.

A distributive power is referred to as a *special* power unless the person who can exercise the power (known as the "donee" of the power given him by the settlor) can himself appoint the trust property to himself when it will be a *general* power. A very wide special power exercisable in favour of everyone but a small excepted class is often referred to as a hybrid or intermediate power, for example a power to add to the class of discretionary beneficiaries anyone except the settlor, his spouse, and past and present trustees.

An exceptional feature of *powers* (arising from the feature that no one has the right to compel trustees to exercise a power) is that they may be made exercisable by the trust instrument in favour of pure abstract non-charitable purposes when a *trust* for such purposes will be void for infringing the beneficiary principle (requiring there to be a beneficiary capable of enforcing the trust if a valid trust is to subsist). In the United Kingdom the courts cannot allow such a trust to take effect as though it were a valid power in order to enable the trustees if they wish to carry out the purposes.[7] Since such purposes may well represent desirable social purposes falling outside the limited field of charitable purposes, it is a pity that the United Kingdom has not adopted legislation enacted in many Canadian Provinces to the effect that a trust for non-charitable

---

[6] *Re Manisty's Settlement* [1974] Ch. 17; *Edge v Pensions Ombudsman* [2000] Ch.602.
[7] *IRC v Broadway Cottages Trust* [1955] Ch. 20 at 36; *Re Endacott* [1960] Ch. 232 at 246.

purposes takes effect as a power for such purposes if they are certain, except with regard to any purpose that is illegal or contrary to public policy.

To the extent that *powers* are not exercised within the specified time (or, otherwise, a reasonable time) then the trustees must distribute the income or capital as the case may be to appropriate trust beneficiaries. Discretionary *trusts* remain exercisable despite the passing of time, though only in favour of such persons as would have been possible beneficiaries if the discretion had been exercised within a reasonable time.[8]

Language Revealing Intent to Create a Trust

Where lawyers are not called upon to draft the trust instrument or to advise the use of the words "upon trust for" the intended beneficiaries, problems can arise as to whether or not some imperative form of words has been used to indicate that someone is to be subject to a legally binding obligation to hold and manage certain property for the benefit of others (or himself and others). Testators who make their own wills may use expressions like "in full confidence that," "in the firm expectation that," "fully trusting that," or "it is my heartfelt desire that" a specified legatee will deal with a legacy in a particular manner. Nowadays, such precatory expressions will not be held to create trusts unless there is something else in the will indicating that the legatee is to be under a legal obligation rather than what, presumptively, is a moral obligation.[9]

Often the uncertainty surrounding a testator's intention to create a trust will involve uncertainty as to the exact subject-matter of the trust, for example "I leave my residuary estate (after payment of debts, expenses and liabilities) to my wife so that she may properly maintain herself and our children, between whom whatever remains should be divided when no longer required on her death." Here, the widow will take an absolute interest rather than a life interest under a trust with or without power for her to have recourse to capital. Such cases involving spouses and issue are not uncommon so that s.22 of the Administration of Justice Act 1982 expressly states, "Except where a contrary intention is shown, it shall be presumed that if a testator devises or bequeaths property to his spouse in terms which in themselves would give an absolute interest to the spouse, but by the same instrument purports to give his issue an interest in the same property, the gift to the spouse is absolute notwithstanding the purported gift to the issue."

A settlor may create a trust by declaring that he himself is to hold

---

[8] *Re Locker's S.T.* [1977] 1 W.L.R. 1323.
[9] *Comiskey v Bowring-Hanbury* [1905] A.C. 84.

certain of his property appropriated on trust for a specific beneficiary or beneficiaries. Thus, a man co-habiting with a woman and discussing with her the money in an account kept by him at a particular bank may tell her, "This money is as much yours as mine". The court will interpret these words as a declaration of trust over the bank account (a chose in action) for the man and woman equally, since it appreciates it is "dealing with simple people, unaware of the subtleties of equity, but understanding very well indeed their own domestic situation".[10]

However, the court is not ready to treat imperfect outright gifts as if they were perfect declarations of trust for the intended donees. So, if a lessee, L, writes on the front of his lease, "This lease I give to Edward from this time forth" and signs this endorsement, this is ineffective to transfer the lease to Edward: a signed, witnessed and delivered deed of assignment is required. If L had signed an endorsement "I hold this lease on trust for Edward", this would be an effective declaration of trust. The courts cannot give effect to L's intention as expressed in the original form of endorsement by treating him as having used the latter form of endorsement: the attempted outright *transfer* is the clearest evidence that L did not intend to *retain* the property and himself be trustee thereof.[11] There is a crucial distinction between saying "I am keeping this for you" and "I am giving this to you".

Nevertheless, if L had earlier settled assets on a trust for Edward and Edward's family, known as "the Edward Family Trust", and L was one of the trustees thereof, then if L wrote a signed note on the lease, "This lease I give to the Edward Family Trust from this time forth" the court will take a liberal view.[12] It will forgive L's mistaken nonsense of regarding the trust as a legal person and treat him as intending to transfer an interest to "the trustees of the Edward Family Trust". Because he is already a trustee of the Trust he can be regarded as transferring the lease from himself as legal beneficial owner to himself as trustee for the Edward family, and subject to the further equitable obligation to transfer the legal title as soon as practicable into the names of himself and his co-trustees. Thus, there would be a valid trust of the lease.

Gifts to Unincorporated Associations

Where a testator intended to benefit an unincorporated association (*i.e.* a club or society not incorporated under the Companies Act

---

[10] *Paul v Constance* [1973] 1 All E.R. 195 at 197.
[11] *Richards v Delbridge* (1874) L.R. 18 Eq. 11; *Milroy v Lord* (1862) 4 De G.F. & J. 264.
[12] *Choithram International SA v Pagarani* [2001] 1 W.L.R. 1, PC.

and so having no legal personality) the courts favour construing the testator's language as revealing that he did not intend to create a trust but intended to make an outright absolute gift. The gift cannot take effect as a gift to the club as such since it has no legal personality, but it will take effect as a gift of cash to the club treasurer to be held by him on a bare trust for the members acting in a general meeting or via their committee, as laid down in the club rules binding the members as a matter of contract law. A gift of shares or land will take effect as a gift to the club trustees to be held, like similar property held by them, on a bare trust for the members acting in a general meeting or via their committee according to the club rules.

A testator's bequest of the proceeds of sale of his residuary estate "for the Hull Judeans (Maccabi) Association in memory of my late wife to be used solely in the work of constructing the new buildings for the Association and/or improvements to the said buildings" was thus held to be an outright gift accruing to the Association's funds available to be used, without distinction between capital and income, for whatever purposes were decided upon under the Association's constitution binding the members as a matter of contract.[13]

This benevolent construction prevented problems arising under special rules governing the validity of a trust. If it had been held that the proceeds of sale had to be set aside as a capital endowment on trust for the income therefrom, or the use of the building built with the proceeds of sale, for ever to be dedicated to the purposes of the Association, then the beneficiary principle and the perpetuity rules would need to be satisfied. Later in this chapter it will be seen that these problems have been mitigated by *Re Denley*[14] and the Perpetuities and Accumulation Act 1964 but it is simpler if these problems never arise.

CERTAINTY OF SUBJECT MATTER

If a settlor wishes to create a trust by declaring himself trustee of some of his own property he must be specific as to which of his property is to be subject to the trust, especially where he is to retain for himself some of the relevant assets identical in nature to the assets intended to be subjected to the trust. It is no use saying "I hold 15 of the 30 cases of Chateau Lafite 1982 in my cellar on trust for X". Until 15 of the cases are marked to show that they are held for X there is no trust obligation, since X cannot identify particular property as held on trust for him so as to trace the proceeds of sale

---

[13] *Re Lipinski's W.T.* [1976] Ch. 235.
[14] [1969] 1 Ch. 373.

thereof or to restrain dealings therewith as in breach of trust.[15] However, if the settlor had said, "I hold all my 30 cases on trust for myself as to half and X as to half" he would validly hold the particular 30 cases on trust for himself and X as tenants in common in equal shares, so that the proceeds of any sale would be held on trust for the two equally and it would be a breach of trust if the settlor claimed to retain for himself more than half.

One would not expect the position to differ if the settlor said, "I hold £1,000 of the £2,000 in my deposit account on trust for X" or "I hold 500 of my 1,000 shares in BF Ltd on trust for X". Until the £1,000 or the 500 shares are isolated apart from the remaining pounds or shares one cannot identify particular property as held on trust: to perfect the imperfect gift in equity, as at law, requires identification of that property as particular property distinct from identical property of the settlor-donor.[16] However, in *Hunter v Moss*[17] the Court of Appeal (perhaps blinded by the merits of the donee, who had done an awful lot for the subsequently ungrateful donor) held: "just as a person can give by will a specified number of his shares in a certain company, so equally he can declare himself a trustee of 50 of his shares in MEL and that is effective to give a beneficial proprietary interest to the beneficiary under the trust." Crucially, this overlooks that *on death* the donor is automatically divested of legal beneficial ownership in all his assets so there can be no problems as to which assets he remains the beneficial owner of, while *in his lifetime* a donor-settlor can only divest himself of his beneficial entitlement to particular assets when he has done everything necessary to identify those assets in which he has created a new equitable interest for the donee so as to relinquish his own beneficial interest therein. Thus, a person can give by will 50 of his 100 gold bars or bottles of Ch. Lafite 1961 to X but, in his lifetime, he cannot declare himself a trustee of 50 of those 100 chattels.

It is submitted that *Hunter v Moss* should not be followed by the English Court of Appeal, just as the Australian courts have not followed it.[18] A true analogy with the testamentary position will, however, arise if a settlor declares himself trustee of 500 of his 1,000 BF Ltd shares for X and of 500 for Y. He has then divested himself of beneficial entitlement to all 1,000 shares, so that X and Y toge-

[15] *Re London Wine Co (Shippers) Limited* [1986] P.C.C. 121; *Re Stapylton Fletcher Ltd* [1994] 1 W.L.R. 1181. Where there is a contract for the sale of goods comprised in a larger mass of such identical goods the Sale of Goods Amendment Act 1995 converts the contract into one for sale of the relevant fraction of the whole to enable title to ascertained property to pass once the purchase price is paid.
[16] *Re Goldcorp Exchange Ltd* [1995] 1 A.C. 74.
[17] [1994] 1 W.L.R. 452. Leave to appeal was refused by the House of Lords but this signifies nothing either way: *Wilson v Colchester Justices* [1985] A.C. 750 at 756.
[18] See *Re Harvard Securities* [1997] 2 B.C.L.C. 369.

ther exclusively have the equitable interest in all 1,000 shares entitling them to demand the transfer to themselves of legal title to all
1,000 shares on *Saunders v Vautier* principles.

Where one is concerned not with shares in a private company but
shares in a public company held by a nominee under the CREST
system of paperless transfer of shares with, say, one million shares
recorded as held for Stockbroker & Co whose records state that
20,000 shares are held for S, S does not actually own 20,000 shares.
He owns a one fiftieth equitable interest in Stockbroker's pool of
one million shares which may amount to a one fifth interest in the
public company's shares held by the nominee. Thus, if he declares
himself trustee of his 20,000 shares this is nonsense, but the court
will be able to avoid such nonsensical construction by construing
him as declaring himself trustee of his one fiftieth interest in
Stockbroker's interest. It would then follow that if he declared
himself trustee of only 10,000 of his 20,000 shares[19] then, because he
does not actually own any shares, the court should construe him as
declaring himself trustee of one hundredth of his interest in
Stockbroker's interest.

Where a settlor in his lifetime transfers property to trustees then,
necessarily, it must be clear what property has been transferred so
as to be held on trust. In a very exceptional case, however, there
may still be a problem. Take a settlor who transfers four houses to
trustees in trust for his wife for life and after her death on trust to
convey to Barbara absolutely those two of the houses which she
selects and to convey the two remaining houses to Charlotte
absolutely. If Barbara predeceases the settlor's wife, without having
selected two particular houses out of the four, it will be impossible
to ascertain the two remaining unselected houses. The trust in
favour of Barbara and Charlotte will thus fail for uncertainty and
the four houses will therefore be held on resulting trust for the
settlor (or his estate if he is dead).[20]

When a settlor makes his will, especially one which he may have
prepared without professional assistance, problems can arise out of
an intention to leave his residuary estate to X who is then expected
to pass on to Y whatever is left at X's death. There are no problems
over leaving the residuary estate to X. Indeed, it is standard practice
after making specific bequests and devises to leave the residue of
one's estate, after payment thereout of debts, expenses and liabilities, to particular beneficiaries. It suffices that the net residuary

---

[19] 10,000 cannot be isolated from 20,000 shares, although in the case of a private
company the share certificate of S for 20,000 shares can be replaced by the
company sending S two share certificates each for 10,000 shares, so that S as
registered legal owner of two 10,000 shareholdings can then declare himself trustee
of one particular 10,000 shareholding.
[20] *Boyce v Boyce* (1849) 16 Sim. 476.

estate will in due course be precisely ascertained after satisfying debts, expenses and liabilities.

The nebulousness of X's obligation to pass on to Y whatever is left of the property X received will normally mean that there is no trust, there being uncertainty of subject-matter and uncertainty of intention to create a trust. Exceptionally, in context it may be that the will could be construed so that X might take a life interest under a trust with remainder to Y absolutely.

Where the settlor and X actually discussed the matter, and it may be that the settlor would not have made his will leaving property to X but for their understanding that X by his will is to pass whatever is left to Y, then equity is prepared to overcome technical difficulties to prevent X fraudulently depriving the settlor and Y of their expectations.[21] There is a floating obligation suspended during X's lifetime which descends upon the property at his death and crystallises into a proper trust. During his life X cannot with intent to defeat the understanding with the settlor make gifts (whether outright or on trusts). X's equitable fiduciary obligation gives Y the equitable right to restrain, or to trace and recover, any such gifts.

CERTAINTY OF BENEFICIARIES

Where there is certainty of intention to create a trust and certainty of subject-matter there cannot be a valid trust for beneficiaries if those beneficiaries are themselves uncertain. In such a case the property will be held on resulting trust for the settlor or his estate if he is dead. If the settlor is alive he can then settle the property on more clearly defined beneficiaries, though he will have suffered the adverse tax consequences of remaining liable for income tax on the property held on resulting trust for him. If the settlor is dead, obviously he cannot return "for a rave from the grave" to remedy the position and make his wishes clearer by settling the property again.

The courts are thus particularly reluctant to find testamentary trusts to be void. It is also significant that in will construction summonses judges of first instance have much leeway: wills always have different contexts in which they fall to be construed, so earlier case law can be distinguished, and parties are expected to treat the judge's decision as final and not appeal, a specific legatee being at risk as to paying the costs of both sides if his appeal fails so that the residuary legatee takes the property. The costs of the first instance case will come out of the testator's residuary estate, and even if the residuary legatee wins an appeal the costs normally will still come

---

[21] *Re Cleaver* [1981] 1 W.L.R. 939 at 1023–1024; *Healey v Brown* [2002] W.T.L.R. 849.

out of the residuary estate because it would be unfair to penalise a specific legatee for the faults of the testator. Where there is an ambiguity a benignant construction should be given if possible *ut res magis valeat quam pereat*: a construction should be chosen that makes the trust valid rather than void.[22]

Where Every Beneficiary Must Benefit

If the terms of the trust require trust property to be divided equally between a number of beneficiaries, it necessarily follows that it must be possible to draw up a complete list of the beneficiaries, so as precisely to ascertain the figure for the denominator by which to divide the trust property. Equal division requires knowing the precise number of persons who are to benefit equally. This is the case whether there is a trust for equal division between beneficiaries or whether there is a power which, *if* exercised by the trustees, *must* be exercised so as to benefit objects equally. The mere fact that a very broad discretionary power *may* in theory be exercised so as to benefit the objects equally does not mean that it must be possible to draw up a comprehensive list of objects just in case the power is so exercised. The very breadth of the power surely reveals that equal division is the last thing intended by the settlor, so that any exercise by the trustees of the power purporting to benefit all objects equally will be void for capriciousness as contrary to any sensible expectation of the settlor: a comprehensive list is thus not required.

If beneficiaries are not intended to benefit equally but the settlor intends every beneficiary to receive some benefit (whether large, medium or small) then, logically, a comprehensive list must be capable of being drawn up if there is to be a valid trust, under which the trustees must have duties to consider the claims of *all* beneficiaries before deciding what amount is appropriate for each and every beneficiary, for example a trust to spend £30,000 on providing gifts of varying values for each and every one of my business associates and customers as a token of my appreciation for them, or a trust to spend £20,000 on providing gifts of varying values for each and every person who has delivered mail to any properties owned at any time by me. In the former example, no list can be drawn up since the concepts of business associates and customers are uncertain, as appears when considering the difference between business associates and business acquaintances and customers and ex-customers. In the latter example, the concept is clear but it will be impossible to draw up a fully comprehensive list, as appears when considering discovering students employed to deliver mail at

---

[22] *IRC v McMullen* [1981] A.C. 1 at 11; *Guild v IRC* [1992] 2 A.C. 310; *Charles v Barzey* [2002] UKPC 68; [2003] 1 W.L.R. 437, para 12.

Christmas over the last 30 years and neighbours who, as good neighbours, have delivered mail wrongly put through their letter boxes, assuming the trust is not restricted implicitly to those delivering mail in the course of their regular employment.

Where Every Beneficiary Need Not Benefit

Where there is a discretionary trust or a discretionary power, so that trustees are only to benefit such persons within a class as they see fit, the question arises whether or not it remains necessary to draw up a comprehensive list of persons eligible to benefit. The answer to this depends upon the position if a discretionary *trust* is not carried out, so that the court is asked to intervene, and whether or not the courts must order equal division on the basis that it can act only on the maxim, "Equality is Equity?" If so, then in all cases of discretionary trusts it will be necessary to draw up a comprehensive list, so that equal division may be possible in the eventuality that the court may have to intervene to distribute the trust property.

This was thought to be the case until the House of Lords in *McPhail v Doulton*[23] by a 3:2 majority made it clear that if trustees fail to carry out discretionary trusts (referred to as "trust powers") then: "the court will do so in the manner best calculated to give effect to the settlor's intentions. It may do so by appointing new trustees, or by authorising or directing representative persons of the classes of beneficiaries to prepare a scheme for distribution, or even, should the proper basis for distribution appear, by itself directing the trustees so to distribute." After all, equal distribution is surely the last thing intended by the settlor.

There is thus now no reason for certainty purposes to distinguish between discretionary trusts and discretionary powers between which there may be a very fine dividing line. This has particular pragmatic sense as appears from considering the practical position of the trustees in the following example.

Property is left on trust, during a specified perpetuity period to pay or apply the income to or for the benefit of such of Sainsbury plc employees or ex-employees and their relatives and dependants (hereinafter called the "Sainsbury Class") as my trustees may see fit from time to time but so that my trustees:

[shall pay or apply any income not so paid or applied within three months of receipt to or for the benefit of such of my issue as my trustees shall see fit from time to time] or
[may pay or apply any income within three months of receipt to

[23] [1971] A.C. 424, discussed in social context p.39 *supra*.

or for the benefit of such of my issue as my trustees may see fit from time to time].

Where the main paragraph is coupled with the first of the two bracketed alternatives there is a discretionary *power* of distribution (exercisable within three months of income being received) in favour of the Sainsbury Class, coupled with a discretionary *trust* in favour of the issue in default of full exercise of the discretionary power. In the case of the second alternative there is a discretionary *trust* in favour of the Sainsbury Class, coupled with a discretionary *power* (exercisable within three months of income being received) instead to benefit issue. If within three months of income being received the power is not exercised in respect of such income, then that income must be distributed between the beneficiaries under the discretionary trust.

Where there is a discretionary fiduciary power the trust bene-ficiaries entitled in default of exercise of the power: "must clearly be entitled to restrain the trustees from exercising the power save among those within the power. So the trustees, or the court, must be able to say with certainty who is within and who is without the power."[24] It is not sufficient that the trustees or the court can say of one or five or six persons that they are clearly within the class of objects if it cannot be said that certain others who may present themselves are or are not within the class. This does not require a comprehensive list to be drawn up so that everyone can see whether or not they are within the beneficial class. It is sufficient that the class description provides a certain test for determining whether *any particular person* who presents himself *is* or *is not* within the class.

Trustees with discretionary fiduciary powers must consider per-iodically whether to exercise the power and so *pro tanto* prevent the trust beneficiaries from benefiting. They must consider the needs of those trust beneficiaries and also survey the range of possible objects of the power and consider the appropriateness of grants to particular objects. This enables the trustees to appreciate the width of the field or the size of the problem before considering in indi-vidual cases whether or not a particular grant is appropriate.[25]

In *McPhail v Doulton* the House of Lords extended the "is or is not" test for certainty of objects of a power to certainty of bene-ficiaries of a discretionary trust. Although trustees *must* carry out discretionary trusts, it is only necessary for them to survey the range of possible beneficiaries in a sensible responsible way and then to consider the appropriateness of grants to particular individuals. A wider and more comprehensive range of inquiry is required for

---

[24] *Re Gulbenkian's S.T.* [1970] A.C. 508 at 525.
[25] See *Re Hay's S.T.* [1982] 1 W.L.R. 202.

discretionary trusts than for discretionary powers but nothing like a comprehensive list of possible beneficiaries is required in either case.

Application of the "Is or Is Not" Test

Take a discretionary trust for employees and ex-employees of a specific company, their relatives and dependants. If there is conceptual certainty then it does not matter that there is evidential uncertainty since the court can always resolve the matter on the evidence presented to it on an application for directions. The above company trust has been held valid in *Re Baden's Deed Trusts (No. 2)*[26] where it was the concept of "relatives" that was carefully considered.

After all, at face value "relatives" means descendants of a common ancestor and one cannot say of any given postulant that he definitely *is* a relative or definitely *is not* a relative. A few persons will prove they are relatives by producing relevant birth and marriage certificates or other sufficient evidence.[27] As to the rest, they may or may not be relatives, depending how far it is possible to research into the past and at some stage (for example using a time-travelling machine yet to be invented) trace common ancestry back to 300 AD or 10,000 BC. Does it matter that one cannot allocate applications for grants into either a "Qualifying File" or "Non-Qualifying File" but must have a "Don't Know File?"

The answer is "No". The crux of the matter is that if one beneficiary, B, who clearly is a relative, objects that the trustees should not have paid money to X because X is not a relative, the burden of proof lies on the trustees to prove X is a relative for otherwise they will be liable for breach of trust.[28] The trustees are under an enforceable duty to make payments only to those who prove they are relatives by birth certificates, marriage certificates or other sufficient evidence. It suffices that there is a "Payable File" containing applications of those who have proved they are relatives while other persons' applications are in a "Non-payable File".

Examples of discretionary trusts or fiduciary powers failing the "is or is not" test include those for "my good friends", "my old

---

[26] [1973] Ch. 9.

[27] DNA testing is now available to prove relationship to millions of others, research indicating that six women of 3000 BC vintage are responsible for a vast number of European descendants. New trusts should be restricted to descendants of a particular known relative alive about 100 years ago. Old originally valid trusts should not be invalidated because concerned with unrestricted relatives: courts should allow powers of appointment to be exercised to favour a narrower workable class or liberally construe relatives as descendants of persons known by the settlor to have been his relatives.

[28] *Re Baden's Deed Trusts* [1972] Ch. 607 at 626.

friends", "persons with whom B has had a social or other relationship", "persons who have moral claims upon me", "persons who my executors and trustees think have helped me or my late husband". There is such an uncertain penumbra of meaning involved in these concepts that the issue of payment or not to an alleged beneficiary is unjusticiable, *i.e.* cannot properly be adjudicated upon according to clear criteria: the trustees cannot with certainty know whether X is or is not a beneficiary, neither can a complaining beneficiary, neither can the court.

Objects of Personal Powers

There is a crucial distinction between powers vested in individuals *qua* individuals (for example where a testator creates trusts and gives his widow a power of appointment in favour of a class of objects) and fiduciary powers vested in trustees. Trustees as fiduciaries are under onerous duties with powers vested in them as such being fiduciary powers, unless expressly stated to be personal powers whose exercise or non-exercise is unchallengeable unless amounting to a fraud on the power. A widow with a personal, as opposed to a fiduciary, power is unhampered by such duties she can release the power, she need never bother considering to exercise it, she can exercise it in favour of the first person she thinks of without needing to consider and survey the range of possible beneficiaries.[29] Of course, she cannot exercise the power in favour of persons outside the class of objects of the power.

What if she has power to benefit any of the testator's friends that he may have forgotten in his will? There is a "core" meaning of friend, though there is an uncertain "penumbra" of meaning at the stage when a friend becomes an acquaintance, which would make a discretionary trust or a fiduciary power in favour of friends void for uncertainty. However, it would seem that a widow may validly exercise her personal power so as to benefit a person within the "core" meaning of friend. Though the courts have not yet considered it, it is possible that she may even benefit someone within the penumbra of meaning of friend so that only an appointment in favour of someone outside such penumbra can be impeached. After all, why should a testator not be allowed to afford his widow the opportunity to exercise her personal power in her discretion among such persons as do not fall outside the penumbra of meaning of friend, especially when he could confer upon her a power to appoint

---

[29] *Re Gulbenkian's S.T.* [1970] A.C. 508 at 518; *Re Hay's S.T.* [1982] 1 W.L.R. 202 at 209; *Mettoy Pension Trustees Ltd v Evans* [1991] 2 All E.R. 513 at 545.

capital to anyone in the world[30] in the hope that she might thereby benefit any of his friends that he might have forgotten?

Trusts for Purposes Benefiting Persons

As will shortly be fully considered, trusts need not be directly for persons but may be for purposes directly or indirectly benefiting persons who have *locus standi* to enforce the trust. In such cases it seems that it must be possible to say of any given person who might seek to enforce the trust that he does or does not have *locus standi* to sue, such trusts being akin to discretionary trusts for the beneficiaries capable of benefiting from implementation of the purposes.[31] As to how certain the purposes themselves have to be, it seems that it must be possible to say whether any activity is or is not within the prescribed purpose or purposes.[32] Thus, in a trust to spend £1 million on worthy causes for the benefit of inhabitants of West Yorkshire, although such inhabitants satisfy the requirement of conceptual certainty, the uncertainty as to what activities are or are not worthy causes will invalidate the trust. Such a trust will also infringe the requirement of administrative workability.

ADMINISTRATIVE WORKABILITY

Closely linked with the requirement of certainty and also the requirement for there to be a beneficiary with *locus standi* to enforce the trust is the requirement that a trust must be administratively workable. As Lord Eldon stated in *Morice v Bishop of Durham*,[33]

"As it is a maxim that the execution of a trust shall be under the control of the court it must be of such a nature that it can be under that control; so that the maladministration of it can be reviewed by the court, or the court itself can execute the trust: a trust, therefore, which in case of maladministration could be reformed and a due administration directed."

Essentially, the terms of the trust must be justiciable: a court must act judicially according to some clear criteria expressly or impliedly provided by the trust instrument or by extrinsic admissible evidence. If such criteria are absent then the court cannot be in a position to control or carry out the trust. The court cannot resort to guesswork, for this is to fulfil a non-justiciable function.

Thus, a discretionary trust for everyone in the world is void for

[30] *Re Hay's S.T.* [1982] 1 W.L.R. 202.
[31] *Re Grant's W.T.* [1979] 3 All E.R. 359 at 368.
[32] *Twinsectra Ltd v Yardley* [2002] UKHL 12 [2002] 2 A.C. 164, paras 16 and 101.
[33] (1805) 10 Ves. 522 at 539–540.

lack of administrative workability even though the class of beneficiaries is certain.[34] The trustees and the court do not have sufficient
definitional criteria to enable the trustees to carry out positive active
duties or to enable the court to "police" or carry out such duties.
There can be no duties and so no trust in a case involving such a
hopelessly wide range of beneficiaries. Where on earth would you
start if you and your fellow "trustees" have everyone in the world
(except the settlor, his spouse, and yourselves) to consider as beneficiaries?

In *R. v District Auditor, Ex p. West Yorkshire MCC*[35] the council
was about to be abolished but had £400,000 unspent. It transferred
the money to trustees on trust to spend it in 11 months as the
trustees might see fit "for the benefit of any or all or some of the
inhabitants of the County of West Yorkshire" in any of the following ways:

(1)   to assist economic development in the county in order to
relieve unemployment and poverty;
(2)   to assist bodies concerned with youth and community
problems;
(3)   to inform all interested and influential persons of the
consequences of the proposed abolition of the council
(and other metropolitan county councils) and of other
proposals affecting local government in the county.

The Divisional Court held that if this were a discretionary trust
directly for West Yorkshire inhabitants, of which there were two
and a half million, it was void for lack of administrative workability, and so could not be enforced by such inhabitants. Essentially, however, the trust was a pure abstract purpose trust and
therefore void for infringing the beneficiary principle since it was
not charitable. It could not be validated as a trust for a purpose
directly or indirectly benefiting persons with *locus standi* to enforce
the trust, since absence of administrative workability prevented
anyone having enforceable rights.

Need Fiduciary Powers be Administratively Workable?

On the basis that while trusts need actively to be carried out powers
do not, since although trustees must consider whether or not to
exercise their powers they may choose not to do so and the court
cannot then intervene to compel them to act positively or itself
exercise the power,[36] courts of first instance have confined the

[34] *Re Hay's S.T.* [1982] 1 W.L.R. 202.
[35] (1985) 26 R.V.R. 24, [2001] W.T.L.R. 785.
[36] *Re Manisty's Settlement* [1974] Ch. 17 at 25.

requirement of administrative workability to trusts. Thus they have upheld a discretionary power to add anyone in the world (except the settlor, his spouse and past and present trustees) to the class of beneficiaries under a discretionary trust[37] and also a discretionary power to appoint trust capital to anyone in the world, except the settlor, his spouse and past and present trustees.[38]

A distinction has thus been created between trusts where there is positive and negative justiciability and fiduciary powers where there is, allegedly, only negative justiciability. An appellate court may yet dispute this fine distinction between trust powers (*i.e.* discretionary trusts) and powers as did Lord Wilberforce for the test for certainty of objects in *McPhail v Doulton*.[39] If the court may intervene negatively to remove a trustee, who spitefully refuses to consider exercising a power in favour of B, or to restrain or invalidate the capricious exercise of a power for reasons which are irrational, perverse or irrelevant to any sensible expectation of the settlor, surely the settlor's expectations must be discerned to discover whether there are justiciable criteria to justify the court's intervention. Where on earth would you start if you and your fellow trustees had a fiduciary power (*i.e.* a power vested in the trustees *ex officio*) to appoint capital to anyone in the world (except yourselves, the settlor and his spouse) or to add anyone (except as aforesaid) to the class of trust beneficiaries? On what criteria could the exercise of such a power be challenged and then be upheld or struck down by the court?

The impossibility of satisfactorily answering these questions becomes even more significant when the case-law reveals that fiduciary powers may be positively exercised by the court as one aspect of the court's inherent jurisdiction to supervise and, if necessary, to intervene in the administration of trusts.[40] In an exceptional case the court does have jurisdiction to intervene to compel the exercise of a power or even itself exercise the power, *e.g.* where persons within the ambit of the power are also beneficiaries and it would be irrational and beyond the expectations of the settlor not to exercise the power to advance capital to a beneficiary or to maintain an infant beneficiary[41] or not to exercise the power to augment the pensions of pensioners and prospective pensioners under a pension scheme trust.[42] Indeed, if a settlor created a trust to accumulate income for a full accumulation period and then to

---

[37] *Re Manisty's Settlement* (above)
[38] *Re Hay's S.T.* [1982] 1 W.L.R. 202; *Re Beatty's W.T.* [1990] 3 All E.R. 844.
[39] [1971] A.C. 424.
[40] *Schmidt v Rosewood Trust Ltd* [2003] UK PC 26, paras 42 and 51.
[41] *Re Lofthouse* (1885) 29 Ch.D 721; *Klug v Klug* [1918] 2 Ch.67.
[42] *Mettoy Pension Trustees Ltd v Evans* [1990] 1 W.L.R. 1587, *Thrells v Lomas* [1993] 1 W.L.R. 456.

distribute the capital (with accumulated capitalised income) between such charities as the trustees chose in their discretion, but the settlor's non-legally-binding letter of wishes contained the wish that the trustees should distribute substantially the whole trust fund before expiry of the relevant period to the settlor's descendants, their spouses and cohabitees under a fiduciary power in their behalf, then it seems the court would order the trustees to exercise their discretion to provide significant benefits for the objects of the fiduciary power or would replace the trustees with new trustees or, if there was insufficient time before expiry of the relevant period to organise replacement trustees with the requisite information to exercise their discretion, the court itself could exercise the power.[43]

FORFEITURE CLAUSES (CONDITIONS SUBSEQUENT)

Settlors sometimes provide for the interest of a beneficiary to be forfeited in some eventualities: the question then arises as to how certain and administratively workable must these eventualities be.

The answer is that for a beneficiary to be divested of his interest on a subsequent contingency that contingency must be conceptually certain, so that the beneficiary and the court can see from the outset precisely and distinctly upon the happening of what event the interest is to be forfeited. Ceasing to reside in a particular place has been held void for uncertainty, while ceasing permanently to reside in a particular place has been upheld, since the concept of permanent residence is sufficiently certain as relevant in establishing domicile for private international law purposes.[44]

Where conditions as to religion are concerned the courts have become less ready to strike down forfeiture clauses. In *Clayton v Ramsden*[45] the House of Lords struck down a provision for forfeiture on marriage to a person "not of Jewish parentage and of the Jewish faith". It was unanimously held that the first limb (and therefore the whole condition) was void for uncertainty and in

---

[43] In *Mettoy Pension Trustees Ltd* [1990] 1 W.L.R. 1587 at 1617–1618, Warner J considered that whether a discretionary trust or a discretionary fiduciary power was concerned the court could intervene to give effect to the settlor's intentions by appointing new trustees or authorising or directing representative persons of the classes of persons capable of benefiting to prepare a scheme for dealing with the trust property or even itself decide how the trust property should be dealt with. This was approved by *Schmidt v Rosewood Trust Ltd* [2003] UKPC 26, paras 42 and 51, so that if a discretionary trust for everyone (except 4 persons) is administratively unworkable so should a discretionary power to appoint to anyone (except 4 persons), although a power to add anyone in the world (except 4 persons) to a class of beneficiaries was accepted as valid by the PC, counsel having accepted such validity. Perhaps letters of wishes may provide workability.
[44] *Re Gape* [1952] Ch. 743.
[45] [1943] A.C. 320.

obiter dicta a 4:1 majority concluded that the second limb was similarly void. Then, in *Blathwayt v Baron Cawley*[46] the House of Lords upheld a condition for forfeiture if someone should "be or become a Roman Catholic". In *Re Tepper's W.T.*[47] a provision for forfeiture if the beneficiaries did not remain within the Jewish faith or married outside the Jewish faith was not inevitably struck down in the light of *Clayton v Ramsden*. Scott J. gave leave to the parties to adduce extra evidence of surrounding circumstance to elucidate the meaning of "the Jewish faith" as used by the testator, having pointed out that in *Clayton* it seemed there was no evidence before the court as to the meaning of Jewish faith. He said[48]:

"The question is what the testator, sitting in his armchair, meant by 'the Jewish faith.' Direct evidence of his intention is not admissible; but I would have regarded as admissible extra evidence of the Jewish faith as practised by the testator and his family. It would, in my view, be well arguable that he meant the Jewish faith in accordance with which he practised his religion. If evidence of that character were allowed it might well be possible to attribute to the expression 'the Jewish faith' a meaning sufficiently certain to enable the *Clayton v Ramsden* test to be satisfied."

Where the condition for forfeiture is conceptually certain, but there may be evidential uncertainty as to whether or not forfeiture has in fact occurred, it will be possible to avoid an application to the court if the trust instrument provides that the opinion of the trustees (or of some third party like a widow) is to be conclusive on the question of forfeiture.[49] If conceptual uncertainty is inherent in the forfeiting condition then, since conceptual uncertainty *ex hypothesi* cannot be resolved by the court, it cannot *a fortiori* be resolved by the court-policed opinion of the trustees under a provision purporting to make such opinion conclusive.[50]

QUALIFICATION CLAUSES (CONDITIONS PRECEDENT)

Settlors sometimes provide that a person will only qualify as a beneficiary if he satisfies some condition or answers to some particular description: the question then arises as to how certain and administratively workable must the condition or description be.

Logically, if the words used are conceptually uncertain it should

[46] [1976] A.C. 397.
[47] [1987] Ch. 358.
[48] *Ibid*, at 377.
[49] *Dundee General Hospitals Board v Walker* [1952] 1 All E.R. 896.
[50] *Re Coxen* [1948] Ch. 747; *Re Jones* [1953] Ch. 135; *Re Wright's W.T.* [1981] L.S.Gaz. 841.

be immaterial whether such words appear as part of a condition subsequent or of a condition precedent: if the condition subsequent would be void for uncertainty why should not the condition precedent be equally void? This is reinforced when one considers that the effect of X qualifying under a condition precedent is to divest Y of the interest that would otherwise be his, and Y and the trustees ought to be able to see precisely and distinctly upon what contingency Y's claim is to be overridden by X's claim.

Case law, for the present however, requires a distinction to be made between conditions subsequent and conditions precedent. A distinction also needs to be made between class gifts and individual gifts. There is a *class* gift where property is held on trust for equal or discretionary distribution between qualifying members of a class, for example £1 million to be distributed as my trustees see fit between such of my siblings' children as marry persons of the Jewish faith and of Jewish parentage. The test for certainty of qualification for discretionary trusts is the *McPhail v Doulton* test that one must be able to say of any given claimant that he is or he is not within the beneficial class, so the above trust will be void as *Clayton v Ramsden* indicates.

There is an *individual* gift where trustees are to give particular property or a specified amount of money to each person who comes within a qualifying class description (for example £5,000 to each of my friends' children who marry persons of the Jewish faith and of Jewish parentage) or to specific ascertained individuals if they satisfy the qualifying conditions (for example Bleak House to my son, Abraham, if he marries a woman of Jewish faith and of Jewish parentage, but if he does not, then for Gideon absolutely). With class gifts the ultimate amounts to be taken by beneficiaries are at first uncertain whilst with individual gifts the amounts are quantified from the outset, although the aggregate value passing to the individuals is uncertain until the number of such individuals is ascertained.

The better view in the case of individual gifts to unspecified members of a class is that the condition or qualification will be void for conceptual uncertainty if one cannot provide a comprehensive list of the individuals who qualify as members of the class.[51] It ought not to be sufficient for the claimant to be able to show that, whatever the conceptual uncertainty of the qualifying wording, he at least has complied with it, being within the narrowest part of the "core" meaning when this is not sufficient for a claimant beneficiary under a class gift. There is an obviously difficult borderline between

---

[51] See Hayton & Marshall, *Commentary and Cases on the Law of Trusts and Equitable Remedies* (11th ed.), pp. 175–177 criticising *Re Barlow's W.T.* [1979] 1 W.L.R. 278.

the "core" meaning and the "penumbra". A qualifying beneficiary has a right to sue the trustee or executor for his gift, while the person entitled to the fund after payment thereout to qualifying beneficiaries has a right to sue the trustee or executor for wrongful payment to non-qualifying beneficiaries. The trustee or executor "between the devil and the deep blue sea" must be able to judge how many persons are beneficiaries he must pay (so that he must pay no one else), and so must the court, but how can this be done, which requires provision of a list, where there is unjusticiable conceptual uncertainty? Even if the narrowest part of the "core" meaning can be certain, why should there be authority in the trustees or the court to distribute the property among a smaller class than that indicated by the settlor? The House of Lords refused to do this in the case of discretionary trusts or discretionary fiduciary powers for classes.[52]

In the case of an individual gift to an ascertained individual (such as my elder son, Abraham), where the person entitled to the property in default of that individual satisfying the condition precedent only has that ascertained individual to worry about rather than an expansive uncertain class, as a concession to human sentiment, one may accept that individual's entitlement if he satisfies the "core" meaning of the concept.[53]

Here pragmatism prevails over logic, so effect is given to the intentions of the settlor/testator as modified by the court. Normally, it is a question of "all or nothing", the court having no power to delete unsatisfactory uncertain words or to rewrite trusts in narrower more certain terminology. The court cannot guess how the settlor/testator would have wanted to rewrite his disposition. If the settlor is still alive and the trusts are void for uncertainty there is a resulting trust which affords him the opportunity to try again using more certain language. If he is dead he cannot try again, so the courts will be more reluctant to declare his trusts void.

THE BENEFICIARY PRINCIPLE

The essence of a trust is that it is an obligation concerning property which is enforceable in the courts which will control the trustees and, in a rare case, even carry out the trust. There must thus be beneficiaries who can apply to the court to enforce their rights. As Millett L.J. states,[54] "If the beneficiaries have no rights enforceable against the trustees there are no trusts". It follows that a trust may be created for the benefit of persons but not for a purpose unless

---

[52] *Re Gulbenkian's S.T.* [1970] A.C. 508; *McPhail v Doulton* [1971] A.C. 424.
[53] *Re Allen* [1953] Ch. 810.
[54] *Armitage v Nurse* [1998] Ch. 241 at 253.

that purpose be charitable, for a purpose cannot sue, but if it be charitable the Attorney General may sue to enforce it.[55]

Where, however, the trust, though expressed as a purpose, is directly or indirectly for the benefit of an individual or individuals it is in general outside the mischief of the beneficiary principle. Exceptionally, where that benefit is so indirect or intangible or the purpose trust is otherwise so framed as not to give those benefited any *locus standi* to apply to the court to enforce the trust, the beneficiary principle will invalidate the trust. The principle invalidates purpose trusts which are abstract or impersonal, like trusts for furthering the purposes of the Socialist Party or of a contemplative order of nuns, the objection being not that the trust is for a purpose but that there is no beneficiary with *locus standi* to enforce the trust, but query whether express appointment of an enforcer with *locus standi* to sue could justify the valid its of a purpose trust that is administratively workable and restricted to a valid perpetuity period (see p.40 above). A *power* to carry out such abstract purposes is valid but the court will not allow what has been construed as a *trust* to take effect as though it were a power in order to enable the purposes to be carried out. Such an approach is allowed in some states in America and in Ontario and this seems preferable as a matter of policy.

In *Re Denley's Trust Deed*[56] Goff J. upheld a trust of land conveyed by a company to trustees so that, until the expiration of a specified perpetuity period, the land should be maintained and used as and for the purpose of a recreation or sports ground for the benefit of employees of the company. Such employees could take out court proceedings to restrain the trustees from improperly using or disposing of the land and for an order that the trustees allow the employees the use of the land for recreational purposes. In a tax case, *Wicks v Firth*,[57] the House of Lords assumed that an educational trust set up by I.C.I. for the award of scholarships within a specified perpetuity period to children of employees of I.C.I. or certain subsidiary companies for full-time study at universities or other comparable establishments was valid. After all, such children could sue to enforce scholarships awarded to them as well as sue to restrain the trustees from distributing funds to persons who were not children of I.C.I. employees or sue to remove the trustees for acting capriciously.

Because beneficiaries with *locus standi* to sue to enforce purpose trusts for their benefit are essentially in a position no weaker than that of beneficiaries under a discretionary trust, Vinelott J. in *Re*

---

[55] *Leahy v Attorney General for New South Wales* [1959] A.C. 457 at 478.
[56] [1969] 1 Ch. 373.
[57] [1983] A.C. 214.

Grant's W.T.[58] opined that *Denley* was simply a discretionary trust for individuals. Whether a trust is regarded as a discretionary trust for individuals or as a purpose trust benefiting individuals with *locus standi* to sue, it will satisfy the beneficiary principle, but the distinction becomes of practical significance when one considers the rule in *Saunders v Vautier* and whether the trust is subject to the rule against remoteness or the rule against inalienability.

The Impact of the Rule in *Saunders v Vautier*

The rule in *Saunders v Vautier* enables beneficiaries of full capacity, where they are all ascertained and between them absolutely entitled to the trust property, to demand to have such property transferred to them and so terminate the trust: the collective absolute owner can do what a sole absolute owner can do. Take the case where trustees hold property on trust to pay the income for 21 years between such of A, B, C, D and E as they see fit and then to distribute the capital between such of R, S, T, U, V, W, X, Y and Z as they see fit. If each is of full capacity, A, B, C, D, E, R, S, T, U, V, W, X, Y and Z can unanimously elect to divide the trust property between themselves as they agree. If each is of full capacity, A, B, C, D and E can for 21 years unanimously elect to take the whole income and divide it between them equally or as they otherwise agree. If each is of full capacity, R, S, T, U, V, W, X, Y and Z can then unanimously elect to take the whole capital and divide it between them equally or as they otherwise agree. If the beneficiaries are a fluctuating body of persons, like present and future employees of a company, then they cannot exercise *Saunders v Vautier* rights because one cannot currently ascertain all the beneficiaries in order to obtain unanimous agreement.

If a settlor settles property *absolutely* on B, aged nine years, and directs that the income shall be accumulated for 21 years and only then paid to B, B, on attaining majority, can terminate the trust and stop the accumulations as the person solely, absolutely and beneficially entitled to the trust property, and so take the trust property and the income therefrom. To prevent B obtaining the trust capital and income before attaining 30, the settlor should have settled property on B *contingent* upon B attaining 30 years of age and directed accumulation of income for 21 years.

What then of the position of a testator who bequeaths to his executors £80,000 "on trust to use the income only for providing holidays for my workaholic solicitor son, Simon, during his life, remainder to his children equally", and £80,000 "on trust to use the income only for educating and maintaining my lazy son, Larry, at medical school until he attains 25 years of age when he should have become a qualified doctor and to pay the capital to him if he obtains the post of Senior Houseman at a hospital in the UK?" Can Simon claim the income as of right and not take holidays: can Larry, aged 21, claim the income as of right till he attains 25 even if he changes to read law or gives up university altogether?

They can do so if the trust is regarded as a trust of income for the benefit of Simon for life and of Larry till he attains 25 years with the purpose of benefiting them in a particular way, since as sane adults they can decide what is for their own benefit and how to use their own income. This accords with the *Saunders v Vautier* philosophy which frustrates a settlor's intentions where an absolutely entitled, fully capable beneficiary prefers to be benefited in a different way.

If, instead, the trust is regarded as coming within a separate category of purpose trust then the income remains with the trustees for them to use only for the specified purposes, so long as such purposes are not void for uncertainty, illegality or public policy, and if the purposes cannot be carried out then the testamentary trust of income fails (so as to accelerate the trust of capital or to be held on resulting trust for the residuary legatee under the will).

However, such a development of the *Re Denley* purpose trust approach would contravene the *Saunders v Vautier* philosophy which really treats as void for public policy any attempt by a settlor to prevent the sane adult beneficiary intended to be benefited without having to satisfy a contingency, from deciding how he wants to be benefited. Thus if Blackacre is held on trust for A for life, remainder to B, and a testator bequeaths £10,000 on trust to be spent on planting trees on Blackacre, then A and B can, instead, elect to take the £10,000 for themselves.[59] In England it seems it will, in practice,[60] not be open to the House of Lords to overturn the *Saunders v Vautier* principle, as a core principle of antiquity.

To avoid such principle and give effect to the testator's intentions regarding Simon and Larry in the above examples, the testator would need to make the payments for purposes conditional or contingent. He should direct the executors to pay income to Simon equivalent to the amount of any sums paid by Simon in each year for holidays personally enjoyed by Simon and to pay income to Larry if Larry is attending a full-time course at medical school, but otherwise to pay the income to X.

Contingent purpose trusts benefiting persons with *locus standi* to enforce the purposes avoid the *Saunders v Vautier* principle unless

---

[59] See *Re Bowes* [1896] 1 Ch. 507, which happens to have been endorsed in *Re Denley* by Goff J. who thus did not contemplate that his decision might be used to subvert the *Saunders v Vautier* philosophy.

[60] *e.g.* approach in *Rhone v Stephens* [1994] 2 A.C 310.

the contingent beneficiaries link up with the persons otherwise absolutely entitled to the trust property. Thus, if a testator bequeaths £250,000 to trustees on trust *if* A, B or C attend fee-paying schools or attend university or receive musical instrument lessons or sports coaching sessions, to pay so far as possible out of income, but with power to have resort to capital, the fees therefor together with attendant travelling and maintenance expenses, but otherwise on trust for the NSPCC, then there would be a valid trust for the benefit of A, B and C, though if they were aged 18, 19 and 20 years, being contingent beneficiaries, they could not claim all the income under *Saunders v Vautier*. However, with the agreement of the NSPCC, income and, indeed, capital could be divided up as agreed unanimously, no one but A, B, C and the NSPCC being interested in the trust fund.[61]

There will also be a valid trust if a testator bequeaths £250,000 to trustees by way of a contingent purpose trust to pay out of income direct to the relevant school treasurer any school fees of his relatives (a fluctuating class) if they attend fee-paying schools until the expiry of 21 years from the death of the last surviving grandchild of the testator alive at the testator's death, with any unexpended income and capital to pass to the NSPCC. Current relatives and the NSPCC cannot prejudice future relatives by agreeing to divide up the capital before the very end of the perpetuity period, by which time the relatives will have lost their bargaining power, so that the capital will then pass to the NSPCC as intended by the testator.

Exceptions to Beneficiary Principle

In *Re Endacott*[62] the Court of Appeal accepted that there are some anomalous cases which, as concessions to human sentiment, provide exceptions to the beneficiary principle. These cases are testamentary trusts for (1) the erection or maintenance of graves and sepulchral monuments; (2) the maintenance of particular animals; (3) the saying of private masses by priests; and (4) the promotion and furtherance of fox-hunting.[63] Harman L.J. said: "These cases stand by themselves and ought not to be increased in number, nor indeed followed, except where the one is exactly like another."

These are said to be trusts of imperfect obligation since the trustees are not obliged to carry out the trusts because the trusts are for purposes which, of course, have no *locus standi* to sue. To the

---

[61] *e.g. Tod v Barton* (2002) 4 I.T.E.L.R. 715.
[62] [1960] Ch. 232.
[63] *Re Thompson* [1934] Ch. 342 where Trinity Hall, the default beneficiary otherwise entitled, only objected *pro forma*, not wishing to offend *alumni* of a "hunting, shooting and fishing" mentality.

extent that the trustees do not actually use the trust property to effect the anomalous purposes under the *power* conferred upon them by the testator, then the beneficiaries otherwise entitled to such property may claim it and also prevent it being used in any other way.

To prevent these anomalous purpose trusts from continuing indefinitely they must be restricted to the perpetuity period of 21 years (or a period of 21 years from the death of the last survivor of specified lives in being at the date of the will). If the testator directs that the executors and trustees are to use the income for the specified purpose "so far as they legally can do so" or "so far as the law allows" then the trust will be regarded as restricted to the perpetuity period of 21 years.[64]

RULES AGAINST PERPETUITY OR ACCUMULATIONS

It has long been English policy to prevent a settlor creating a trust fund for persons or for purposes that will enable the settlor to rule the living from the grave (for example by requiring his descendants if they are to benefit to take his surname, to be Catholics, and not to marry persons who are not Catholics or who are of a stigmatised racial or ethnic origin) for an excessively long period, and that will take capital out of the category of entrepreneurial risk capital into safe trust capital for too long. There are two mutually exclusive rules against perpetuity: (1) the rule against remoteness of vesting applicable only to trusts for persons; and (2) the rule against inalienability, otherwise known as the rule against purpose trusts of excessive duration. The Perpetuities and Accumulations Act 1964 has radically reformed the rule against remoteness (so that one can wait and see what happens) but does not apply to the rule against inalienability applicable to purpose trusts (which must be applied at the outset to make void such trusts as infringe it).

The Rule Against Purpose Trusts of Excessive Duration

If property is left on trust to be applied indefinitely for the purpose of maintaining a tombstone or a testator's pet animals and their issue, then the trust fund is tied up for ever and the income therefrom is inalienable since it must be applied for the purposes. Although the actual trust property within the fund may change regularly, as certain investments are sold and other investments purchased with the proceeds of sale, the fund itself has forever to be set aside as a capital endowment fund to support the purposes for ever. Such a non-charitable purpose trust will be void: to be valid it

---

[64] *Re Hooper* [1932] 1 Ch. 38.

must be clear from the outset that persons will become absolutely entitled to the trust property by the end of the perpetuity period of 21 years or of 21 years from the death of some specified life in being at the creation of the trust. Charitable purpose trusts are exempt from the rule since they are for the public benefit and are to be encouraged to continue for ever.

The Rule Against Remoteness of Vesting

Where property is set aside as endowment capital on trusts to use the income therefrom so that persons may have successive interests therein over a lengthy period, it will be necessary after the first few interests for subsequent persons' interests to be contingent upon their birth if nothing else. To restrict such subsequent persons' interests, a contingent future interest was held to be void unless at the creation of the trust it was *absolutely* certain that the contingency would be satisfied, so that the interest would become vested in interest (though not necessarily vested in possession), within the perpetuity period of 21 years from the death of some expressly or impliedly specified life in being at the creation of the trust. If T died, leaving his estate to W for life, then for S for life, then for T's grandchildren who attain 21 years of age, W has a life interest vested in possession (a right of present enjoyment), S has a life interest vested in interest (a present right to future enjoyment) and grandchildren under 21 have contingent interests (a present right to stop breaches of trust but only maturing into a right to future enjoyment of the trust property if the contingency is satisfied, which must be the case, if at all, within 21 years of the deaths of their parents who are implied lives in being).

A future interest is said to be vested in interest once the person or persons entitled to the interest are ascertained and the interest is ready to take effect forthwith upon the ending of all the preceding interests. For the purposes of the rule against remoteness, the size of a beneficiary's interest must also be ascertained before the interest is regarded as vested. Thus at common law a gift to trustees for such of the children of X who attained 25 years was void (if X were still alive and no child had attained 25 so as to close the class of children). A child, born later, might attain 25 more than 21 years after the death of X and any existing children, and the size of the share of each child could not be ascertained till then.

Many harsh results flowed from the principle that a contingent future interest is void if it might possibly, by any stretch of the imagination, vest outside the perpetuity period. Accordingly, the Perpetuities and Accumulations Act 1964 radically reformed the rule against remoteness so that now where such a contingent future interest would be void at common law one "waits and sees", so that such interest is valid until it becomes absolutely certain that it must vest in interest, if at all, outside the perpetuity period of 21 years from the death of statutory lives in being or of a period not exceeding 80 years specified as the perpetuity period in the trust instrument.

Special provisions apply where there is a class of beneficiaries like grandchildren of X or members of a club. Thus if a testator by will leaves his cricket field and pavilion to trustees to hold on trust solely for the members from time to time of Slogworthy Cricket Club, one waits and sees if the club is dissolved within the period of statutory lives in being plus 21 years for the then members (absolutely entitled under the *Saunders* v *Vautier* principle) will divide the property between themselves. Otherwise, at the end of the period persons can still become members and obtain an interest, so s.4(4) of the 1964 Act will apply to exclude such future persons from the class of beneficiaries and the, say, 49 members at the expiry of the period will take absolute vested *Saunders* v *Vautier* interests in the trust property. Hopefully, they will all agree (after buying out any dissentients) that the property should be vested in four club members on a bare trust to be administered for current members according to the rules of the club.

There are also special provisions for discretionary trusts for beneficiaries intended to have unequal benefits. At the end of the statutory perpetuity period the property is held on a resulting trust for the settlor or his estate by virtue of s.3(3) of the 1994 Act. It would seem that the *Re Denley* type of purpose trusts for people should be regarded as subject to the rule against remoteness (not the rule against inalienability which would otherwise invalidate many of such trusts) and where the beneficiaries are intended to benefit unequally under the trustee's discretion and not ultimately to be treated as absolute owners, it would seem that s.3(3) will apply.

The 1964 Act is unsatisfactory in requiring a two stage approach. First, one checks whether the contingent future interest is absolutely certain to vest in interest within the common law period of 21 years from the death of a person whose life is causally related to any event necessary to vesting. If it must so vest it is valid at common law. Otherwise, one proceeds, secondly, to "wait and see" and treat the interest as valid until it becomes certain that the contingent gift must vest in interest outside the period of 21 years from the death of a person within a statutory list of measuring lives.

The statutory list, which is arbitrary and both over-inclusive and under-inclusive, was chosen to replace common law lives under the misapprehension that common law lives were only those lives that necessarily validated a gift so that no such measuring lives existed when a gift was void. A statutory list (including potential beneficiaries and their parents and grandparents) was thus required for those cases where a gift was void at common law.

However, consider gifts on trust for the first grandchild of A to marry, or for such of A's grandchildren as attain 21 years, or for such of A's grandchildren alive 50 years after my death. The causally related lives in being are A, his children and grandchildren living at the date of the gift.[65] A is causally related because A can affect the identity of beneficiaries by fathering a child who begets a child, while A's children can affect the identity of beneficiaries by begetting children. A's existing grandchildren are causally related because they may satisfy the condition precedent and claim the prize. All three gifts are void at common law. It is theoretically possible for all lives in being other than A to expire within a week, for A to father X in a year's time and himself die a year later, and for X to beget a child who goes on to satisfy the relevant contingency more than 21 years after the death of A, the last surviving life in being.

Rule Against Accumulations

Originally, the period during which trust money could be tied up so as to accumulate at compound interest was co-extensive with the perpetuity period for the rule against remoteness. Members of Parliament, fearful of the economic and social consequences of such hoarding of income for a period that might exceed 100 years and fearing for what their fathers might do with the property they hoped to produce income for themselves, ensured that income can now only be accumulated and added to capital (whether under a trust or a power to accumulate) for one of the following six possible periods under the Law of Property Act 1925, s.164 (replacing the Thellusson Act 1800) and the Perpetuities and Accumulations Act 1964, s.13:

(1) the life of the grantor or settlor;
(2) 21 years from the death of the grantor, settlor or testator;
(3) the duration of the minority or respective minorities of any person(s) living or conceived at the death of the grantor, settlor or testator;
(4) the duration of the minority or respective minorities only of any person(s) who under the instrument directing the accumulations would, for the time being, if of full age, be entitled to the income directed to be accumulated;
(5) 21 years from making of the disposition;

---

[65] See J. Dukeminier (1986) 102 L.Q.R. 250.

(6)   the duration of the minority or the respective minorities of any persons in being at the date of the disposition.

If an excessive accumulation infringes the perpetuity period it is wholly void: if it is within that period but in excess of the six accumulation periods, it is cut back to the nearest appropriate period of the six and only the excess is void.

Independently, s.31 of the Trustee Act provides for income to be accumulated during a beneficiary's minority save to the extent used for the maintenance, education or benefit of such beneficiary.

The economic and social fears of accumulation have proved groundless so that in Eire and Northern Ireland it is possible to accumulate for the whole common law perpetuity period, while in the Isle of Man and in Jersey (both obviously part of the United Kingdom) it is possible to accumulate for the whole statutory perpetuity period of 80 and 100 years respectively. It would make obvious sense if English law allowed accumulations up to the 80-year statutory perpetuity period. Indeed, the English Law Commission in its April 1998 Report No. 251 has recommended a compulsory perpetuity period of 125 years during which it will be permissible to accumulate income.

JUDICIAL LEEWAY FOR BENIGN VALIDATING CONSTRUCTION

Many questions of validity of trusts hinge upon the construction of the wording in the trust instrument. If the words "for any purposes connected with the education and welfare of children" are construed disjunctively as covering two distinct purposes, the trust will be a void non-charitable purpose trust since all the property is not devoted exclusively to educational purposes (which are charitable), but if those words are construed conjunctively so that the welfare purposes must also be educational then the trust will be a valid charitable trust.[66] A benevolent conjunctive approach was taken to trusts for "charitable and benevolent" purposes.[67] If a testator leaves his residuary estate on trust for "those who have only received small legacies" this will be void for uncertainty unless "small" can be given a meaning in the context of a will, for example if there are two classes of legatees one receiving legacies over £1,000 and the other receiving legacies of no more than £200.[68]

As discussed earlier in this Chapter, where a testator left his residuary estate to the trustees on trust "for the Hull Judeans

---

[66] *Attorney General of Bahamas v Royal Trust Co.* [1986] 1 W.L.R. 1001, in which, however, it was not possible to take the conjunctive approach.
[67] *Re Best* [1904] 2 Ch. 354.
[68] *Re Steel* [1979] Ch. 218.

(Maccabi) Association in memory of my late wife to be used solely in the work of constructing the new buildings for the Association and/or improvements to the said buildings" it was not construed as a capital endowment trust for the purpose of the club so that the trust capital converted into the new club house must be held for ever for the purposes of the club. It was merely an outright gift accruing to the club's funds subject to the members' contractual rights thereto under the club's constitution.[69] Such benign construction saves many dispositions to unincorporated associations which have no legal personality, being merely a collection of members joined by contract for the fulfilment of some purpose.

Where there are two possible constructions due to an ambiguity of wording then a construction should be chosen that makes a trust valid rather than void.[70] Thus a discretionary trust for Cambridge students or for Manchester United Fans could be restricted to students registered with Cambridge University and to members of Manchester United Supporters' Club.

---

[69] *Re Lipinski's W.T.* [1976] Ch. 235.

[70] *IRC v McMullen* [1981] A.C. 1 at 11; *Guild v I.R.C.* [1992] 2 A.C. 310, where "similar purpose in connection with sport" was restricted to a charitable purpose; *Re Hetherington* [1989] 2 All E.R. 129; *Charles v Barzey* [2002] UKPC 68, para 12.

CHAPTER FOUR

Charitable Trusts

FAVOURED TREATMENT

Trust Law

The policy of upholding charitable trusts in the public interest means that charitable purposes need not be certain, as long as the settlor revealed a general charitable intention, and are valid even if consisting of pure abstract purposes which may continue for ever. Where there is such an initial general charitable intention or where property has been effectively dedicated to a charitable organisation or purpose which subsequently fails, then the property will be applied *cy-près* by the court or the Charity Commissioners for some closely allied organisation or purpose to the exclusion of the settlor or his heirs. A trust instrument may provide in certain events for trust income to pass over from one charity to another charity and so on to other charities indefinitely without restriction to a perpetuity period. There is no limit on the number of trustees of a charitable trust and such trustees can act by a majority (though for private trusts unanimity is required unless otherwise authorised by the trust instrument).

Tax Treatment of Charities

Generally, charities (whether trusts or corporations) are exempt from income tax (other than for dividend income), capital gains tax, corporation tax, inheritance tax and stamp duty. Where trading income (as opposed to investment income) is concerned a charity is only exempt from tax:

(1) if the purpose or one of the primary purposes of the charity is to carry on the particular trade; or

(2) if the work in connection with the trade is mainly carried out by the beneficiaries.

If substantial trading is being carried on which is not within the exemption (and the realisation of donated goods is not a trade) then the charity will form a company to carry on the trade and have the company covenant to pay its net profits to the charity for a period capable of exceeding three years. The company deducts the covenanted payment from the chargeable profits liable to tax so that no tax is payable. It must deduct from the gross covenanted payment income tax at the basic rate before making the payment to the charity and must account to the Revenue for the tax so deducted: the charity is then entitled to claim repayment of this tax. Gift aid may now be used to transfer profits of the company to the charity. In the case of council tax rates from April 1, 1993, 80 percent mandatory relief applies to land which is occupied by or used by a charity and wholly or mainly used for charitable purposes: discretionary relief is available for the other 20 per cent if the local authority sees fit.

The exemption from income and capital taxes applies only to the extent that the income or capital is applied to charitable purposes only. While a trust for the education of children in the United Kingdom is a charitable trust, no tax exemptions will be available if the trustees operate the trust as a private trust for the benefit only of the children of A, B and C. To prevent misuse of fiscal privileges the Finance Act 1986 has special anti-avoidance measures restricting relief where payments are made to overseas bodies (for example to "launder" company profits through "tame" off-shore charities) without taking reasonable steps to ensure that the payments are then used for charitable purposes and where non-arm's-length loans or investments are made which cannot be shown to be for the benefit of the charity. Where the charity loses tax exemption this can affect the position of those who have made covenants in favour of the charity.

Tax Incentives to Donors

Basic and higher rate income tax relief is available (via deduction at source and via submission of tax returns respectively) for individuals' charitable covenants capable of exceeding three years (and the lump sum representing four annual payments may be forthwith deposited and one-quarter of the debt released each year). Companies obtain similar corporation tax relief for such covenants. The charity can recover from the Revenue the amount of basic rate tax or corporation tax deducted at source by the individual or the company. Individuals and companies can also make one-off Gift Aid donations which have the same effect as if paid under a qualifying covenant. Where their employer has a recognised payroll deduction scheme, individuals can also make donations to a charity. Such donations are deductible expenses of the individual and are paid gross to an approved charitable agent to pay the selected charity.

Transfers to charities are exempt from inheritance tax and are taxed on a no-gain no-loss basis for capital gains tax so that no such tax is payable by the donor.

CHARITABLE STRUCTURES

Once a charity goes much beyond direct handouts to the needy it is necessary for there to be some institutional structure to carry out charitable purposes. With the decline of the Church's power and the breakdown of feudal relationships and the beginnings of capitalism, the charitable trust emerged in the sixteenth century as the means of carrying out philanthropic desires. Between 1540 and 1660 almshouses increased in number from 40 to 750 and grammar schools from 30 to 540. The Chancery Court enforced charitable trusts as part of its jurisdiction over trusts and developed rules favourable to the enforcement of charitable trusts. In 1601 the Statute of Charitable Uses was enacted as part of the Poor Law Code to provide for an administrative system of supervision of charitable trusts: the terms of its preamble are still referred to today in ascertaining whether or not a trust is charitable.

In the eighteenth century, while trusts of endowment capital continued to be set up for the income to be used for charitable purposes, many new charitable projects were undertaken by voluntary societies raising money by subscriptions from members and from the public. Such societies were unincorporated associations governed by the contracts binding the members. Some societies had an endowment but many operated as collecting charities being free to spend funds without any distinction between capital and income. The unincorporated association is the governing form but its constitution will usually declare that its property is to be held on trust for its purposes by designated trustees since it has no legal personality and so cannot itself hold property.

Since the Companies Act 1862 those associated with a charitable purpose can instead form a company limited by guarantee (available where profits cannot be distributed to members). Such a company has legal personality distinct from its management committee or its members and so can hold property and enter into contracts. It also has the advantage of limited liability. A small unincorporated charity will often form a company to carry on its activities when the scale of its activities has significantly increased. A special simple procedure is available under ss.50–55 of the Charities Act 1993 (replacing the Charitable Trustees Incorporation Act 1872) for the Charity Commissioners to grant a certificate of incorporation to the trustees of the charity (as opposed to the charity itself), so making title-holding simple, but the individual trustees remain liable as if no incorporation had been effected, a major weakness. However, ss.29 and 30 of the Charities Act 1992 in arranging for the Official Custodian for Charities to divest himself of trust property other than land, enable such property to be vested in a nominee company on behalf of the trustees. Whatever the structure of a charity it may perform subsidiary ancillary trading functions through its trustees or management committee holding the shares in a company limited by shares and registered under the Companies Act 1985 (or 1948 or 1929): such a company can then covenant to pay its profits to the charity so that tax relief is available.

Less usual structures for carrying out charitable purposes include the following: a society registered under the Friendly Societies Act 1974 or registered and incorporated under the Friendly Societies Act 1992; a society, like a housing association, registered under the Industrial and Provident Societies Acts 1965–1975; and a corporation established by statute, royal charter, or Church Measure having statutory effect. The Cabinet Office Strategy Unit has recently recommended the introduction of the Charitable Incorporated Organisation to be available for old and new charities.

THE CHARITY COMMISSION

Under the Charities Act 1993 (and since 1853) there is a Charity Commission established with five Commissioners dealing with charities in England and Wales. In Northern Ireland powers comparable to those of the Commission are exercised by the Department of Finance, while in Scotland the Inland Revenue are effectively the determining body for charitable status, but the Lord Advocate has a supervisory role under the Law Reform (Miscellaneous Provisions) (Scotland) Act 1990.

The Charity Commissioners' functions are to promote the effective use of charitable resources by encouraging better methods of administration, by giving charity trustees advice and by investigating and checking abuses. They have power to investigate and remove trustees and transfer the trust assets to other similar charities. They are under duties to maintain a register of charities, to receive annual reports and accounts, and make them available for public inspection, and to make schemes modernising the purposes and improving the administrative machinery of charities. With the Attorney General's consent the Commissioners may also take legal proceedings on behalf of charities or compromise such proceedings. The Commission is an independent non-ministerial government department responsible to the Home Secretary directly. He is responsible for appointing the Commissioners, making statutory instruments under the 1993 Act, laying the Commissioners' Annual Report before Parliament, supervising and auditing the general efficiency of the Commission and the financial resources allocated to it. He cannot direct the Commissioners about the exercise of their statutory functions: no Parliamentary questions can be addressed to him about their actions in particular cases. The Commission is thus responsible only to the courts in applying the law of charity.

The Annual Report of the Charity Commissioners for 2001-2002 reveals that (leaving aside about 120,000 exempted charities on which see p.115 below) there were then 185,948 registered charities with a total annual income exceeding £26 billion p.a. and total assets exceeding £70 billion. There are over a million charity trustees and over 563,000 paid employees. It is estimated that unpaid charitable work in relationship to direct services is valued at over £8.1 billion, fund-raising £6.6 billion, and administration £790 million. There has been much concern in recent years over the abuse of charitable status and the fact that, after carrying out its main functions, the Commission has had little resources to devote to monitoring and investigating charities. The Woodfield Efficiency Scrutiny, 1987, and the Public Accounts Committee's Monitoring and Control of Charities, 1988, recommended stronger powers to investigate and monitor possible abuse. The Charities Act 1993 provides these stronger powers as well as criminal penalties for trustees that fail to produce annual returns and accounts. The 1992 Act has special provisions controlling public charitable collections as well as private fund raising, while the 1993 Act disqualifies certain unsatisfactory types of person from the capacity to be a trustee of a charity, for example if convicted of a crime of dishonesty or deception, or removed from office as trustee of a charity by order of the Commissioners or the court, or if an undischarged bankrupt.

Extra funding from the Government in 1993 and 2002 has strengthened the Commission significantly so that it can fulfil a more pro-active role. The Government obviously has a special interest in the proper supervision of charities since charities have such extensive tax reliefs and since government departments and statutory bodies make annual grants to charities exceeding £2,000 million. It also wishes to encourage charitable giving so as to reduce the demands on government funds, and to this end members of the public need to have confidence that their donations will be well spent. The Charity Commission has a vital role in ensuring that charitable funds are properly employed. About 100 out of 600 staff are now engaged in monitoring and investigatory tasks. The Public Accounts Committee and the National Audit Office keep the commission on its toes.

REGISTRATION AS A CHARITY

A charity, whatever its structure, must be registered (with conclusive presumption that it is a charity for tax privileges) unless it is an exempt charity or an excepted charity. Exempt charities are large institutions which were exempt from the Commissioners' jurisdiction prior to the 1960 Charities Act because other statutory arrangements for supervision existed, for example most universities, Eton, Winchester, the Church Commissioners and institutions administered by them, major museums, charitable societies registered under the Friendly Societies Act or the Industrial and Provident Societies Acts.

Excepted charities cover tiny charities with less than £1,000 per annum income from property, registered places of worship and charities excepted by order or regulations, for example non-exempt universities, voluntary schools, scout or guide funds, many religious charities.

Where draft *inter vivos* trusts are concerned there is much scope for negotiations with the Commission so as to modify the trusts so that they may be accepted as charitable. In doubtful cases the Commission consults with the Revenue and an informal appeal by way of written submissions may be made to the Commissioners. Thereafter, a formal appeal may be made to the court by the disgruntled trustees or the disgruntled Inland Revenue, as the case may be. Disgruntled trustees hardly ever appeal, since legal aid is not available, and the vast majority of philanthropic organisations at this stage have very scanty resources. Trustees must therefore amend their trusts as indicated by the Commission. The Cabinet Office Strategy Unit has recently recommended the establishment of a new independent tribunal to enable trustees to challenge the Commission's decisions at a reasonable cost.

In testamentary trusts where the beneficiary entitled in default of the validity of the alleged charitable trust alleges that the trust is not charitable and is void, it is quicker and cheaper for such beneficiary or the Attorney General to apply by originating summons directly to the Chancery Division of the High Court for a ruling rather than apply to the Charity Commission and then appeal to the court. Costs will normally be payable out of the deceased's residuary estate. If the ruling is favourable the charity will then be registered.

WHAT ARE "CHARITABLE" PURPOSES?

Introduction

To be charitable, purposes must fall within the spirit and intendment of the preamble to the Statute of Charitable Uses 1601 and so be (a) for relief of poverty, (b) for advancement of education, (c) for advancement of religion, or (d) for other miscellaneous purposes beneficial to the community which the law recognises as charitable,[1] or fall within the Recreational Charities Act 1958 by providing facilities for recreation or other leisure-time occupation in the interests of social welfare. Except in the case of the relief of poverty, it is also necessary that the purposes have an element of public benefit, namely they must provide a benefit of a tangible nature for the public at large or a sufficient section thereof. Even then, the purposes may be disqualified from charitable status if they involve profit distribution to participants or are substantially political or contain an overt element of self-help.

Preamble to 1601 Act

The preamble is as follows:

"Whereas lands, tenements, rents, annuities, profits, hereditaments, goods, chattels, money and stock of money, have been heretofore given, limited, appointed, and assigned as well by the Queen's most excellent majesty, and her most noble progenitors, as by sundry other well disposed persons: some for relief of aged, impotent, and poor people, some for maintenance of sick and maimed soldiers and mariners, schools of learning, free schools, and scholars in universities; some for repair of bridges, ports, havens, causeways, churches, sea banks and highways; some for education and preferment of orphans; some for or towards the relief, stock or maintenance of houses of correction; some for marriages of poor maids; some for supporting, aid, and help of young tradesmen, handicraftsmen, and persons decayed; and others for relief or redemption of prisoners or captives, and for aid or ease of any poor inhabitants concerning payment of fifteens, setting out of soldiers and other taxes; which lands, tenements, rents, annuities, profits, hereditaments, goods, chattels, money, and stocks of money, nevertheless, have not been employed according to the charitable intent of the givers and founders thereof, by reason of frauds, breaches of trust, and

---

[1] *Commissioners of Income Tax v Pemsel* [1891] A.C. 531 at 583 per Lord Macnaghten.

negligence in those that should pay, deliver and employ the same."

In legislative and historical context the Act was intended to be almost wholly confined to purposes which would operate for the benefit of the public as a whole and for reducing the burden of parish poor relief and other parochial obligations on ratepayers: the purposes were to benefit the poor and not the rich except where necessarily incidental (see Francis Moore's 1607 Reading on the 1601 Statute). However, the actual wording of the preamble when divorced from its context enabled nineteenth century courts to separate trusts for the relief of poverty from trusts for the advancement of education or of religion or of objects of general public utility.

This broadening of the meaning of charitable enabled the courts to strike down charitable testamentary trusts of land or charitable *inter vivos* trusts of land created within 12 months of the settlor's death since such charitable trusts were void under the Mortmain and Charitable Uses Act 1736 (unless in favour of the universities and colleges of Oxford and Cambridge or the schools, Eton, Winchester and Westminster). This Act was to prevent the disinheritance of families of testators (except in a specially good cause!). A trust for the publication of the works of Joanna Southcott who claimed she was pregnant by the Holy Ghost and would give birth to a second Messiah was thus held charitable so that *it was void*.[2] The sentiment underlying the 1736 Act of not allowing charity to take property away from a testator's family led to the requirement that if the gift was initially impossible or impracticable then the property reverted to the testator's estate to pass to his family, unless there was a general charitable intention present when the property would be applied *cy-près* for closely allied charitable purposes. The 1736 Act was repealed but substantially re-enacted by an 1888 Act of the same title. All such restrictions on charitable dispositions were repealed by the Charities Act 1960.

A new expanded definition of charity

The Cabinet Office Strategy Unit has recently recommended that Lord Macnaghten's fourfold classification of charity should be expanded so that "a charity should be defined as an organisation which provides public benefit and has one or more of the following purposes:

(1) the prevention and relief of poverty;

(2) the advancement of education;

[2] *Thornton v Howe* (1862) 31 Beav14.

(3) the advancement of religion;
(4) the advancement of health[3];
(5) social and community advancement[4];
(6) the advancement of culture, arts and heritage;
(7) the advancement of amateur sport;
(8) the promotion of human rights, conflict resolution and reconciliation;
(9) the advancement of environmental protection and improvement;
(10) other purposes beneficial to the community."

Trusts for Relief of Poverty

Poverty is not confined to those who are destitute: it includes those who have to "go short" in the ordinary meaning of that term, due regard being had to their station in life and so forth, for example distressed gentlefolk, ladies of limited means, members of the Savage Club who have fallen on evil days. There is no absolute income level beyond which one cannot be poor (for example the bottom of the scale of taxable income or some point on the legal aid scale) though this would be more egalitarian. A trust cannot be for the relief of poverty if it may also benefit the rich.[5]

Trusts for the relief of poverty are irrebuttably presumed to be for the public benefit so that a trust for a person's poor relations is a valid charitable trust as is a trust for poor employees and ex-employees of a company.[6] However, if the trust is not for the relief of poverty amongst such a class of persons but is really for benefiting particular private persons (for example for the children of A and B for their relief in needy circumstances) albeit with relief of poverty as the motive, it is regarded as a non-charitable private trust.

Trusts for Advancement of Education

Education has a broad meaning extending beyond establishing or maintaining schools, universities, libraries, museums, teaching posts, and scholarships to the advancement of research, to cultural fields, such as music, drama, dancing and the fine arts, and to intellectual and physical games associated with the educational aims of schools and universities. However, charitable educational pur-

---

[3] Including the prevention and relief of sickness, disease or of human suffering.
[4] Including the care, support and protection of the aged, people with a disability, children and young people.
[5] *Re Gwyon* [1930] 1 Ch. 255 (where any schoolchild could qualify for a pair of knickerbockers with "Gwyon's Present" on the waistband).
[6] *Dingle v Turner* [1972] A.C. 601.

posed do not extend to political propaganda masquerading as education, for example a trust for the study and propagation of Marxism or of the reasons for abolishing vivisection or of the need for Disarmament. The purpose of changing the law or government policy cannot be a charitable purpose.[7] Schools can be run out of charitable trust funds if non-profit-making or if profits are ploughed back into school purposes.[8] Student unions, ancillary to the educational purposes of their universities, are charitable.[9]

Some allegedly educational objects can be rejected as conferring no tangible benefit on a section of the public, for example the training of spiritualistic mediums, the maintenance of the testator's studio and his pictures therein as a public museum where the pictures are atrociously bad and have no public utility nor educative value. However, a trust of money to be "applied towards finding the Bacon-Shakespeare manuscripts" in the belief that Bacon wrote Shakespeare's plays was upheld as involving valid educational research: such research "must either be of educational value to the researcher or must be so directed as to lead to something which will pass into the store of educational material or so as to improve the sum of communicable knowledge in an area which education may cover—education extending to the formation of literary taste and appreciation".[10]

A trust for the advancement of education will not be a valid charitable trust unless the possibility of benefiting thereunder is open to a section of the public. In *Oppenheim v Tobacco Securities Trust*[11] the House of Lords held that the eligible class of beneficiaries cannot constitute a section of the public if the nexus between them is a personal link with a particular person, for example a common ancestor or common employer. Thus a trust for the education of children of employees or ex-employees of the British American Tobacco Co. Limited or any of its subsidiary or allied companies was not charitable even though current employees exceeded 110,000.

This formal personal nexus test leads to certainty but it may also be manipulated so that while a trust for the education of children of employees of Cadbury-Schweppes plc will be non-charitable, a trust

<hr/>

[7] *Southend v Att-Gen* [2000] WTLR 1199; *National Anti-Vivisection Society v IRC* [1948] A.C. 31.

[8] *Abbey Malvern Wells Ltd v Minister of Local Government* [1951] Ch. 728, *Customs & Excise v Bell Concord Educational Trust* [1989] 2 All E.R. 217.

[9] *London Hospital Medical College v IRC* [1976] 1 W.L.R. 613, *Att-Gen v Ross* [1986] 1 W.L.R. 252. Political campaigning by charities is not possible unless subordinately in furtherance of, and ancillary to, their main purpose: see Charity Commission CC9.

[10] *Re Hopkins' W.T.* [1965] Ch. 669 at 680.

[11] [1951] A.C. 297.

for the education of children of inhabitants of Bourneville (many of
whom are employees of Cadbury-Schweppes) will be charitable and
valid. In *Dingle v Turner*[12] their Lordships in *obiter dicta* indicated
that a more flexible approach concerned with the substance of the
matter ought to be appropriate, taking into account the number of
potential beneficiaries and the purposes of the trust, but they disagreed on whether or not a relevant consideration was the settlor's
intention to take advantage of fiscal privileges and create "fringe
benefits" for those associated with the settlor. The purists considered that fiscal considerations should be irrelevant to the question of charitable or non-charitable, the fiscal privileges having
developed long after charitable trusts had developed with their
trusts law privileges, while the realists thought that fiscal considerations had to be examined since they were such a major factor
in a modern context.

Can one avoid application of the personal nexus test by creating,
say, a trust for the advancement of the education of children resident in the United Kingdom, but then expressly direct the trustees
that they must give a preference to children of employees of Super
plc provided the total income so devoted shall not exceed 75 per
cent of the total available income each year? Logically, since there is
a duty—as opposed to a mere power—to prefer the private class,
there is much to be said for treating the trust as severable into a
non-charitable private trust as to 75 per cent and a charitable trust
as to 25 per cent, but logically one may also view the private class as
subsumed within the public class. The High Court and the Charity
Commissioners pragmatically have treated such a trust as charitable, but have left it open to the Revenue to charge tax on the
charitable funds to the extent they are not used for charitable
purposes because the trustees operate the trust as a private trust for
a private class.[13] In practice, it is safer for settlors to rely on the
discretion of their chosen trustees rather than have an express
preference stated in the trust deed which may put the Revenue on
inquiry.

Trusts for the Advancement of Religion

Since the Statute of Charitable Uses 1601 was concerned with the
better marshalling of assets directly or indirectly intended for the
relief of poverty, it does not refer to trusts for the advancement of
religion. It merely refers *inter alia* to the repair of bridges, ports,
causeways, *churches*, seabanks and highways since the parish, the

---

[12] [1972] A.C. 601.
[13] *Re Koettgen* [1954] Ch. 252; *IRC v Educational Grants Association* [1967] Ch. 123
and 993; Annual Report of Charity Commissioners, 1978, paras 86–89.

authority responsible for such repairs, was also the authority responsible for looking after the poor. However, the courts soon held that the equity of the Statute extended to trusts advancing orthodox religion and long regarded as charitable.

Religious toleration has come on apace since then so that nowadays trusts for the advancement of a variety of religions, denominations and sects are accepted as charitable, so long as they contain some genuine form of faith in and worship of a god or gods, and so long as they are not regarded as inculcating doctrines adverse to the very foundation of all religion or subversive of all morality. Trusts for the advancement of the following religions are charitable: the Plymouth or Exclusive Brethren, Buddhism, Islam, Judaism, the Sikh faith and the Unification Church ("the Moonies"), but Scientology is not regarded as a religion and neither is Freemasonry. Bodies which seek to develop ethical and moral standards, but on a wholly humanistic—or atheistic—footing, will not be held to advance religion, though a humanistic body may qualify under the fourth category of charitable purposes.[14]

Some fine distinctions are drawn in the case law. A gift to a vicar "for his work in the parish" is charitable[15] but not a gift to a vicar and churchwardens "for parish work", since in the latter instance there is nothing expressly or impliedly to restrict the work exclusively to work of a religious and charitable nature. The maintenance of a particular grave or tomb is not a charitable purpose if not part of the fabric of a church, but the upkeep of a churchyard, including its graveyard, is a charitable purpose. A gift for the saying of masses in public is charitable, since such is part of religious services tending directly or indirectly towards the instruction or edification of those members of the public in attendance. A trust for the saying of masses in private has not that justification, and is not as yet regarded as charitable simply on the basis that the money paid to the priest celebrating mass assists in the endowment of priests, whose duty and function it is to advance the teaching of the Roman Catholic Church.[16] The doctrinal belief of that Church in the benefits of saying masses in the interests of its deceased members is not susceptible of proof and so cannot sway the court in determining whether saying masses is for the benefit of the public or a sufficient section thereof. It is the court and not the Church that determines what is or is not for the public benefit.

In *Gilmour v Coats*[17] the House of Lords held that a trust for the

---

[14] *Re South Place Ethical Society* [1980] 1 W.L.R. 1565.
[15] *Re Simson* [1946] Ch. 299 *cf. Farley v Westminster Bank* [1939] A.C. 430.
[16] *Re Hetherington* [1990] Ch. 1.
[17] [1949] A.C. 426. Ireland being a good Catholic country, its courts uphold gifts to contemplative orders: *Bank of Ireland Trustee Co. Ltd v Att.-Gen.* [1957] I.R. 257 confirmed by the Irish Charities Act 1960, s. 45(1).

benefit of a Carmelite community of cloistered nuns was not charitable since the public benefit test was not satisfied. No tangible benefit was conferred directly or indirectly upon the public. The benefits of intercessory prayer, while part of doctrinal belief, were "manifestly not susceptible of proof"; the alleged edification of a section of the public by the example of the pious spiritual life of the nuns was "too vague and intangible to satisfy the prescribed test"; the availability of such cloistered life to take any women of the Catholic faith out of the worldly community was not to be regarded as benefiting the public or a section thereof (despite educational scholarships for Founders's kin or open to public competition being charitable).

However, where persons who live in the secular world and mix with their fellow citizens attend at places of worship and then, uplifted, return to the secular world, the courts are entitled to assume that some benefit accrues to the public even though the worshippers (for example the members of the Catford Synagogue) are not in themselves a section of the public but a private class.[18] Since then, *Dingle v Turner*[19] has blurred the distinction between a public and a private class, Lord Cross saying: "A trust to promote some religion among the employees of a company might perhaps safely be held to be charitable provided that it was clear that the benefits were to be purely spiritual."

The strict *Gilmour v Coats* approach to cloistered bodies within "mainline" religions contrasts sharply with the presumption that the religious writings of dubious value of Joanna Southgate (a "foolish and ignorant woman" who believed herself with child by the Holy Ghost) and of Harold Hobbs (a retired builder of fundamentalist Calvinist and pacifist beliefs) are charitable as conferring a tangible benefit on the public.[20]

Trusts for Other Purposes Beneficial to the Community

A purpose is not *ipso facto* charitable merely because it is beneficial to the community: it must also fall within the spirit and intendment of the preamble to the 1601 Statute, taking into account decided cases and analogies with such cases.[21] Thus, the provision of crematoria is charitable, by analogy with the provision of burial grounds, by analogy with upkeep of churchyards, by analogy with the preamble's repair of churches.[22]

---

[18] *Neville Estates Limited v Madden* [1962] Ch. 832.
[19] [1972] A.C. 601.
[20] *Re Watson* [1973] 1 W.L.R. 1472.
[21] *Williams Trustees v IRC* [1947] A.C. 447.
[22] *Scottish Burial Reform and Cremation Society v Glasgow Corporation* [1968] A.C. 138.

Despite such authority, Russell L.J. and Sachs L.J. in *Incorporated Council of Law Reporting v Attorney General*[23] took the view that proceeding by analogy was unnecessary (as accepted by counsel for the Attorney General) where the object cannot be thought otherwise than beneficial to the community and of general public utility, for such object should be presumed charitable unless there are special grounds for holding it to be outside the equity of the 1601 Statute. Subsequently, Dillon J. took the justifiable view that this was contrary to authority, so the proper approach remained that of analogy from the preamble or decided cases.[24] However, the Privy Council recently stated,[25] "Russell L.J.'s appoach has much to commend it".

Within this miscellaneous category of charitable trusts are trusts for the relief of the aged, the infirm, the promotion of health, recreational facilities and public amenities, social rehabilitation, distress resulting from calamities, the protection of human life, limb and property and of the environment, the upholding of the nation and its established structure, the benefit of a locality, animal welfare, and, most recently, the promotion of community participation in healthy recreation by the provision of facilities for playing sport. Thus pure sport for members of a private club is charitable so long as costs of membership are reasonable and the sport requires healthy exercise.

The test of whether those eligible to derive benefit constitute a sufficient section of the public for the trust to be charitable is even more strict than that for educational trusts. This appears from *IRC v Baddeley*[26] which concerned trusts for the religious, moral, social and physical well-being of persons resident in West Ham or Leyton who were Methodists or likely to become Methodists. The social and recreational element vitiated the trust as a charity, but Viscount Simonds and Lord Somervell further held that the eligible persons were not a section of the public. The case concerned a form of relief accorded to a selected few out of a large number equally willing and able to take advantage of it: the beneficiaries were a "class within a class". There was no justification for restricting the broadly defined purposes of general public utility to persons of a particular creed. After all, a trust to build a bridge for the use of Methodists only could not be a charitable trust of general public utility. While there must be a sensible relationship between the benefit conferred and the class chosen to receive it, Lord Reid

---

[23] [1972] Ch. 73.
[24] *Re South Place Ethical Society* [1980] 1 W.L.R. 1565.
[25] *Attorney General of Cayman Islands v Wahr-Hansen* [2001] 1 A.C. 75 at 82.
[26] [1955] A.C. 572.

dissented, considering the class to be a section of the public; and the other two Law Lords expressed no opinion on the point.

Since then the House of Lords in *Dingle v Turner*[27] has taken a more flexible line and has indicated that the question whether the beneficiaries constitute a section of the public rather than a fluc-tuating body of private individuals:

> "is a question of degree and cannot be by itself decisive of the question whether the trust is a charity. Much must depend on the purpose of the trust. It may well be that, on the one hand, a trust to promote some purpose, prima facie charitable, will constitute a charity even though the class of potential beneficiaries might fairly be called a private class and that, on the other hand, a trust to promote another purpose, also prima facie charitable, will not constitute a charity even though the class of potential bene-ficiaries might seem to some people fairly describable as a section of the public."

As a result the Charity Commissioners have registered as chari-table a London Welsh association trust for the benefit of Welsh people in London, by creating a community centre in London for promoting the moral, spiritual and educational welfare of Welsh people, on the basis that Welsh people in London constituted a sufficient section of the public. In Northern Ireland[28] a testamentary gift to set up the Presbyterian Residential Trust to found, or help to found, a home for old Presbyterian persons has been upheld. While each of the four heads must be approached differently, there was a paramount public purpose of assisting the aged which was not negatived by selecting the aged from Presbyterians who constituted a section of the public.

If purposes would be charitable if carried out in England but are purposes exclusively carried out abroad they are still charitable unless it would be contrary to English public policy.[29]

Recreational Charities Act 1958

Uncertainties raised by what was said in cases like *IRC v Baddeley*[30] when dealing with social and physical well-being were thought to jeopardise the charitable status of certain organisations with a social element but which had hitherto been assumed to be chari-table, for example village halls, community centres, women's

---

[27] [1972] A.C. 601.
[28] *Re Dunlop* [1984] N.I. 408
[29] *Re Carapiet's Trusts* [2002] W.T.L.R. 989, paras 30–31 (the advancement in life of Armenian children).
[30] [1955] A.C. 572.

institutes, the National Playing Fields Association. The Recreational Charities Act 1958 was therefore passed to remove such uncertainties but without otherwise disturbing the law, so that section 1 emphasises that nothing is to derogate from the principle that a trust to be charitable must be for the public benefit. Otherwise: "it shall be and be deemed always to have been charitable to provide, or assist in the provision of, facilities for recreation or other leisure-time occupation if the facilities are provided in the interests of social welfare." This social welfare requirement is not satisfied unless:

"(a) the facilities are provided with the object of improving the conditions of life for the persons for whom the facilities are primarily intended; and
(b) either;
　　(i) those persons have need of such facilities by reason of their youth, age, infirmity or disablement, poverty or social and economic circumstances; or
　　(ii) the facilities are to be available to the members or female members of the public at large."

In *IRC v McMullen*[31] a restrictive view was taken of (a) and (b) by Walton J., Stamp and Orr L.JJ, who considered that the Act only applied to the class of persons intended to be benefited (for example young persons) if the class were deprived or disadvantaged in such a way as to have a special need for recreational facilities. Bridge L.J. disagreed, holding that the Act could be used to uphold a trust to provide such facilities for pupils of schools and universities in the United Kingdom even though such beneficiaries could not be said to be a deprived class, since he considered that it is not only the deprived who can have their conditions of life improved. His liberal view has been endorsed by the House of Lords in *Guild v IRC*[32] upholding as charitable a trust for the benefit of the Sports Centre in North Berwick.

Trusts with Mixed Charitable and Non-Charitable Purposes

A discretionary trust for mixed charitable and invalid non-charitable purposes will fail, since for a trust to be a valid charitable trust it must be for exclusively charitable purposes. A trust for charitable or benevolent purposes is thus void[33] for uncertainty and infringement of the beneficiary principle and the rule against inalienability. If it had been for charitable and benevolent purposes (*i.e.* confined

---

[31] [1979] 1 W.L.R. 130.
[32] [1992] 2 A.C. 310.
[33] *Chichester Diocesan Board v Simpson* [1944] A.C. 341.

to benevolent purposes that are charitable) the trust would have been valid. If it had been a testamentary residuary gift for part to be used for charitable purposes and part for benevolent purposes then, on the basis of equality being equity, half would be a valid charitable trust and half a void non-charitable purpose trust. Whether "and" is used conjunctively or disjunctively is a question of construction in context, so that a bequest of residue on trust "for any purposes connected with the education and welfare of Bahamian children" has been held by the Privy Council disjunctively to cover either welfare purposes or education purposes, so that the whole residuary bequest was void.[34]

Judicial intervention has saved some religious trusts from the above rigorous rules. Where there is a gift for a religious purpose which could be carried out in a way which is beneficial to the public (*i.e.* by public masses) but could also be carried out in a way which would not have a sufficient element of public benefit (*i.e.* by private masses) the gift is construed as a gift to be carried out by the methods that are charitable, all non-charitable methods being excluded.[35]

THE *CY-PRÈS* DOCTRINE

Initial Failure of Charitable Trust

If a non-charitable trust cannot take effect and so fails at the outset, there arises a resulting trust for the settlor or his estate if he is dead. However, if a charitable trust cannot take effect but the settlor had a general or paramount charitable intention, then the trust property will be applied *cy-près* to some other charitable purposes as nearly as possible resembling the original purposes, under a scheme formulated by the court or the Charity Commissioners. If the settlor did not have the requisite general or paramount charitable intention then a resulting trust arises, the courts originally being most reluctant to disinherit heirs in favour of charity.

Judges have much leeway in determining whether or not there actually has been an initial failure of the charitable trust and whether or not a general or paramount charitable intention existed. Where property is left on trust for a particular body which existed at the date of the will but ceased to exist before the testator's death, such trust will normally fail unless, which is most unlikely, a general charitable intention can be found. Exceptionally, where the body had a capital endowment which passed to another body carrying out, *inter alia*, purposes of the first body, the court may treat the

---

[34] *Attorney General of Bahamas v Royal Trust Co.* [1986] 1 W.L.R. 1001.
[35] *Re White* [1893] 2 Ch. 41; *Re Hetherington* [1990] Ch. 1.

testator's gift as augmenting the endowed funds, irrespective of which body happens to hold such funds, so that the gift does not fail.[36]

In the case of gifts to bodies which never existed, the courts are ready to infer a general charitable intention, but it is rather rare for the courts to infer such an intention where the gift was to a body which existed at the date of the will, but not at the testator's death, or where the gift was for a purpose which, though possible and practicable at the date of the will, has ceased to be so by the testator's death.[37]

The refusal of the trustees to accept all the terms of a trust may make the trust fail at the outset where, exceptionally, the identity of the trustees is crucial to the carrying out of the trust: normally, equity will not allow a trust to fail for want of a trustee. Thus, if the London College of Music is to be trustee of trusts establishing musical scholarships at the college and the trusts for British boys are restricted to orphans from two institutions (who would, anyway obtain local authority financial assistance which would be reduced *pro tanto* by the amount of the scholarships), the college may refuse to accept the trusteeship if the trusts are so restricted. The court may hold this to be the rare case where the identity of the trustees is vital, so the trust fails, but then may find a general charitable intention exists, which enables a *cy-près* scheme to be made whereby the offending restrictions are deleted from the trusts.[38]

Subsequent Failure of Charitable Trust

Where at the testator's death the designated charitable body existed or it was not then impossible or impracticable to carry out the designated charitable purposes, then the gifted property has become charitable property to the perpetual exclusion of the testator's residuary legatee or next-of-kin. Thus, without the need to prove any general charitable intent the *cy-près* doctrine is available upon any subsequent failure of the trusts. The concept of subsequent failure has been extended by s.13 of the Charities Act 1993 to cover, for example, cases where the original purposes in whole or in part have, since they were laid down, ceased to provide a suitable and effective method of using the property available by virtue of the gift, regard being had to the spirit of the gift, for example if in 1640 a residuary bequest was made to pay the vicar out of the income five shillings a year to support him in his work in the parish with the rest

[36] *Re Faraker* [1912] 2 Ch. 488.
[37] *Re Spence's W.T.* [1979] Ch. 483.
[38] *Re Woodhams* [1981] 1 W.L.R. 493.

of the income to provide bread for the poor in the parish, and the annual income is now £8,000 having been £1 in 1641.[39]

The position for outright *inter vivos* gifts to charitable bodies or for charitable purposes is the same. Once the charity for which the fund was raised has been effectively brought into action the fund is to be regarded as permanently devoted to charity to the exclusion of any resulting trust for the subscribers.[40]

[39] *cf. Re Lepton's Charity* [1972] Ch. 276.
[40] *Re Ulverston & District New Hospital Building Trusts* [1956] Ch. 622.

CHAPTER FIVE

The Settlor

TRANSFER OF PROPERTY TO BE HELD ON TRUST

There cannot be a trust until property has been subjected to the terms of a trust. Normally, the settlor transfers property to the trustees, but he may make himself trustee of certain property by, so to speak, transferring property from his right hand to his left hand, so that it is clear which of his own property has now been appropriated to be held by him on trust for others. A "spes" or hope of acquiring property in the future is not itself property and so cannot be the subject-matter of a gift or trust. B cannot assign (although he can contract to assign) whatever he hopes to inherit on his father's death, or whatever he hopes will be appointed to him as an object of a power of appointment, to trustees for X and Y nor can he declare himself trustee thereof for X and Y.[1] Where, after a life interest for A, B has the remaining interest in capital absolutely or contingent on being alive at A's death or on attaining 30 years, B has a proprietary interest which he can assign or declare trusts of.

Due Formalities Must Be Observed

Where a settlor, S, wants to settle property on beneficiaries by transferring it to trustees he must make sure that the property is effectively transferred to trustees. Money given by cheque will not be effectively transferred till the cheque is cleared, since it could be stopped before then or there might be no funds in the account to satisfy the cheque. Chattels can be transferred by delivery, with

---

[1] *Re Ellenborough* [1903] 1 Ch. 697; *Re Brooks' S.T.* [1939] 1 Ch. 993.

intention to make a gift, or by deed. Legal estates in freehold or leasehold land need to be transferred by deed or a registered land transfer form and equitable interests therein by signed writing. Full legal title to registered land or to shares in a private company only passes when the transferee becomes registered as the new proprietor of the land (which is when all the relevant documents have been delivered to the appropriate district registry) or as the new share-holder. Equitable title, however, in such land or shares passes as soon as the transferor has done everything which it is obligatory for *him* to do, for example executing the appropriate transfer form and delivering the appropriate land or share certificate to the trans-feree.[2]

Where S declares that he is henceforth holding his property on trust for others no formalities are required unless the property is land when, at some stage, signed written evidence must be produced if the trust is to be enforced: see s.53(1)(b) of the Law of Property Act 1925 which saves S from the perils of oral evidence being (mis)used to deprive him of his land. Where S has an equitable interest in property (other than land) under a trust and declares that he holds it on sub-trust for successive beneficiaries or for discre-tionary beneficiaries, so that he retains an active role (for example in keeping "an even hand" between a life tenant interested in income and a remainderman interested in capital) then no formal-ities are needed. If S simply declared he held such interest for a person of full capacity, X, absolutely, then it seems X could directly sue the head trustee, T (joining S as co-defendant so that he would be bound by the decision), so that T would be holding the property for the benefit of X and not S. It follows that, in substance, S's declaration of sub-trust would amount to an assignment of his interest to X, with S dropping out of the picture: such assignment must actually be in signed writing or be void under s.53(1)(c) of the Law of Property Act 1925, which is concerned with providing a paper trail to enable whoever are the trustees to know conclusively to whom their duties are owed, *i.e.* to know who can sue them.

Where S has an absolute equitable interest under a trust, of which T is trustee, what formalities must be observed if S tells T to hold the trust property on trust for X instead of S? The result of S's instruction is that S drops out of the picture, S being responsible for his interest passing to X, so that S has assigned his interest. His instruction to T must therefore be in signed writing (so that T and his successor trustees know where they stand without any problems of oral evidence) or be void under s.53(1)(c) of the Law of Property Act 1925.[3]

---

[2] *Re Rose* [1952] Ch. 499; *Mascall v Mascall* (1984) 49 P. & C.R. 119.
[3] *Grey v IRC* [1960] A.C. 1.

Does the position change if, instead, S tells T to transfer the trust property to Y absolutely and T does so? Yes. T's transfer to Y absolutely at S's instigation destroys or overreaches S's equitable interest in that property and T's trusteeship function in respect of that property, so there is no question of there being any assignment of S's equitable interest within s.53(1)(c).[4] If the last example were extended one step further, so that S told T to transfer the trust property to Y[5] who had agreed to hold on trust for Z, then S may be said to be responsible for disposing of his interest to Z, and signed writing to needed to enable Y, his executor and his successor trustees to know where they stand without any problems of oral evidence, so avoiding the mischief against which s.53(1)(c) is directed.

Where S has an absolute equitable interest under a trust of which T is trustee, but the terms of the trust give T or Mrs S a special power of appointment in favour of, say, S's grandchildren, and it is either T or Mrs S who, pursuant to such power declares that T is henceforth to hold on trust for G1 and G2 equally, instead of for S, this amounts to the creation of a new equitable interest in favour of G1 and G2 and is not a disposition of a subsisting equitable interest within s.53(1)(c).[6] The declaration may be effective, therefore, even if it is not in signed writing, unless land is the subject-matter when written evidence within s.53(1)(b) is required. If, instead of T or Mrs S acting in the above fashion, S himself had orally told T to hold on trust for G1 and G2 equally, then this would amount to S disposing of his subsisting equitable interest and so would be void for failing to be in signed writing as required by s.53(1)(c).[7]

Since the Finance Act 1985, stamp duty, a tax on documents not on oral transactions, is no longer payable *ad valorem* on gifts. There is thus no longer the need to try to arrange matters to be effected orally, especially when there is the danger that the transaction might fall within s.53(1)(c) and so be ineffective to the income tax disadvantage of S.

The Settlor's Obligations Under Covenants

A covenant is a promise contained in a signed, witnessed and delivered deed. At common law if A covenants to pay C £50,000 or to transfer to C Picasso's "Guernica" on C's 25th birthday, then, on attaining 25, C can sue A for £50,000 or for damages of the value of Guernica as the case may be. In equity C cannot obtain specific

---

[4] *Vandervell v IRC* [1967] 2 A.C. 291.
[5] Technically, this was the position is *Grey v IRC* where T and Y happened to be the same persons, holding some property on trust for S and some on trust for S's grandchildren.
[6] *Re Vandervell (No. 2)* [1974] 2 Ch. 269.
[7] *Grey v IRC* [1960] A.C. 1.

performance of A's promise and thus obtain Guernica itself since equity only enforces proper bargains for value and not voluntary unilateral promises even if in a formal deed: "Equity will not assist volunteers" (*i.e.* donees) unless they actually are beneficiaries under a trust of the property in question. While the common law primitively might regard a deed as having magical effect, equity, as a subsequent, sophisticate gloss on the common law, enforced only proper contracts and, even then, only if common law damages were inadequate, as where the subject-matter of the contract was unique like a specific painting or a specific piece of land.

C's common law right to sue A on A's covenant is known as a chose in action. It is a type of property that C can transfer to T1 and T2 on trust for D or, instead, C can declare that he himself henceforth holds the covenant on trust for D. Then T1 and T2—or C—hold the covenant on trust for D, just as they would hold Blackacre on trust for D if C had validly transferred it to T1 and T2 for D or had validly declared himself trustee of it for D. The fact that there is, what is known as, a completely constituted trust (or equitable gift) of the covenant or of Blackacre means that D can enforce it even though he is a mere donee or volunteer. After all, in the vast majority of trusts the beneficiaries are volunteers but have enforceable rights against the trustees in respect of property effectively vested in the trustees on trust for the beneficiaries, whether that property consists of land, shares, equitable interests, copyrights, covenants or other choses in action.

Where an outsider has covenanted with C, and C then assigns the benefit of this covenant to trustees on trust for D, it is obvious that the trustees, or failing them, D (who will need to join the trustees as co-defendants with the covenantor) can enforce this covenant so as to benefit D.

Where it is C himself who covenants with T to transfer property to T on trust for D, the position requires further analysis. Everything hinges on the intention of C which, if not expressed, will depend upon whether the covenant is contained in a one covenant deed or is a minor provision in the middle of a lengthy deed, *e.g.* a marriage settlement, creating forthwith a trust of certain property. If C is regarded as having, for example, covenanted to pay £60,000 to T on D's 30th birthday or to transfer to T whatever C may inherit upon the death of his father *to the intent that the benefit of the covenant shall henceforth be held on trust* for D, then there will be an immediate binding trust *of the covenant* which is property held on trust for D.[8] Thus D, though a volunteer, has enforceable rights to the covenant held on trust for him: there is said to be a completely constituted trust of the covenant.

---

[8] *Fletcher v Fletcher* (1844) Hare 67.

If, however, there is no express or necessarily implied intent to create an *immediate trust of the covenant* but, instead, only an intent (in the context of a lengthy deed) to create a trust of the £60,000 or of the property inherited on the death of C's father when C gets round to transferring it to T after D's birthday or C's father's death, then there can be no trust of such property till transferred to T.[9] Since nothing is held on trust for D he has nothing to enforce: there is said to be no completely constituted trust of the covenant.

What then of C's covenant with T in such a case: can T enforce it at common law? Well, as just seen, T does not hold the covenant on trust for D, and he obviously does not hold the covenant for his own personal benefit, so he can only hold it (and its fruits, like damages) on resulting trust for C. If C refuses to pay up, so T then tries to sue C at common law this will mean that T, holding the covenant on a bare trust for C, is disobeying his absolutely entitled beneficiary: then equity has an exceptional reason to intervene and prevent T from so suing.[10]

The general rule is that equity will not frustrate a volunteer suing at common law. Thus if C, T and D were all parties to the deed in which C covenanted with T and also with D, then D as a covenanting party can sue at common law and obtain damages (but equity will not make a specific performance order where D is a mere volunteer).[11] The position changes if C, T and D were all parties to a contract. Where D provided contractual consideration for the promise he can, of course, sue and obtain damages at common law, but if such would be inadequate due to the special nature of the property to which the promise related he can obtain specific performance in equity.

Where C's lengthy settlement transferred property to T in consideration of marriage and contained the common covenant to transfer to T any property C might inherit on his parents' deaths (so as to keep the family "nest egg" intact) then C's issue are treated as within the marriage consideration, so that as beneficiaries who have provided consideration they may enforce the promise in the covenant.[12] If, however, C's wife died without issue, and the statutory next-of-kin, who were beneficiaries entitled in default of such issue, tried to enforce the promise they would fail, having neither common law contractual rights nor rights in equity since equity will not assist volunteers where there is no completely constituted trust.[13] Of course, if C had carried out his promise and so had completely

---

[9] *Re Kay's Settlement* [1939] Ch. 329; *Re Cook's S.T.* [1965] Ch. 902.
[10] *Hirachand Punamchand v Temple* [1911] 2 K.B. 330; *Ingram v IRC* [1997] 4 All E.R. 395 at 424. Note Contracts (Rights of Third Parties) Act 1999 s.3(2).
[11] *Cannon v Hartley* [1949] Ch. 213.
[12] *Pullan v Koe* [1913] 1 Ch. 9.
[13] *Re Plumptre's M.S.* [1910] 1 Ch. 609.

constituted the trust of the property to which his promise related, then if his wife and issue subsequently died the default beneficiaries could as beneficiaries enforce their rights to such property.

Only the Settlor (or His Agent) Can Constitute a Trust

At common law only the donor or his authorised agent can make an effective gift. If A has bought a ring for his girlfriend, C, and it is being altered ready for collection on Friday, A may request his friend, B, to collect it and deliver it to A on Friday evening, so that A can give it to C on her birthday on Saturday. A tells C about this. She happens to meet B in the street returning from the jeweller. She asks B to let her have the ring so that she can wear it and go round to A's flat as a surprise for him on Saturday lunchtime. She is told by B that he is not supposed to let her have the ring but she dances off with it on her finger.

As it happens, while away on the Friday A discovers that C has been unfaithful to him, so he decides she is not to have the ring. He is furious when B tells him that C now has the ring. He phones C to tell her that their relationship is over and she must return the ring to him. She refuses, saying that since she has the ring she is keeping it: possession is nine-tenths of the law. He tells her that if she does not return it he will sue her and she will have to return it or pay him its value. He is in the right, since a gift requires an authorised delivery by the donor or his agent pursuant to the donor's intention to make a gift: there had been no authorised delivery.

Equity follows the law so that only the settlor or his authorised agent can constitute or "perfect" a trust of the settlor's property. What happens then if A transfers property to Barclays Bank on trust for C and covenants to transfer to the bank whatever he might subsequently inherit on his father's death; his father then makes a will appointing the bank to be executor thereof and bequeathing £100,000 to A; and, on his father's death, the bank takes out a grant of probate to the father's estate and so clearly obtains title to £100,000 that is part of such estate? Can the bank switch the £100,000 held under its executorship "hat" to be held under its trusteeship "hat"? It can do so only if A authorises this: otherwise A can claim the £100,000 for himself and not honour his promise.[14] After all, C is merely a volunteer and equity will not assist volunteers unless they have rights in property under a completely constituted trust thereof as seen in the preceding section hereof.

---

[14]   *Re Brooks' S.T.* [1939] 1 Ch. 993, overlooked in *Re Ralli's W.T.* [1964] Ch. 288.

THE INFLUENCE OF THE SETTLOR

Generally, the trust is the equitable equivalent of the common law gift though it is much more flexible, since the beneficiaries may be unborn or unascertained, and it then has a continuing effect that requires the subject-matter to be managed for a considerable period for the benefit of the beneficiaries. Sometimes, however, the trust results from a contract, as where employer and employee contract that a certain percentage of the employee's salary is to be paid by deduction at source to a pension fund trust to which the employer is to contribute an amount of double the employee's contribution, with the employer to have the right to reduce its contributions where the pension fund has capital surplus to its marginal requirements as certified by an actuary.

Once a settlor has transferred property to trustees then, like an outright donor of property to a donee, he has no rights left in respect of such property. He cannot enforce the trust[15] since it is only the beneficiaries (or the Attorney General for charitable purpose trusts) who have the equitable rights that the courts can enforce. In practice, the trustees will usually listen to what he has to say but they must exercise their own independent minds: if he tells them to appoint £10,000 to B pursuant to their powers in this behalf and they do so automatically without exercising their own discretion, the appointment will be void.[16]

A settlor may, however, reserve to himself in the trust instrument certain powers, though he needs to be aware that some of them may involve disadvantageous consequences so far as tax is concerned or in the event of his bankruptcy. He may reserve power to revoke the trust, in whole or in part, without prejudice to benefits received by the beneficiaries prior to such revocation. He may reserve powers to remove the trustees and appoint new trustees, or powers to delete persons from, or add persons to, the designated class of beneficiaries, or powers to make appointments of income or of capital to such of the beneficiaries as he sees fit. He may reserve powers of veto, or a requirement of consultation, before the trustees exercise their powers to appoint income or capital amongst discretionary beneficiaries, or before the trustees exercise their powers of investment, or before the trustees change the law governing administration of the trust to a foreign law and appoint foreign trustees in place of themselves. He may even reserve to himself the role of discretionary portfolio manager employed by the trustees and subject to light regulation by them (that ensures he cannot thereby

---

[15] *Re Astor's S.T.* [1952] Ch. 534 at 542; *Bradshaw v University College* [1987] All ER 200 at 203.
[16] *Turner v Turner* [1984] Ch. 100.

benefit himself and his spouse as if he were sole beneficial owner and the trust a sham trust).

Instead of reserving powers of the above types to himself he may confer some of them on a person commonly called the "protector", who knows the settlor and the beneficiaries well, especially where the trustees are professional trustees without much familiarity with the settlor and the beneficiaries. Alternatively, he may provide that these powers are only to pass to the protector on his death or earlier mental incapacity. In simpler cases it may well be that after his death the settlor stipulates that his widow is to have certain powers or, where many shares in the family company are held by the trust, that whoever is managing director shall have certain powers. In a complex case the protector may even be a company controlled by the settlor or members of his family.

To guide the protector or the trustees after his death, when many discretions will fall to be exercised, the settlor will usually provide a letter of wishes that is to have no binding legal force but which is expected to be taken very seriously into account especially in case a beneficiary alleges that the trustees have not exercised their fiduciary powers bona fide for the purposes for which the settlor conferred the powers. However, the trustees, after considering the letter of wishes, can properly decide that circumstances have changed since the letter was written so that they do not follow the letter of wishes but take another course of action.

The settlor may also be a trustee or sole trustee, and even a beneficiary as well, but it is impossible for him to be sole trustee and sole beneficiary: S cannot hold on trust for S, since a person cannot have rights against himself, but S and T can hold on trust for S and T as in the case of co-owned houses.[17] Where S happens to be a beneficiary or trustee then he has additional rights or duties as such, but he needs to be aware that his additional capacity might have disadvantageous consequences so far as tax is concerned or in the event of his bankruptcy.

BORDERLINE BETWEEN TRUST AND AGENCY OR PARTNERSHIP

There must come a stage when the settlor's influence or control is so excessive that the trustees must in substance be treated merely as agents administering and distributing his property as he wants. This arises where, as a matter of form or as a matter of substance the trustee, T, holds the capital and the income arising therefrom to the order of the settlor, S, who remains beneficial owner of the property he transferred to T. However, despite a power of revocation

[17] *Re Cook* [1948] Ch. 212.

reserved by S in a trust for S for life, remainder to his children equally unless by will he appoints the capital unequally between them in such shares as he sees fit, or remainder on a discretionary trust for the descendants of S, such a trust is perfectly valid. There is a crucial difference in form between property *now* held to the order of S and property held for the benefit of others *until* S formally orders whatever remains of it to be held to his order. However, if S and T ignore this formal distinction so that, as a matter of substance, T from the outset deals with the trust property as directed by S, the formal trust will be treated as a sham trust, the real trust being one for S.[18]

Where the trustees merely invest trust funds the question of partnership cannot arise since "partnership is the relation which subsists between persons carrying on a business in common with a view of profit": s.1 of the Partnership Act 1890. Trustees of unit trusts which invest in shares to provide dividends and capital growth for unit holders are thus merely co-owners of the investments held on trust for the common benefit of the unit holders.[19]

If, however, a trust fund is set up so that the trustees can deal in or speculate in widgets, commodities, or stocks and shares, so Schedule D trading is being carried on for income tax purposes, then there may be a partnership if this business is carried on by, or on behalf of, those sharing the net profits, for example if the four trustees are the four beneficiaries or if the trustees can only deal within parameters directed by the beneficiaries (acting unanimously or via a committee), when all these persons will be regarded as partners and liable for each other's acts in the course of the partnership.

THE SETTLOR AND THE REVENUE OR HIS HEIRS

As revealed by the last section, the settlor has to be aware that the Revenue or his heirs may intervene to claim that he has created no trust but an agency or partnership relationship. They may invoke principles of trust or of property law to claim that no effective trust at all has been created or that the settlor has failed to dispose of all his interest in the settled property. Here the Revenue's purpose will be to establish that the settlor or his personal representatives, if he is dead, are still entitled to capital or income of the trust property and so are properly assessable to tax in respect of it. If the settlor is

[18] *Rahman v Chase Bank (C.I.) Trust Co Ltd* [1991] Jersey L.R. 103; "When is a Trust not a Trust" D.J. Hayton (1992) 1 J.Int. Trust & Corp. Pl. 3.
[19] *Smith v Anderson* (1880) 15 Ch.D. 247. Generally, see K.F. Sin, *The Legal Nature of the Unit Trust* (Clarendon, Oxford, 1997).

dead, his heirs or creditors may claim that the trust property remained part of his estate available to them.

As a matter of tax law the Revenue may also invoke anti-avoidance provisions in Pt XV of the Income and Corporation Taxes Act 1988 to treat trust income as the settlor's income, for example if income or capital is paid out to minor children of the settlor or if the settlor and his spouse are not entirely excluded from benefiting under the settlement.

BORDERLINE BETWEEN TESTAMENTARY AND LIFETIME DISPOSITIONS

If a settlor, S, transfers property to a trustee, T, on trusts under which in S's lifetime income is payable to S and then, on his death capital passes to S's children equally, this is a valid form of trust taking effect forthwith, even if S reserves a power of revocation or T has a power to appoint capital to S and, in considering whether or not to exercise it, is directed to consider the interests of S to the exclusion of the interests of S's children. However, if in S's lifetime capital and income are held to the order of S and, on S's death, whatever remains is to pass to S's children equally, this is a testamentary disposition requiring compliance with the formalities of the Wills Act 1837 (requiring two witnesses, while a deed requires only one witness). After all, S remains absolute beneficial owner of the assets transferred to T.

If S in his lifetime opens a joint bank account in the name of S and B, with S to have withdrawal rights upon his signature alone and B to have such rights only upon both signatures, so that on S's death B will be entitled to everything in the account by virtue of the *ius accrescendi* of the joint tenancy, there is no testamentary disposition by S. The creation of the joint tenancy by S is a lifetime disposition of a fluctuating and defeasible interest, which automatically accrues to the survivor by virtue of the feature that distinguishes a joint tenancy from a tenancy in common.[20]

The essence of the joint account[21] is that it is a simple way to achieve the same as would be achieved by S transferring assets to T on trust for S for life, remainder to B, but with power for S to revoke the trust in his lifetime wholly or partly from time to time. For this very reason the joint account with the bank could be one under which in S's lifetime the money can only be withdrawn by S, the money remaining to accrue to the survivor of S and B.

---

[20] *Young v Sealey* [1949] Ch. 278; *Re Figgis* [1969] 1 Ch. 123; *Russell v Scott* (1936) 155 C.L.R. 440 (Australia); *Lynch v Burke* [1995] 2 I.R. 159.

[21] Which may extend beyond cash to securities: *Aroso v Coutts & Co* [2001] W.T.L.R. 797.

CHAPTER SIX

The Trustees

Trustees have many duties which are strict and onerous except to the extent that the trust instrument moderates them to a greater or lesser extent. The trust instrument may qualify or restrict trustees' duties as much as the settlor wishes so long as his wishes are not uncertain, illegal or contrary to public policy and do not negate the very existence of a trust relationship. Thus, one cannot exclude the duty to act in good faith (namely honestly and not recklessly) nor the duty to provide accounts for the beneficiaries: "if the beneficiaries have no rights against the trustees there are no trusts."[1]

Trustees' duties are either equitable duties (for example to exercise reasonable care, to diversify investments unless the settlor intended otherwise, to provide accounts promptly) or fiduciary duties. A fiduciary must act in good faith, must not act for his own benefit or the benefit of a third person without the informed consent of those to whom he owes his fiduciary duties, must not (unless clearly authorised by those persons or the trust instrument) put himself in a position where his self-interest conflicts with his fiduciary duty or if in such a position must prefer his fiduciary duty over his self-interest, must not act for two principals or two trusts without authorisation and if an actual conflict of duty arises he must cease to act for one principal or trust and preferably both.[2] Breach of fiduciary duty connotes disloyalty or infidelity: mere incompetence is not enough.[3]

---

[1] *Armitage v Nurse* [1998] Ch. 241 at 253, CA. The Pensions Act 1995, however, restricts what a company-settlor can insert in the company's pension trust.
[2] *Bristol & West B.S. v Mothew* [1996] 4 All E.R. 698 at 712, CA.
[3] *ibid.*

Where a trustee is in breach of his fiduciary duty of undivided loyalty or otherwise does what he is not authorised to do he becomes strictly liable to account for profits[4] or losses,[5] but the court at trial can see if such breach was subsequently remedied or authorised as may occur in the case of commercial trusts. Thus, a trustee holding money on trust to pay it over to X only upon security being provided for repayment may pay it over without obtaining security. However, if security is provided a few weeks later then the breach is remedied. If the client for whom the trustee is a bare trustee then, upon the borrower's request, agrees that the security can be released by the trustee, any loss flowing from the debt being unsecured cannot be recovered. However, if the trustee knowing that a request by the borrower to exchange the original "certificate" for a new "Bond" is to switch for the secured debt an unsecured debt and does not make this crucial point clear to the client when obtaining the client's agreement, then the trustee remains liable to the client for loss arising from the debt being unsecured.[6]

Where a trustee merely does badly what he is authorised to do, then his accounts will be surcharged with the amount of money that would have been there but for the trustee's breach of trust. Thus, where a solicitor received the lender's money on trust to pay it over on completion of a purchase of land in return for a mortgage over that land, but the solicitor pays out the money without obtaining the mortgage till four weeks later, then the loss arising from the land being sold for £one million less then the amount of the loan due to a fraudulent scheme can only be recovered if it is proved that but for the four weeks opportunity provided by the breach of trust the mortgage fraud could not have been carried out.[7]

Trustees automatically have many powers which may be extended or qualified by the trust instrument, so long as the relevant trust clause is not uncertain, illegal or contrary to public policy (for example a power to accumulate income for 80 years contravenes English but not Jersey or Isle of Man rules). Many extra powers are usually conferred by well-drafted trust instruments, so that the trustees end up, for investment purposes, having all the powers of a natural person acting as the beneficial owner of the trust property but without detracting from their equitable or fiduciary duties to the trust beneficiaries.

---

[4] *Boardman v Phipps* [1967] 2 A.C. 46.
[5] *Hodgkinson v Simms* (1994) 117 D.L.R. (4th) 161.
[6] *Youyang Pty Ltd v Minter Ellison* [2003] H.C.A. 15.
[7] *Target Holdings Ltd v Redferns* [1996] A.C. 421.

DUTIES OF TRUSTEES

Summary of Main Duties

Before looking at some specific duties in more detail it may help to see that trustees' main duties are as follows:

1. To bring and keep under their control the trust property which must be kept separate from their private property and from any other property of which they are trustees unless they are authorised to "pool" trust property with other trust property in a large segregated pool of assets. Originally, they had to keep the property in their joint names but they are now (under the Trustee Act 2000) authorised to keep it in the name of any nominee or custodian.

2. To safeguard the value of the trust fund by investing in investments authorised under the trust instrument or otherwise under the Trustee Act 2000.

3. To administer the trust honestly and impartially for the benefit of all the beneficiaries and so keep "an even hand" or "fair balance" between those beneficiaries currently entitled and those entitled in the future; except that in the case of discretionary trusts it is meaningless to speak of a duty to act impartially: the trustees are entitled to prefer some beneficiaries over other beneficiaries, so long as such preference is not based upon irrational or improper factors.

4. To account strictly to the beneficiaries, distributing income to those entitled to it and capital to those entitled to it, and keeping accounts and trust documents (but not those relating to how the trustees came to exercise their discretions) available for inspection by the beneficiaries.

5. To consider the exercise of their powers and if they decide to exercise them, to do so honestly and not capriciously or perversely to any sensible expectation of the settlor nor mistakenly overlooking a material factor. Powers or discretions conferred on trustees must be exercised unanimously unless the trustees are expressly authorised by the trust instrument to act by a majority (or are trustees of a charitable trust or a pensions trust).

6. Not to put themselves in a position where there is a sensible possibility that their self-interest may conflict with their fiduciary duty (or where one fiduciary duty may conflict with another fiduciary duty) so that they cannot

profit from their position without authorisation nor deal with themselves.

7. To exercise such care and skill as is reasonable in the circumstances, having regard in particular:

    (a) to any special knowledge or experience that he has or holds himself out as having, and

    (b) if he acts as trustee in the course of a business or profession, to any special knowledge or experience that it is reasonable to expect of a person acting in the course of that kind of business or profession.

8. Each trustee must act personally except to the extent delegation to other trustees or to agents is authorised under the Trustee Act 2000: a "sleeping trustee" will be liable for the acts of his "active" co-trustees.

9. If a trustee commits a breach of trust he is personally liable for:

    (a) any profit or property acquired by him through the breach, there being a concomitant proprietary liability under a constructive trust;

    (b) any loss caused by his unauthorised acts, *e.g.* in disposing of trust assets; and

    (c) any diminution in what should be the value of the trust fund but for his breach of trust, as explained in Chapter 1.

Investments

The trustees must invest the trust capital and also trust income that is not required to be distributed forthwith. The trust instrument will almost always confer very broad express powers of investment on the trustees, although the Trustee Act 2000[8] now enables a trustee to "make any kind of investment that he could make if he were absolutely entitled to the assets of the trust". It used to be thought that "investing" in "investments" required the purchase of income-producing assets, so that further authorisation was required to permit the purchase of non-income-producing assets expected to provide capital growth, especially if a beneficiary was to be allowed to have gratuitous use of such assets.[9] It thus became common to confer power to purchase assets, whether or not income-producing, and to allow beneficiaries interested in income to have gratuitous use of such assets.

[8] s.3 "general power of investment" restricted to assets other than land, s.8 conferring power to acquire land in the UK for investment or occupation by a beneficiary or for any other reason.

[9] *Re Power* [1947] Ch. 572; *Re Wragg* [1919] 2 Ch. 58.

Nowadays, in the light of modern portfolio investment theory concerned with the risk level of the entire portfolio (rather than the risk attaching to each investment in isolation) and with returns reflecting income yield and capital appreciation,[10] it is likely that making "investments" should cover purchase of non-income-producing assets when balanced by income-producing assets.[11] No one could then complain if the beneficiary interested in income had the gratuitous use of a non-income-producing asset. However, out of caution it is wise to confer on trustees express power to invest *or otherwise apply* trust assets in the acquisition of any asset anywhere, whether or not income-producing.[12] Of course, trustees must remember that even if they do have power to acquire a particular asset they can still be liable for breach of trust in exercising such power if they failed to exercise the degree of care expected of persons investing not for themselves but for the benefit of others.

Unless they are very knowledgeable or otherwise reasonably consider it unnecessary or inappropriate in the particular circumstances, the trustees before exercising their broad investment powers must obtain and consider expert advice from some appropriately qualfied person, *e.g.* one authorised under the Financial Services and Markets Act 2000, having given such person sufficient information to enable proper advice to be given. A person carrying on business as trustee and acting as his own discretionary portfolio manager will himself need to be authorised under the 2000 Act and comply with regulations made thereunder.

In exercising express powers of investment or the statutory powers (*e.g.* in the case of trusts arising under an intestacy or a home-made will) trustees must from time to time review the trust investments and consider whether, having regard to the standard investment criteria, they should be varied.[13] These criteria are (a) the suitability to the trust of investments of the same kind as any particular investment proposed to be made or retained and of that particular investment as an investment of that kind, and (b) the need for diversification of investments of the trust, in so far as is

---

[10] *Cowan v Scargill* [1985] Ch. 270; *Nestle v National Westminster Bank* [2000] W.T.L.R. 795 at 802 per Hoffmann J., Lord Nicholls in (1995) 9 Trust LI.71 at 73; I.N. Legairo (2000) 14 trust L.J. 75.

[11] By *Cook v Medway Housing Society* [1997] S.T.C. 90 at 98 investing in investments covers the "laying out of money in anticipation of a profitable capital or income return", and see Explanatory Notes to Trustee Act 2000, paras 22 and 23, based on Law Com No 260 "Trustees' Powers and Duties" p.22 n.56; but the Charity Commission, surprisingly, in CC14 considers the purchase of non-income producing paintings or antiques as speculative trading and not investing.

[12] Further specific power must be conferred if trustees are to be able to "gear up" the trust fund by borrowing on the security of trust property in order to purchase further property: *Re Suenson-Taylor's Settlement* [1974] 1 W.L.R. 1280.

[13] Trustee Act 2000 s.4.

appropriate to the circumstances of the trust. Where a majority shareholding in the settlor's family company is to be the main asset of the trust the trust instrument will normally make it clear that the shareholding is not to be sold unless the circumstances are exceptional.[14]

Management of the portfolio of trust assets is nowadays such a complex matter that trustees will often delegate this to an agent as permitted by Trustee Act 2000[15] if not expressly authorised in the trust instrument. Before such a delegation the trustees must prepare a policy statement and must include a term in the contract with the agent that he will secure compliance with the policy statement as revised or replaced from time to time.[16] Unless it is reasonably necessary for the trustees to do so, they must not have contractual terms permitting the agent to appoint a substitute, or restricting the liability of the agent or his substitute to the trustees or any beneficiary, or permitting the agent to act in circumstances capable of giving rise to a conflict of interest.[17] The trustees, subject to contrary intention in the trust instrument,[18] must exercise the statutory duty of care in selecting, contracting with, and supervising their agents, removing and replacing them if necessary.[19]

Holding a Fair Balance Between the Beneficiaries

Trustees must keep a fair balance between the beneficiaries, in particular those entitled to capital and those entitled to income. In contrast, executors in realising a deceased's estate and discharging liabilities thereof are under a duty to consider the estate as a whole and are under no duty to consider the effect between the legatees so as to hold the balance fairly between them.[20]

Incidentally, a special feature of the relationship between executors and "legatees" (as a compendious expression covering legatees of bequests of personal property, devisees of devises of land, and next-of-kin inheriting on whole or partial intestacy) is that whatever property comes to the executor *virtute officii* comes to him in full ownership without distinction between legal and equitable interest: the whole property is his, subject to his fiduciary obligation to wind up the deceased's estate in the proper manner.[21] No legatee has any beneficial equitable interest in the assets being

---

[14] *e.g Public Trustee v Cooper* [2001] WTLR 901.
[15] s.11-13.
[16] s.15.
[17] s.14.
[18] s.26, Sch.1 para.7.
[19] s.21, 22, 23.
[20] *Re Hayes' W.T.* [1971] 1 W.L.R. 758.
[21] *Commissioner of Stamp Duties v Livingston* [1965] A.C. 694.

administered: he has an equitable right (a chose in action) to have the estate properly administered so that he will ultimately receive his due entitlement. This chose in action may be disposed of by will or by lifetime disposition.[22] If the testator left his residuary estate after payment of debts, expenses and liabilities to his executors on trust for A for life, remainder to B absolutely, A and B only obtain an equitable proprietary interest under a trust when the executors have wound-up the estate by paying off all debts, expenses and liabilities.[23] At such stage where land is involved the executors ought formally to execute a written document, known as an assent, vesting legal title to land in themselves in their new capacity as trustees.[24]

Some special rules have evolved to protect successive beneficiaries. In the above testamentary trust of residue for A for life and then B absolutely, it would obviously be unfair to charge debts, expenses and liabilities exclusively to the interest of A or of B. Thus, the rule in *Allhusen v Whittell*[25] prescribes a method for treating such payments as coming partly from income and partly from capital subject to the testator's contrary intent. Where the testator's residuary personal property held for A for life and then B absolutely comprises unauthorised investments or non-income producing investments like reversionary interests, so that A is receiving too much or too little income then the rules in *Howe v Dartmouth*[26] and *Re Earl of Chesterfield's Trusts*[27] apply (subject to contrary intent) so that the investments must be sold in order that the proceeds can be invested in authorised investments. Till such sale A's excess income over a fair rate must be apportioned to capital, while if A received no income then on sale of a reversionary interest or on a reversionary interest falling into possession (as where S settled on A for life and then B absolutely S's reversionary interest in property settled on W for life, remainder to S, and W died 15 years later) A must be compensated out of capital for the income he ought to have received.

The above-mentioned rules do not apply to lifetime trusts of necessarily specific property, where the trustees are expressly or implicitly authorised to retain such property but have power to sell such property pursuant to their duty to keep a fair balance between the beneficiaries. Thus, if the property consists just of shares in a company which is only producing a 2 per cent return, due to

---

[22] *Marshall v Kerr* [1995] 1 A.C. 148 at 157–158.
[23] For inheritance tax purposes however A and B have interests from the date of the testator's death: Inheritance Tax Act 1984, s. 91.
[24] *Re King's W.T.* [1964] Ch. 542.
[25] (1867) L.R. 4 Eq. 295.
[26] (1802) 7 Ves. 137.
[27] (1883) 24 Ch.D. 643.

company policy concerned with pursuing high capital growth in share values, then the shares ought to be sold and the proceeds invested in shares or gilts producing a fairer income return unless the income beneficiary otherwise desires[28] (as where she has sufficient income, taking other sources into account, and the remainderman is her son whom she wishes to benefit). The trustees must take into account the income needs of the life tenant or the fact that the life tenant was a person close to the settlor and a primary object of the trust whereas the remainderman is a remote relative or a stranger.[29] Thus, the trustees need not adhere to any mechanical rule for preserving the real value of the capital if the life tenant was the widow of the settlor or testator who had fallen upon hard times and the remainderman was a wealthy cousin or charity.

As far as trust expenditure is concerned: "Trustees are entitled to be indemnified out of capital and income of their trust fund against all obligations incurred by the trustees in the due performance of their duties and the due exercise of their powers. The trustees must then debit each item of expenditure either against income or against capital. The general rule is that income must bear all ordinary outgoings of a recurrent nature, such as rates and taxes and interest on charges and encumbrances. Capital must bear all costs, charges and expenses incurred for the benefit of the whole estate."[30] For convenience of administration trustees may be given the administrative power in cases of doubt to determine what expenditure should be attributed to capital and what to income. Where, however, the power expressly enables trustees to discharge out of income expenses that clearly ought to be charged to capital then this may be regarded as a distributive power for swelling capital at the expense of income, so that income beneficiaries do not have an interest in possession for inheritance tax purposes.

Traditionally, the concept of capital and income (the "tree" and "fruit of the tree") and the need to balance the interests of those beneficiaries interested in capital and those in income seem fundamental to trust law. However, there is no trust law reason why a settlor should not expressly require the trust assets to be invested as a single unit, without regard to income returns and capital growth as separate entities, and provide that a percentage (*e.g.* four per cent) in each year of the total value of the trust assets (comprising income and capital) shall be paid to B for the rest of B's life or be distributed among a discretionary class of beneficiaries for the

---

[28] *Re Smith* (1971) 16 D.L.R. (3d) 130, 18 D.L.R. (3d) 405. For the converse case of too high an income for the life tenant see *Re Mulligan* [1998] 1 N.Z.L.R. 481.

[29] *Nestle v National Westminster Bank* [2000] W.T.L.R. 795 at 803.

[30] *Carver v Duncan* [1985] A.C. 1082 at 1120, *per* Lord Templeman. The flexible power in Trustee Act 2000 s.31(1) in the light of s.39 must be exercised fairly between income and capital beneficiaries.

duration of a perpetuity period (or used for a particular charitable purpose for ever). Trustees' investment considerations can then be divorced from the "even hand" or "fair balance" requirements.

Due Consideration of Their Powers

Where there are discretionary *trusts* over income then the trustees must distribute the income, though they have power to select which persons amongst the class of beneficiaries are to receive income in such amounts as they choose. If the trustees fail to exercise their discretion the trusts over income remain exercisable despite the passing of time, though only in favour of such persons as would have been within the beneficial class if the discretion had been exercised within a reasonable time.[31]

Where trustees merely have a *power* of appointment of income amongst a class of objects, then if they do not exercise that power within a reasonable time of receiving the income in question, such income must pass to the beneficiary entitled in default of appointment, the power ceasing to be exercisable in relation thereto.[32]

It is necessary for trustees to appreciate that they have a discretion whether or not to exercise a fiduciary power, that they must consider from time to time whether or not to exercise such power, and they must then consciously exercise this discretion by deciding to do nothing or to act in pursuance of such discretion.[33] Once there is a conscious exercise of discretion the court will not interfere unless it can be shown that the particular purported exercise of the power is unauthorised on a proper construction of the terms of the power or that the trustees acted in bad faith, oppressively, corruptly or perversely to any sensible expectation of the settlor,[34] or would not have acted as they did had they not mistakenly taken into account considerations which they should not have taken into account or had they not mistakenly failed to take into account considerations which they ought to have taken into account.[35]

In *Re Hastings-Bass*[36] the trustees only had power to advance assets out of their trust into a new trust if for the benefit of B, so that the advancement would have been void in equity if not for the benefit of B due to mistakenly overlooking the effect of the rule

[31] *Re Locker's S.T.* [1977] 1 W.L.R. 1323.
[32] *Re Allen-Meyrick's W.T.* [1966] 1 W.L.R. 499.
[33] *Turner v Turner* [1984] Ch. 100.
[34] *Edge v Pensions Ombudsman* [2000] Ch. 602; *Re Hay's Settlement Trusts* [1982] 1 W.L.R. 202; *Re Manisty's Settlement* [1974] Ch.17.
[35] *Re Hastings-Bass* [1975] Ch.25 at 41; *Mettoy Pension Trustees Ltd v Evans* [1991] 2 All E.R. 513 at 552–555.
[36] [1975] Ch. 25.

against remoteness. Because that rule only made void the remainders after B's life interest and the advancement to trustees for B for life saved estate duty as intended, the advancement was upheld because the trustees would still have made the advancement to B for life even if they had known the remainders to be void. Normally, a mistake makes the disposition voidable,[37] *e.g* where the settlor made a second settlement on a child, believing it to be the first settlement on that child, forgetting she had years earlier made a settlement on that child, or where a life tenant under a protective trust released his interest to his children interested in the capital absolutely after his life interest, mistakenly believing this transferred absolute equitable ownership to them, rather than activating a discretionary trust for himself and his children for the rest of his life.[38]

Most surprisingly, in two cases[39] where trustees were not mistaken as to the effect of the documents they deliberately executed, but were mistaken as to the unfortunate tax consequences,[40] the High Court held them to be void (so that trustees alone of all taxpayers can undo what they did and also save themselves from liability for negligence to the beneficiaries) because the trustees would not have executed the particular documents if they had not overlooked the disastrous tax consequences.

It is submitted that not only were the Courts wrong to allow mistakes as to disadvantageous consequences to permit intervention by the Courts, but, as held in *Re Barr's Settlement*,[41] the documents should only have been held voidable, so that there should have been examination of whether or not any of the usual bars to equity setting aside dispositions should apply.

In the context of pension trusts where the beneficiaries are also settlors who have earned their rights as deferred remuneration and so have legitimate expectations that their trustees when called upon to decide matters (like whether there is permanent disablement to justify an early retirement pension or whether someone was a deceased member's partner to receive a pension) will, like bodies subject to judicial review, not make a decision that no reasonable body could possibly make, the courts have been prepared to hold that if the trustees failed to take account of a material consideration and that consideration "might" (not "would") materially have

---

[37] On voidable in equity see *Cloutte v Storey* [1911] 1 Ch. 18 at 30-32.

[38] *Hood v Mackinnon* [1909] 1 Ch. 476; *Gibbon v Mitchell* [1990] 1 W.L.R. 1304; *AMP (UK) plc v Barker* [2001] W.T.L.R. 1237 at 1260, *Anker-Petersen v Christensen* [2002] W.T.L.R. 313 at 330-331.

[39] *Green v Cobham* [2000] W.T.L.R. 1101; *Abacus Trust Co Ltd v NSPCC* [2001] W.T.L.R. 953.

[40] Such would not be operative mistakes for rectifying or setting aside documents: see note 38 cases.

[41] [2003] 1 All E.R. 763, [2003] W.T.L.R. 149.

affected their decision, then the decision is void (like decisions void[42] for *Wednesbury*[43] unreasonableness in judicial review).

This is justifiable for pension trusts but for private family trusts a discretionary decision of trustees should only be *voidable* if the trustees mistakenly failed to take into account a material consideration and *would*[44] have acted differently but for such mistake.

Strict Duty to Distribute Trust Property to Right Persons

Trustees are strictly liable if they fail to distribute the trust property to the right person[45] (for example on termination of a trust or under the exercise of a power of appointment) except to the extent that the trust instrument excludes such strict liability (for example by providing the trustees are not to be liable so long as they act honestly) or the court wholly or partly relieves the trustees from liability. The court can do this where the trustees show they acted honestly and reasonably and ought fairly to be excused for the breach of trust and for omitting to obtain the directions of the court in the matter in which the breach was committed.[46]

In cases of doubt as to the claim, share, existence or identity or legitimacy of a beneficiary, the trustees should submit the matter to the court for determination by a claim under Part 64 of the Civil Procedure Rules. The court has a central paternalistic role to play wherever the trustees need advice or assistance. Specific statutory protection[47] is accorded to trustees (and personal representatives) where they distribute property without notice of legitimated or adopted persons, whose existence affects entitlement to such property, or where they distribute property after protecting themselves under s.27 of the Trustee Act 1925 by advertising for claims of creditors or persons born out of wedlock ranking as beneficiaries and then not receiving any such claims.

Duty to Act Gratuitously Unless Authorised to Charge

Trustees, unless specifically authorised by the trust instrument or by statute, have no right to charge for their time and trouble for, otherwise, out of self-interest "the trust estate might be loaded and

---

[42] *Stannard v Fisons Pension Trust Ltd* [1999] I.R.L.R. 27, *AMP (UK) Ltd v Barker* [2001] W.T.L.R. 1237, *Hearn v Younger* [2002] W.T.L.R. 1317.

[43] *Associated Provincial Picture Houses Ltd v Wednesbury Corporation* [1948] 1 K.B. 223; R.Davern, pp.438-442 of DJ Hayton (ed), *Extending the Boundaries of Trusts and Similar Ring-Fenced Funds* (Kluwer, 2002).

[44] *Re Green Trust* [2003] W.T.L.R. 377, para 29.

[45] *Eaves v Hickson* (1861) 30 Beav 136; *Re Hulkes* (1886) 33 Ch.D. 552.

[46] Trustee Act 1925 s.21.

[47] *e.g.* Adoption Act 1976, s.45; Legitimacy Act 1976, s.7.

made of little value".[48] Even where friends are prepared to act gratuitously as original trustees, a properly drafted trust instrument should contain a charging clause expressly authorising reasonable remuneration of trustees since successor trustees may not be prepared to act gratuitously. However, the court has an inherent jurisdiction to authorise a trustee to receive remuneration prospectively or retrospectively or to increase the level of remuneration authorised by the trust instrument.

"In exercising that jurisdiction the Court has to balance two influences. The first is that the office of trustee is, as such, gratuitous; the Court will accordingly be careful to protect the interests of the beneficiaries against claims by the trustees. The second is that it is of great importance to the beneficiaries that the trust should be well administered. If, therefore, the Court concludes, having regard to the nature of the trust, to the experience and skill of a particular trustee and to the amounts which he seeks to charge when compared with what other trustees might require to be paid for their services, and to all the other circumstances of the case, that it would be in the interests of the beneficiaries to increase the remuneration, then the Court may properly do so."[49]

The Trustee Act 2000[50] has revolutionised the position so that (unless prohibited by the trust instrument) a EU trust corporation[51] can charge for all its services as trustee, while a trustee who acts in a professional capacity,[52] but is not a trust corporation or a trustee of a charitable trust or a sole trustee, can receive reasonable remuneration out of the trust funds for services as trustee if each other trustee has agreed in writing that he should be remunerated: it matters not that the particular services sought to be remunerated are capable of being provided by a lay trustee as opposed to a professional trustee.[53]

Duty Against Self-Dealing: a Disability

Not only is there the logical, practical impossibility of T selling or

---

[48] *Robinson v Pett* (1734) 3 P. Wms. 249 at 251.
[49] *Re Duke of Norfolk's S.T.* [1982] Ch. 61 at 79, *per* Fox L.J; *Foster v Spencer* [1996] 2 All E.R. 672.
[50] ss.28, 29, 30.
[51] See p.163 below.
[52] "Acts in the course of a profession or business which consists of or includes the provision of services in connection (a) with the management or administration of trusts generally or a particular kind of trust, or (b) any particular aspect of the management or administration of trusts generally or a particular kind of trust": s.25(5).
[53] ss.28(2), 29(4).

leasing or mortgaging property to himself, there is an obvious conflict of interest where a trustee purchases trust property from himself and his co-trustees. Such a purchase is voidable *ex debito justitiae*, however fair the price, at the instance of any beneficiary[54] unless the purchase was authorised by the trust instrument, or by the court, or by s.68 of the Settled Land Act 1925, or was made pursuant to a contract or option arising before the trusteeship arose,[55] or was acquiesced in by the complaining beneficiary, or unless very exceptional circumstances exist so as to take the purchase out of the mischief underlying the rule as in *Holder v Holder*.[56] Similarly, a trustee should not sell his own property to the trust unless authorised.

A trustee can purchase the equitable interest of a beneficiary if he observes the "fair-dealing" rule and shows: "that he has taken no advantage of his position and has made full disclosure to the beneficiary, and that the transaction is fair and honest."[57] If all the equitable interests are so acquired then the trustee will have acquired the trust property itself. The position will be the same where T is trustee of Trust A and of Trust B and assets of Trust B are purchased for Trust A so that the latter's beneficiaries become interested in those assets.

Duty Not to Profit From the Trust

To maintain confidence in the trust institution and to ensure that the beneficiaries receive impartial disinterested assistance from trustees, a trustee is strictly liable to account for any profit made by using trust property or his position as trustee, unless authorised by the trust instrument or by the fully informed beneficiaries, all being of full capacity. It is a strict prophylactic rule to ensure that the trustee cannot be swayed by considerations of personal interest, so it matters not that the trustee acted honestly and in the beneficiaries' best interests, that the beneficiaries benefited as well as the trustee, that otherwise the beneficiaries would not have obtained the benefit and that the benefit was obtained by virtue of the trustee using his own assets, skill and judgment,[58] though the court in its exceptional jurisdiction may authorise payment to him for his special services. The beneficiaries are entitled to the profit without the need for them to go into detailed evidence particularly within the trustees' knowledge to see if the trustees can justify themselves.

---

[54] *Tito v Waddell (No. 2)* [1977] Ch. 106.
[55] *Re Mulholland's W.T.* [1949] 1 All E.R. 460.
[56] [1968] Ch. 353.
[57] *Tito v Waddell (No. 2)* [1977] Ch. 106.
[58] *Boardman v Phipps* [1967] 2 A.C. 46; *Chan v Zacharia* (1984) 154 C.L.R. 178.

The rule extends to other persons in a fiduciary relationship[59] since they, too, must not place themselves in a position where there is a sensible possibility that their self-interest may conflict with their fiduciary duty. Generally, one can say that a fiduciary relationship exists between A and B where A is entitled to expect that B will act in A's (or in their joint) interest to the exclusion of his own separate interest. In *Boardman v Phipps*[60] the solicitor to the trustees was held liable to account for profits made when he took over and reorganised a company in which the trust had a significant minority shareholding with the result that the trust's shareholding appreciated in value as did the shares he purported to purchase for himself. He learnt about the opportunity when representing the trust at a private meeting with the directors of the company. The trust had no power to purchase further shares in the company unless so authorised by the court in an application under s.57 of the Trustee Act 1925. At a certain stage in the solicitor's plan he would not have been able to give impartial advice to the trustees as to seeking court authorisation so that they, instead of he, could make large profits, so dashing the cup of profit from his lips.

Since the solicitor was good for the money, an order that he personally account to the trust for the profits made by him was satisfactory. However, the beneficiaries could successfully have claimed that the solicitor held his shares in the company on constructive trust for the beneficiaries, subject to his lien for the cost of acquisition of the shares, since the general principle is "that which is the fruit of the trust property or of the trusteeship is itself trust property"[61] (for example where a trustee uses the trust shareholding in a company to have himself appointed a director—or fails to use it to prevent himself being appointed a director—he is constructive trustee of the director's fees[62]).

Indeed, if a fiduciary exploits his position to take a bribe or secret commission for his own benefit, the Privy Council[63] has held that that will forthwith be held on constructive trust for the persons to whom the fiduciary owes his duties, so that property purchased with such money will be capable of being traced and held on constructive trust.

[59] *e.g.* company directors *I.D.C. v Cooley* [1972] 1 W.L.R. 443; *Regal Hastings Limited v Gulliver* [1967] 2 A.C. 134.

[60] [1967] 2 A.C. 46.

[61] *Swain v Law Society* [1982] 1 W.L.R. 17 at 36, *per* Oliver L.J.; *Korkontzilas v Sonlos* (1997) 146 D.L.R. (4th) 214.

[62] *Re Gee* [1948] Ch. 284.

[63] *Attorney General of Hong Kong v Reid* [1994] 1 A.C. 324; rejecting *Lister v Stubbs* (1890) 45 Ch.D. 1.

Duty of Care

As seen, a trustee was strictly responsible to see that the trust property was distributed to the right persons, irrespective of mistake fraudulently induced by others, but s.61 of the Trustee Act 1925 is now available for the court to excuse honest and reasonable acts which *may* be breaches of trust: the court does not have to decide that a breach of trust actually *did* occur before granting relief.

Otherwise, an unpaid trustee is expected to exercise the objective care and skill that a prudent man of business would exercise in the management of his own affairs,[64] except that he must invest only as a prudent man of business would invest not for himself but for persons for whom he feels morally obliged to provide.[65] In selling property such as land a trustee, bound in honour, but not in law (formal written contracts not having been exchanged), to sell to X, is under a duty to consider and explore other offers and so "gazump" in order to get the best possible price for the beneficiary.[66] In the case of professionally qualified trustees like solicitors, accountants and fund managers who are paid to act as trustees they must exercise that degree of care and skill which could reasonably be expected of such professional people acting as experts in their own particular fields.[67] Persons who carry on business as professional trustees, like bank trust companies, and advertise themselves as having special expertise as such must meet the subjective higher standards they set themselves up as having.[68] The case law reflected in the above propositions is now largely codified in the Trustee Act 2000[69] so that a trustee "must exercise such care and skill as is reasonable in the circumstances, having regard in particular (a) to any special knowledge or experience that he has or holds himself out as having, and (b) if he acts as a trustee in the course of a business or profession, to any special knowledge or experience that it is reasonable to expect of a person acting in that kind of business or protection." The circumstances include acting gratuitously or for reward and that the trustee is investing for others and not himself; but it would seem that if a lay trustee has special knowledge or experience above that of the ordinary prudent businessperson then he will be held to the higher standard.

The court will be very reluctant indeed to excuse paid trustees from an actual or possible breach of trust under s.61 of the Trustee

---

[64] *Speight v Gaunt* (1883) 9 App.Cas. 1.
[65] *Re Whiteley* (1886) 33 Ch.D. 347 at 355; *Cowan v Scargill* [1985] Ch. 270.
[66] *Buttle v Saunders* [1950] 2 All E.R. 193.
[67] *Bartlett v Barclay's Bank Trust Co. Ltd* [1980] Ch. 515 at 534.
[68] *ibid*; *Re Waterman's W.T.* [1952] 2 All E.R. 1054; Lord Nicholls (1995) 9 Trust L.I. 71 at 73.
[69] s.1.

Act unless the trustees were justifiably misled by a skilful forgery. However, it may well be that the trust instrument contains a clause exempting the trustees from liability in certain circumstances. Indeed, a clause exempting a trustee from liability for losses unless resulting from his own actual fraud has been upheld: a trustee can be exempted from liability for negligence (gross or ordinary) but cannot be exempted from his duty to act honestly and not recklessly.[70] A deliberate breach of trust would seem to be dishonest as taking a risk to the prejudice of another's known rights, but in special circumstances where a reasonable person in the shoes of the trustee would consider the deliberate breach to be in the best interests of the beneficiaries as a whole, the trustee may rely on the exemption clause if having such genuine honest belief.[71] A power for trustees to invest as if they were absolute owners merely confers very wide powers of investment. It does not protect the trustees against the liability for an investment which is a breach of trust because it is one that a prudent man of business would have eschewed.[72]

In making investment decisions which may have differing consequences for differing classes of beneficiaries the trustees must act fairly, but their overriding duty is to invest (taking account of modern portfolio theory[73]) in order to obtain the maximum financial return consistent with their duty to take as much care as a prudent businessman would take if investing for persons for whom he feels morally obliged to provide,[74] a "safety-first" standard encouraging inactivity. Non-financial criteria, such as ethical or ecological criteria, can only be taken into account if investments are equally suitable from the financial viewpoint.[75] Charitable trustees, however, should have an ethical investment policy which excludes companies whose objects conflict with the purposes of the charity and which enables them to balance the risk of financial detriment from excluding certain investments against the risk of their work being hampered if such investments would alienate some of those who support the charity financially or make potential recipients of aid unwilling to be helped because of the source of the charity's money. Charitable trustees can also exclude certain types of investment (for example in armaments, gambling, alcohol or tobacco or in countries where unfair discrimination prevails or where torture is practised) on ethical grounds, but only so long as this does not involve a risk of

[70] *Armitage v Nurse* [1998] Ch. 241.
[71] *Walker v Stones* [2001] Q.B. 902 (HL appeal pending).
[72] *Bartlett v Barclays Bank Trust Co. Ltd* [1980] Ch. 515.
[73] See p.143 above.
[74] *Cowan v Scargill* [1985] Ch. 270.
[75] Megarry V-C. in *Equity, Fiduciaries and Trusts* (T.G. Youdan ed., Carswell, 1989) pp. 149–159.

significant financial detriment because an adequate width of alternative investments remains open.[76] There is normally little difficulty in showing that there is such adequate width.

With family trusts and pension trusts the object is to provide financial benefits to individuals, so maximising financial returns with prudence as the key.

> "If the courts abandon the criteria of best financial interests they have no standard by which to control the trustees' investment policies other than the purely subjective one of whether they agree with the morals or politics of the trustees. But charitable trusts do provide criteria, other than financial interests, by which to assess their investment policies. They exist to further charitable purposes. The grant of bounty has to be assessed by reference to such purposes, and so should the investment policy."[77]

If the courts trust the trustees to make controversial moral judgments when giving away charitable moneys, should they not equally trust them when investing such moneys?

To avoid problems the trust instrument can expressly exclude certain types of investment and expressly require certain considerations to be taken into account: it can also expressly reduce the standard of care to that of a prudent businessman investing on his own behalf or exempt the trustees from liability for loss unless acting recklessly or dishonestly. Indeed, it can oust the duty of care, *e.g.* by stating that the duty of the trustee is to invest, apply or speculate with the Trust Fund as if he were the exceptionally wealthy absolute beneficial owner thereof who could afford to lose the whole Trust Fund without it affecting his standard of living in any way whatsoever.

Duty to Act Personally and Not Delegate

"*Delegatus non potest delegare*" ("a delegate is not able to delegate") with the sanction of automatic vicarious liability for the wrongfully authorised delegate's acts or defaults was the starting point, but management functions may now be collectively delegated under the Trustee Act 2000 to any appropriate agent as discussed at p.144 above.

The managerial or distributive discretions of an individual trustee may be delegated under s.25 of the Trustee Act 1925 (as substituted by the Trustee Delegation Act 1999) which confers on a trustee a

---

[76] *Harries v Church Commissioners* [1992] 1 W.L.R. 1241, CA, rejected plaintiff's policy involving excluding 37 per cent by value of U.K. listed companies but trustees' exclusion of 13 per cent acceptable.

[77] R. Nobles [1992] Conv 117–118.

general power to delegate any or all of his discretions under trusts or powers for a period not exceeding 12 months. Such delegation must be made by power of attorney attested by a witness. The donee of such a power of attorney can be the only other co-trustee of the donor of power. But two trustees or a trust corporation are still needed for executing deeds transferring land and giving receipts for capital money,[78] (so overreaching co-ownership equitable interests) so a sole donee trustee will then need to appoint a co-trustee unless such donee be a trust corporation. This is a United Kingdom or EU corporation formed to act as a professional trustee and having a share capital of £250,000 (or its equivalent) with at least £100,000 (or its equivalent) thereof paid-up in cash. The donor of the power is automatically vicariously liable for the acts or defaults of the donee: this is a very significant sanction.[79]

In the case of trusts of land the trustees may, by s.9 of the Trusts of Land and Appointment of Trustees Act 1996, revocably delegate by power of attorney any of their functions relating to the land to the beneficiary currently entitled to income without any automatic vicarious liability. There will be personal liability, however, if they break their duties of care in reviewing the delegation and in revoking the delegation if need be where the beneficiary is not up to the task of managing the trust property.[80]

POWERS OF TRUSTEES

The power to apply to the court for advice and the statutory powers of investment and of delegation have already been dealt with in considering the duties of trustees. Trustees have other statutory powers to assist them in administering the trust, and a trust instrument will usually confer further powers. Trustees have statutory powers to compound liabilities and settle claims,[81] to give receipts to purchasers of trust property,[82] to fix the value of trust property,[83] to concur with co-owners of land in disposing of trust property to advantage,[84] to partition trust property between co-owning beneficiaries,[85] and to insure trust property against loss or damage, payment of premiums coming out of income or capital.[86]

---

[78] Trustee Delegation Act 1999 s.7.
[79] s.25(7) Trustee Act 1925 as substituted by s.9 of TDA 1999.
[80] Trusts of Land and Appointment of Trustees Act s.9A inserted by Trustee Act 2000 s.40, Sch.2 Pt II, para.47.
[81] Trustee Act 1925, s.15.
[82] *ibid.* s.14.
[83] *ibid.* s.22(3).
[84] *ibid.* s.24; Trustee Act 2000 s.8(3).
[85] Trusts of Land and Appointment of Trustees Act 1996 s.7; *Rodway v Landy [2001] Ch. 703.*
[86] Trusts Act 1925 s.19 as substituted by Trustee Act 2000 s.34.

There is no statutory authority specifically placing a duty upon trustees to insure the trust property but it is difficult to see how, in many circumstances, failure to insure could be consistent with the trustees' general duty to take care of the trust property,[87] except where the cost of premiums is disproportionately high or there are major liquidity problems.

Besides administrative powers, trustees have statutory distributive powers of maintenance and of advancement, which affect the entitlement of beneficiaries to income or capital, and may well also have express distributive powers of appointment.

Section 31 of the Trustee Act 1925 enables trustees properly to maintain beneficiaries who are minors. It creates a *trust* to accumulate income with *power*, instead, to use the income for the maintenance, education or benefit of a minor for whom trustees hold property on trust, whether his interest is vested or contingent, for example a trust of stocks and shares for X's grandchildren contingent upon attaining 30 years of age or for B (aged five years) absolutely. If someone has a prior entitlement to income (for example a life interest) before the minors (for example X's grandchildren or B) then there is no income available to which section 31 can apply. Once the minor becomes an adult then thereafter the income (or his share thereof) must be paid to him even if his interest in capital is contingent on some later qualifying event, for example attaining 30 years of age or marrying. Any income accumulated during his minority, because not applied for his maintenance, education or benefit, may be used as if current income at any time during minority, but on majority it is irrevocably part of the capital as capitalised income and so passes as capital to those entitled to capital (so a grandchild of X who dies before attaining 30 will lose his share of income accumulated before he attained 18 to those who attain 30 even if they were not alive when the accumulation occurred). Three months before a minor attains 18, the trustees should consider whether or not to use accumulated income as current income to benefit him before he attains 18.

Section 32 of the Trustee Act 1925 enables the trustees to pay or apply up to half a beneficiary's prospective share of capital to him whether his share is contingent or (if a minor) vested. Thus, if a grandparent settles £220,000 on a trust for such of his grandchildren as attain 30 years of age and there are currently two grandchildren, aged 10 and 13 years old, the trustees may pay out £50,000 to cover five years school fees of the elder grandchild. If he dies aged 20 and further grandchildren are born, nothing can be done about the lost £50,000 earlier applied for his benefit. If a prior

---

[87] *Re Betty* [1899] 1 Ch.821 at 829; *Kingham v Kingham* [1897] 1 I.R. 170 at 174; *Pateman v Heyen* (1993) 33 N.S.W.L.R. 188.

life interest subsists (for example to my son for life, remainder to his children if they attain 30 years) then no advancement can be made without the written consent of the life tenant who will lose the income produced by that part of the capital which is advanced. The life tenant has an absolute right to refuse to consent to an advancement unless the trust instrument varies the statutory power to allow the trustees to make an advancement without the life tenant's consent. There will be no need for this if the trust instrument gives the trustees a power to appoint capital as they see fit.

Trustees have a right to reimburse themselves or pay out of the trust property all expenses properly incurred.[88] They have a lien on capital and income for their expenses (including debts duly payable in their capacity as trustees to third parties) in priority to the claims of the beneficiaries. They have a right to remuneration for their services if authorised by the trust instrument or the court or under the Trustee Act 2000.

When exercising their powers in dealing with third parties (for example when contracting to buy or sell property) the trustees are personally liable to those third parties as discussed in Chapter 1.

LIABILITY OF TRUSTEES

Trustees are jointly and severally liable for breach of trust since trusteeship is a joint office *par excellence*. One trustee may thus find himself replacing the whole loss or more than his share of the loss. In such a case he will have a right of contribution from the others so that they are equally liable unless he was guilty of a fraudulent breach of trust. For those who became trustees after the Civil Liability (Contribution) Act 1978 came into force on January 1, 1979, such Act prescribes a general right of contribution and the amount of the contribution recoverable from a person is to be: "such as may be found by the court to be just and equitable having regard to the extent of that person's responsibility for the damage in question." The Act is primarily concerned with tortious and contractual damages. In the case of trustees the court continues to exercise its discretion along the old equitable guidelines of equal liability: such sanction serves a useful salutary function for breach of a joint obligation *par excellence*. However, where trustees and dishonest accessories in a breach of trust or other fiduciary duty are jointly and severally liable there is scope for the court to apportion blameworthiness.[89]

The 1978 Act does not affect any right of indemnity against loss.

---

[88] Trustee Act 2000, s.31(1).
[89] *Dubai Aluminium Co Ltd v Salaam* [2002] UKHL 48 [2003] 1 All E.R. 97; *Arab Monetary Fund v Hashim* (No 9) 1994 *The Times*, October 11, 1994.

A trustee can obtain an indemnity so as to throw the whole loss on his co-trustee in three exceptional instances. First, if his co-trustee has exclusively benefited from the breach of trust (for example used trust money for his own purposes) so that such co-trustee would be unjustly enriched if he could get the other trustee to repay part of the losses he had caused.[90] Secondly, if his co-trustee happens to have a beneficial interest under the trust, such co-trustee-beneficiary must assume sole liability to the extent of the value of his beneficial interest, so he indemnifies the other trustees to the extent of such interest.[91] Thirdly, an indemnity is available if his co-trustee is someone with special qualifications, like a solicitor, on whom he could reasonably be expected to rely and whose advice and strong influence caused his passive participation in the breach of trust.[92] This equitable exception is not now so significant since under s.61 of the Trustee Act 1925 in such a case it is likely that the court will exercise its power to excuse the trustee for the breach of trust brought about by his co-trustee. Whenever the court excuses a trustee from liability for breach this inevitably throws the burden on his co-trustee(s).

Where a trustee commits a breach of trust at the instigation or request or with the written consent of a beneficiary the court has power under s.62 of the Trustee Act 1925 to make such order as seems just for impounding all or any part of the beneficiary's interest by way of indemnity to the trustee. To obtain further protection as of right, especially in view of the weak protection accorded by the Limitation Act, a trustee should obtain a personal indemnity from the beneficiaries where he is embarking upon a breach of trust to assist them. Alternatively, he should obtain the court's approval for his proposed actions under s.57 of the Trustee Act which enables the court to authorise transactions which it considers expedient.

If a beneficiary instigates, consents to, or concurs in a breach of trust prior to its occurrence or he releases the trustees from liability or acquiesces in the breach after its occurrence he may not sue the trustees. Other beneficiaries may do so. Thus, if the life tenant persuades the trustees in breach of trust to pay him £50,000 capital and the remaindermen then force the trustees to replace the £50,000, the trustees may themselves personally keep the income therefrom till the death of the life tenant.[93]

Trustees, excluding persons whose wrongful conduct in the first place led to the equitable obligation of accountability as a con-

[90] *Bahin v Hughes* (1886) 71 Ch.D. 390.
[91] *Chillingworth v Chambers* [1896] 1 Ch. 685.
[92] *Re Partington* (1887) 57 L.T. 654.
[93] *Fletcher v Collis* [1905] 2 Ch. 24.

structive trustee being placed upon them,[94] have only a limited opportunity to plead the Limitation Act 1980 against beneficiaries. No limitation period at all applies where the beneficiary's action is (1) in respect of any fraud or fraudulent breach of trust to which the trustee was a party or privy, or (2) to recover from the trustee trust property or the proceeds thereof in the trustee's possession, or previously received by him and spent for his own benefit[95] or (3) in respect of the trustee's breach of the rules against self-dealing (concerned with acquiring the trust property) or fair dealing (concerned with acquiring the beneficiaries' equitable interests).[96] In these cases only the doctrine of "laches"[97] is available to the trustees where there has been a substantial lapse of time and the circumstances are such that it would not be equitable to allow the claim to be brought.

Otherwise, a claim by a beneficiary against a wrongdoer-constructive trustee[98] or in respect of an honest breach of trust or to recover property in the hands of a third party not implicated in the breach (for example an innocent donee[99]) must be brought within six years of accrual of the right of action.[1] Significantly, a right of action is not deemed to accrue to any beneficiary entitled to a future interest (for example a remainder after a life interest) until the interest falls into possession (for example on the life tenant's death).[2] Furthermore, if any fact relevant to the plaintiff's right of action has been deliberately concealed by the defendant or if the action is for relief from the consequences of a mistake the period of limitation does not begin to run until the claimant has discovered the concealment or mistake or could with reasonable diligence have discovered it.[3]

[94] *Paragon Finance plc v Thakerar* [1999] 1 All E.R. 400 at 408–414, *DEG-Deutsche v Koshy* [2002] B.C.L.C. 478, para.287; in this category are dishonest facilitators of breaches of trust and dishonest dealers with trust property for their own benefit.
[95] Limitation Act 1980, s.21(1).
[96] *Tito v Waddell (No. 2)* [1977] Ch. 106 at 248–250.
[97] *ibid. Lindsay Petroleum Co. v Hurd* (1874) L.R. 5 P.C. 221 at 239–240.
[98] See n.94 above.
[99] *Re Blake* [1932] 1 Ch. 54 at 62–63; *Taylor v Davies* [1920] A.C. 636 at 652–653.
[1] Limitation Act 1980, s.21(3); *Re Robinson* [1911] 1 Ch. 502.
[2] *ibid.* In *Armitage v Nurse* [1998] Ch. 241 at 261, Millett L.J. pointed out that a beneficiary under a discretionary trust or an object of a power does not obtain an interest until receiving something from the trustees so that their liability is usually open-ended.
[3] Limitation Act 1980, s.32(1).

APPOINTMENT, RETIREMENT AND REMOVAL OF TRUSTEES

Appointment

The settlor appoints the original trustees of which there cannot be more than four in the case of trusts of land.[4] New or additional trustees may be appointed under an express power contained in the trust instrument (reserving such power to the settlor for example) or, in default, by exercise of the statutory power in s.36 of the Trustee Act 1925 or by the court under s.41. However, a trustee is not discharged from his trust unless there will be either a trust corporation (within the European Union) or at least two persons to act as trustees in his place,[5] unless only one trustee was originally appointed and no English land is trust property, or unless the trust instrument authorises otherwise[6] for property other than English land (only a trust corporation or two persons being capable of giving a valid receipt for capital money arising on the disposition of English land).[7]

Section 36 confers the power to appoint new trustees on the surviving or continuing trustee(s) or the personal representatives of the last surviving or continuing trustee: trustees hold trust property as joint tenants so that by the *ius accrescendi* on one trustee's death the property passes to the surviving trustee(s). The section 36 power is exercisable where a trustee is dead, remains outside the United Kingdom for more than 12 months, wishes to retire, refuses to act or is unfit or incapable of acting. The remaining outside the United Kingdom ground is often expressly excluded by the trust instrument but non-resident trustees may be appointed even if there is no such exclusion. The court will not interfere with the appointment by trustees of non-resident trustees unless this is so inappropriate that no reasonable trustee could entertain it.[8]

Where it is inexpedient, difficult or impracticable to appoint without the assistance of the court, then the court may make an order appointing new trustees under section 41.

Retirement

A trustee may retire if a new trustee is appointed in his place under

---

[4] Trustee Act 1925, s.34.
[5] Trustee Act 1925, s.37(1)(c), as amended by the Trusts of Land and Appointment of Trustees Act 1996, Sch.3, para.3(12).
[6] *London Regional Transport Pension Fund Trust Co Ltd v Hatt* [1993] R.L.R. 227 at 260-262; *Adam and Co v Theodore Goddard* [2000] W.T.L.R. 349.
[7] Trustee Act 1925, s.14, Law of Property Act 1925, s.27.
[8] *Richard v Mackay* (1990) 1 Offshore Tax Planning Review 1; 1997 Trust L.I. 123.

section 36 above.[9] If no new trustee is appointed, if a trust corporation or at least two persons remain as trustees and consent to
the retirement, then a trustee can retire by executing a deed to this
effect.[10]

Removal

Removal of a trustee is possible if there are grounds under section
36 for appointing a new trustee in his place. Otherwise, if the trust
instrument does not confer a power of removal of trustees on
anyone (for example a settlor or a protector), recourse must be
made to the court to replace him with another trustee under section
41 or simply to remove him (without replacement) under its
inherent jurisdiction. However, if all the beneficiaries interested in
the trust property are ascertained and of full capacity, they can,
under s.19 of the Trusts of Land and Appointment of Trustees Act
1996, compel the trustees to retire and appoint as new trustees the
persons specified by the beneficiaries.

Vesting Trust Property in New and Continuing Trustees

Where a new trustee is appointed by deed, the deed operates
automatically to vest all the trust property in the new and the
continuing trustees as joint tenants for the purposes of the trust,
except where the trust property is registered land, or stocks and
shares, or leasehold land liable to forfeiture if consent to the
assignment has not been given, or a mortgage of land.[11] In these
four exceptional cases the standard procedure for transferring such
property must be used to vest title in the new body of trustees. If
needed the court has wide powers to make vesting orders.[12]

SPECIAL TYPES OF TRUSTEE

Custodian Trustees

It is possible for there to be a custodian trustee and managing
trustees. The trust property and trust documents are conveniently
held by the custodian trustee, while the management of the trust
property and the exercise of discretions and powers exercisable by
the trustees under the trust instrument are carried out by the

[9] *Adam and Co v Theodore Goddard* [2000] W.T.L.R. 349 at 355 criticised by F.
Barlow in [2003] Conv.15 in historical context.
[10] Trustee Act 1925, s.39, as amended by Sch.3, para.3(13) of the 1996 Act.
[11] Trustee Act 1925, s.40.
[12] *ibid.*, ss.44, 51.

managing trustees. All sums payable to or out of the income or capital of the trust property must be paid to or by the custodian trustee, who may however direct that income be paid to the managing trustees or to the life tenant. The Public Trustee and trust corporations may be appointed custodian trustees.

Custodian trustees must do as directed by the managing trustees unless requested to do something they know amounts to a breach of trust, and are not vicariously liable for the acts or defaults of the managing trustees.[13] Exceptionally, custodian trustees of unit trusts have to take reasonable care to ensure that the manager acts in accordance with the Regulations for Collective Investment Schemes.

Trust Corporations

A trust corporation can, on its own, give a valid receipt for capital monies on a sale of land: otherwise, two trustees are necessary. The following are trust corporations: the Public Trustee; the Treasury Solicitor; the Official Solicitor; certain charitable corporations; corporations appointed by the court to act as trustees; and corporations constituted under United Kingdom law or the law of an EU State and empowered to undertake trust business and having an issued capital equivalent to at least £250,000, of which £100,000 or its equivalent has been paid up in cash.

The Public Trustee

The Public Trustee was established by the Public Trustee Act 1906 as a corporation sole available where persons might have difficulty finding someone willing to act as trustee. He cannot accept charitable trusts, trusts involving the carrying on of a business, or the administration of insolvent estates. He can act as personal representative, trustee, custodian trustee or judicial trustee.

Judicial Trustees

The Judicial Trustees Act 1896 established judicial trustees to provide a middle course in cases where the administration by ordinary trustees had broken down and it was not desired to put the trust to the expense of a full lengthy administration by the court. The court appoints judicial trustees if application is made in that behalf. The judicial trustee, often a troubleshooting accountant, is an officer of the court, which makes it easier for him to obtain the court's guidance whenever he needs it.

---

[13] Public Trustee Act 1906, s.4(2).

CHAPTER SEVEN

The Beneficiaries

RIGHTS OF THE BENEFICIARIES

The duties of the trustees, as discussed in the last Chapter, are owed to the beneficiaries who have correlative rights. One may summarise the principal rights of the beneficiaries as follows:

(1) To have the trust property brought and kept under the control of the trustees, but separately from their private property or from any other property of which they are trustees (unless a "pooling" arrangement is authorised so that there exists a segregated pool of intangible assets proportionately belonging to various trusts or to the trustee personally and various trusts).

(2) To have the trust fund properly invested in such fashion that a fair balance is kept between the beneficiaries.

(3) To see the trust accounts and from time to time have them checked, and to require the trustees to account for benefits due to beneficiaries.

(4) To have the trustees consider whether or not to exercise their discretions and to challenge the exercise of a discretion apparently exercised not in good faith but capriciously or perversely or mistakenly.

(5) To require the trustees to make good any breach of trust, causing loss of income or of capital, caused by the trustees' dishonesty or inexcusable[1] lack of competence, and

---

[1] Not excusable under the Trustee Act 1925, s.61.

to account for any unauthorised profits they may have made from the trust.

(6) To apply to the court[2] for the removal of an unsatisfactory trustee, or for specific guidance on a question affecting their rights, or for appointment of a judicial trustee or for the court to administer the trust.

(7) To bring proceedings as claimant against a tortious or contractual wrongdoer and join the trustees as co-defendants, but only where the trustees wrongfully refuse to act as claimants against the wrongdoer to recover damages on behalf of the trust.

(8) If all the beneficiaries are in existence and of full age and sound mind, to terminate the trust and to direct the trustees what to do with the trust assets.

(9) To ask the court under the Variation of Trusts Act 1958 to approve a variation of the trust's terms on behalf of potential beneficiaries who are unable to give their consent because unborn, incapable, or unascertained, when the remaining beneficiaries (other than contingent discretionary beneficiaries under a protective trust) have agreed on what variation should be made, and where such variation would benefit those who are unable to give their consent.

(10) To sell, give away or otherwise dispose of their own beneficial rights under the trust (if in signed writing satisfying s.53(1)(c) of the Law of Property Act 1925 or an exempted CREST disposition), and to consent to a breach of trust or to authorise, so far as their interest is concerned, what would otherwise be a breach of trust, though this may render their interest liable to be impounded by the trustees in the court's discretion under s.62 of the Trustee Act 1925 if the trustees are held liable to some other beneficiary for such breach.

(11) To trace and so either obtain an equitable lien (or charge) over, or a proportionate equitable interest in, the trust property or its traceable product if such be wrongfully in the hands of anyone who is not a purchaser for value of legal title in good faith without notice of the breach of trust.

(12) To sue a third party as jointly and severally liable with the trustees where the third party dishonestly assisted a breach of trust or dishonestly dealt with trust property for his own benefit.

---

[2] See Ch. 8 below.

(13) To sue a third party to prevent him being unjustly enriched at the beneficiaries' expense by a breach of trust.

FUNDAMENTAL RIGHT TO MAKE TRUSTEE ACCOUNT

As Millett L.J., stated,[3] "There is an irreducible core of obligations owed by the trustees to the beneficiaries and enforceable by them which is fundamental to the concept of a trust. If the beneficiaries have no rights enforceable against the trustees there are no trusts." In the latter situation, if the trustees are not to be regarded as themselves absolute beneficial owners, they will hold the property transferred to them by the settlor on resulting trust for the settlor.

The beneficiaries' rights to enforce the trust by making the trustees account for their conduct, with the correlative duties of disclosure of trust documents (with supporting information) thereby imposed on the trustees, are at the core of the trust concept.[4] The trustees must find and pay a beneficiary with a fixed interest in income (for example a life tenant) or a fixed interest in capital (for example a remainderman), while in the case of a discretionary trust the trustees are under a duty to take such steps as are reasonably practicable to make a discretionary beneficiary aware that he be such, so that he can make out a case to them for a payment in his favour.[5] Indeed, without knowledge that he is a beneficiary a person cannot be in a position to make the trustees account for their stewardship of the trust property.[6] Therefore, even discretionary beneficiaries and beneficiaries with a future interest have a right to make the trustees produce accounts for their inspection and verification with a view to falsifying the accounts or surcharging the accounts[7].

Indeed, the Privy Council has recently made clear that not only beneficiaries under a discretionary trust but also objects of a fiduciary power of appointment "have a right to have their claims properly considered by the trustees. But if the discretion is exer-

---

[3] *Armitage v Nurse* [1998] Ch. 241 at 253.
[4] "The irreducible core content of trusteeship" D.J. Hayton in A.J. Oakley (ed.) *Trends in Contemporary Trust Law* (Clarendon, Oxford, 1996); *Schmidt v Rosewood Trust Ltd* [2003] UKPC 26.
[5] *Re Manisty's Settlement* [1974] Ch. 17 at 25; *Re Baden's Deed Trusts* [1973] Ch. 9 at 20, 27.
[6] *cf. Scally v Southern Health Board* [1992] 1 A.C. 294 at 306–307.
[7] *Armitage v Nurse* [1998] Ch.41 at 261 (but time does not begin to run against a discretionary beneficiary or an object of a power of appointment until s/he has received some trust property absolutely or a limited interest in possession therein); *Chaine-Nickson v Bank of Ireland* [1976] I.R. 393; *Lemos v Coutts & Co.* [1992–1993] C.I.L.R. 460; *Att.-Gen. of Ontario v Stavro* (1995) 119 D.L.R. (4th) 750; *Re Murphy's Settlements* [1999] 1 WLR 282 (right of discretionary beneficiary to make settlor tell beneficiary name and address of offshore trustee).

cisable in favour of a very wide class the trustees need not survey mankind from China to Peru if it is clear who are the prime candidates for the exercise of the trustees' discretion".[8]

Courts can enforce the rights of discretionary beneficiaries or objects in various ways, *e.g.* an order requiring the trustees to consider the exercise of their discretion and in particular to consider a request from a person within the ambit of the discretion; an order requiring the trustees to disclose trust accounts and other trust documents with supporting information; an appointment of new trustees in place of wrongdoing trustees; an order directing representative persons of the classes of beneficiaries or objects to prepare a scheme of distribution or should the proper basis for distribution appear, by itself directing the trustees so to distribute.[9]

The right to disclosure of trust documents etc. is one aspect of the court's inherent jurisdiction to supervise, and if necessary to intervene in, the administration of trusts[10] but it is not an absolute right. The court retains a discretion to find the circumstances so exceptional that no relief should be granted[11] or that only some classes of documents should be disclosed (whether completely or in a redacted form) or that some safeguards should be imposed (whether by undertakings to the court, arrangements for professional inspection or otherwise) to limit the use which may be made of documents or information disclosed under the court's order.[12]

Where the trustees prepare documents revealing their input into the exercise of their discretions and such documents contain material upon which their reasons for exercising their discretions were or might have been based, then such documents do not have to be disclosed if beneficiaries request them.[13] The trustees are entitled to confidentiality as to their deliberations (which could well embitter or embarrass beneficiaries or objects of powers). However, if their conduct cries out for an explanation or otherwise the beneficiaries or objects can raise a plausible case of misconduct by the

---

[8] *Schmidt v Rosewood Trust Ltd* [2003] UKPC 26, para.41.

[9] *ibid*, paras 42 and 51. For direct court intervention see *Mettoy Pension Trustees Ltd v Evans* [1990] 1 W.L.R. 1587, *Thrells v Lomas* [1993] 1 W.L.R. 456, *Klug v Klug* [1918] 2 Ch. 67, *Re Lofthouse* (1885) 29 Ch. D. 921; p.95 above.

[10] *ibid*, para.51.

[11] *e.g. Rouse v IOOF Australia Trustees Ltd* (1999) 73 S.A.S.R. 484, [2000] W.T.L.R. 111.

[12] *Schmidt v Rosewood Trust Ltd* [2003] UKPC 26; [2003] 2 W.L.R. 1442, para.54.

[13] *Re Londonderry's Settlement* [1964] Ch. 594; *Wilson v Law Debenture Trust Corp* [1995] 2 All E.R. 337, but in pension trust cases the Pensions Ombudsman has ruled that it now is maladministration to fail to give reasons to a claimant for rejecting his claim (*e.g.* to an early retirement pension), ordering the trustees to supply copies of materials considered by them and their reasons: *Allen v TKM Pension Trust Ltd* (PO Decision L00370, 25 April, 2002, and see PO Annual Report 2001-2002 pp.6-7).

trustees, so that litigation has been commenced against them, then under the Civil Procedure Rules claimants are entitled to obtain standard disclosure of documents that can advance or hinder either party's case, while subsequent application can be made for specific disclosure of documents not earlier disclosed.

Indeed, if desirable to assist fair and expedient resolution of a dispute, pre-action disclosure can be ordered by the court of documents that would be subject to standard disclosure once the action had been commenced.[14]

Letters of wishes (including memoranda of the settlor's wishes prepared by the trustees) are often prepared by settlors to provide important non-legally-binding guidance for trustees with a very broad range of flexible powers.[15] These letters have such legal significance, trustees being obliged to take them into account even if not ultimately implementing them, that they should probably be regarded like the trust instrument and so disclosed on request to beneficiaries or objects (subject to covering up any confidential matter not relevant to the requester). Without knowledge of the material in the letter it may not be possible to know what are the purposes for which the settlor conferred extensive flexible powers, so that it becomes impossible to allege that the trustees exercised their discretion not in accordance with the purposes for which the powers were conferred but perverse to any sensible expectation of the settlor: it thus becomes impossible to monitor the exercise of the trustees' distributive functions. However, as one can still monitor the investment managerial side of the trusteeship, it may be that if the settlor expressly made his letter confidential to the trustees then they could justifiably refuse to show it to beneficiaries or objects unless administrative unworkablility arose.[16]

If a settlor wishes particular persons to be kept in the dark and work hard and not keep pestering the trustees for money to lead a sybaritic life, then he can make them objects of a personal power of appointment, *e.g.* stipulating that the trustees are not obliged to consider the exercise of the personal power from time to time or to inform the objects they are such and that the trustees are not obliged to disclose the trust instrument or other trust documents to the objects, whose only rights are to retain whatever may happen to be appointed to them, which the trustees should achieve in untraceable fashion so far as possible.

---

[14] CPR r.31.16.As pointed out in *Scott v National Trust* [1998] 2 All E.R. 705 at 719, "If a decision taken by trustees is directly attacked in legal proceedings, the trustees may be compelled either legally (through discovery or subpoena) or practically (in order to avoid adverse inferences being drawn) to disclose the substance of the reasons for their decision".

[15] See Underhill & Hayton, *Law of Trusts & Trustees* (16th ed) pp.680-685.

[16] *Re Rabbaiotti's Settlement* [2000] W.T.L.R. 953; and see p.96.

EQUITABLE RIGHT TO TRACE

A Proprietary Remedy

Where there is a breach of trust the beneficiaries have a personal claim to make the trustees personally accountable for losses or profits as the case may be. If the trustee is bankrupt then the personal claim, like personal claims of other creditors, will only entitle the beneficiary to restoration to the trust fund of a percentage dividend after realisation of the bankrupt's estate so the claim may be worthless. However, beneficiaries under a trust have an equitable proprietary right for the trust fund to be kept segregated for their benefit, so that it does not form part of the bankrupt trustee's estate available for creditors generally.

The beneficiaries can claim not just the original trust property remaining in the trustee's hands and authorised transpositions of such property into new investments held by the trustee. If the trustee in breach of trust appropriated trust funds (or took a bribe[17]) to buy a Picasso for himself then the beneficiaries can claim the Picasso as part of the trust fund. If he sold it and bought a flat with the proceeds and regularly used the rent from leasing out the flat to make an instalment purchase of a Porsche, then the beneficiaries can claim the flat and the Porsche. If he makes a gift of the flat to his wife and of the Porsche to his mistress, then the beneficiaries can still recover these assets and may obtain an interlocutory injunction against the wife and mistress to preserve the property (or even other property purchased with the proceeds of sale of the flat or the Porsche) until trial of the action.

If the traced property is worth more than the trust property from which it is derived, the beneficiaries will claim the whole or an appropriate proportion of the traced property is held by its owner on constructive trust for the beneficiaries as part of their trust fund. If the traced property is worth less, then the beneficiaries will claim an equitable lien or charge over it as security for part of their personal claims in respect of the breach of trust.

The beneficiaries' equitable right to the traced property or a lien over it via the tracing process binds everyone but a bona fide purchaser for value of a legal interest without notice (actual, constructive or imputed) of the circumstances generating the beneficiaries' right to trace,[18] but, of course, the proceeds of any such sale may be traceable. The tracing process is of no assistance if such proceeds are dissipated (for example spent on a holiday, a racehorse

---

[17] *Attorney General of Hong Kong v Reid* [1994] 1 A.C. 324 at 331.

[18] *Foskett v McKeown* [2001] 1 AC 102. It was also pointed out (pp 113, 129-130) that the tracing process may be used in support of legal rights.

that dies) so that tracing is physically impossible. It has been suggested[19] that the doctrine of tracing does not extend to tracing value into a previously acquired asset of the defendant whose own credit worthiness enabled him to become full legal beneficial owner without full payment, so that payment with trust money of a debt due in respect of such an asset should amount to dissipation of the money. However, there is much to be said for the view that payment of the outstanding balance of the purchase price by the wrongdoing trustee should be regarded as delayed payment of part of the purchase price, thereby enabling a proportionate proprietary interest in the asset to be claimed,[20] regardless of whether or not the defendant at the time of the purchase intended[21] to pay the balance of the purchase price out of the trust moneys that he would later misappropriate. Equity should not allow the wrongdoing defendant to deny the beneficiaries' claim that throughout he acted in their best interests and so intended to purchase the valuable asset with trust money from the outset.

Finally, the tracing process is of no assistance if exceptional circumstances exist so as to raise the defence of change of position "available to a person whose position has so changed that it would be inequitable in all the circumstances to require him to make restitution, or alternatively to make restitution in full"[22] (for example where the innocent donee of canvass that is trust property is a famous painter who paints a picture on the canvass). The defence is not available to wrongdoers which will include defendants with actual, "Nelsonian" or "naughty" knowledge that the property is not theirs to dispose of,[23] but it is available to a defendant merely guilty of negligence.[24]

Mixing of Trust Money with Trustee's Own Money

Where a trustee, T, wrongfully pays trust money into his private bank account and then money is drawn out, there is a presumption invokable by the beneficiaries that T acted honestly and used his own money first.[25] Thus, if £1,000 is withdrawn to pay off debts so as to become untraceable it is presumed as far as possible that this

[19] *Bishopsgate Investment Management Ltd v Homan* [1995] Ch. 211 at 221.
[20] L. Smith, *Law of Tracing* (Clarendon, Oxford (1997)), pp.146–152, 353–356.
[21] *Bishopsgate Investment Management Ltd v Homan* [1995] Ch. 211 at 216–217; *Foskett v McKeown* [1997] 3 All E.R. 392 at 409.
[22] *Lipkin Gorman v Karpnale Ltd* [1991] 2 A.C. 548.
[23] *Papamichael v National Westminster Bank* [2003] 1 Lloyd's Rep. 341, para 209.
[24] *Dextra Bank & Trust Co Ltd v Bank of Jamaica* [2002] 1 All E.R. (Comm) 193; *Niru Battery Manufacturing Co v Milestone Trading Ltd* [2002] EWHC 1425 (Comm); [2002] 2 All E.R. (Comm) 70.
[25] *Re Hallett's Estate* (1880) 13 Ch.D. 696.

was T's own money, leaving the trust money intact. However, if the £1,000 had been used to purchase shares that have doubled in value the beneficiaries will be able to claim these shares as representing their £1,000.[26] Since T himself was responsible for the wrongful mixing of moneys that makes his money indistinguishable from the beneficiaries' money, he cannot allocate profitable transactions to himself and losses to the beneficiaries nor can he disprove or complain of the beneficiaries' allocation of profits to themselves and losses to him. Equity does not allow the wrongdoing trustee to deny the beneficiaries' claim that he acted in their best interests and not his own.

If T's £2,000 and the beneficiaries' £3,000 were used to purchase a £5,000 asset, then if the asset appreciated in value the beneficiaries would be entitled to 3/5 of it; although if the asset depreciated the beneficiaries would have an equitable charge on it for their £3,000 and interest thereon.[27]

Trustee Mixing Two Trust Funds

Where T purchases property using moneys from two different trusts (for example £2,000 of Trust A and £3,000 of Trust B) then the two trusts share the property in the proportions in which they contributed to the purchase (2:3) whether the property appreciates or depreciates.[28]

Where the trust moneys have been mixed in the same current (as opposed to deposit) bank account, one needs to consider the rule in *Clayton's Case*[29] which, as between banker and customer, treats payments out of an account as being made in the same order as payments in: "First in, first out." Thus, if the paying-in order is (1) £1,000 from Trust A (2) £2,000 from Trust B (3) £3,000 from Trust C and then (4) £2,000 is withdrawn to pay for a holiday and later (5) £4,000 is withdrawn to pay for shares now worth £6,000, under *Clayton's Case* the £2,000 is treated as withdrawn from Trust A and partly from Trust B. Thus, the £4,000 invested in shares represents £1,000 of Trust B and £3,000 of Trust C. Poor Trust A has lost all its money, while Trust B has shares worth £1,500 and Trust C has shares worth £4,500. However, if the shares worth £6,000 were divided between Trusts A, B and C in the original £1,000, £2,000, £3,000 proportions each trust would recover its original moneys. This latter approach has been adopted in New Zealand, New South

[26] *Re Oatway* [1903] 2 Ch. 356.
[27] *Re Tilley's W.T.* [1967] Ch. 1179; *Foskett v McKeown* [2001] 1 A.C. 102.
[28] *Foskett v McKeown* [2001] 1 A.C. 102.
[29] (1816) 1 Mer. 572.

Wales, Jersey and Ontario, while the English Court of Appeal[30] has unthinkingly applied *Clayton's Case* until 1992 in deciding *Barlow Clowes International Ltd v Vaughan*.[31] Woolf and Leggatt L.JJ. (but not Dillon L.J.) there indicated that the rule of convenience in *Clayton's Case* based on presumed intention would be ousted in such a case in favour of a just pro rata distribution that the parties would be presumed to prefer once their moneys had been pooled, without knowing how the vagaries of chance might subsequently affect such moneys. It has now been said[32] that "it might be more accurate to refer to the exception that is, rather than the rule in, *Clayton's Case*."

Third Party Innocently Mixing Trust Funds With His Own

If the third party is a bona fide purchaser of a legal interest without notice the beneficiaries have no rights against him. However, if he is an innocent volunteer (*i.e.* donee) the position of his fund *vis-à-vis* the beneficiaries' trust fund is the same as that of one trust fund and another trust fund as discussed in the preceding two paragraphs, so that the innocent donee and the beneficiaries will have proportionate shares in the asset traced to the donee.[33] However, where such donee would have been able to acquire the asset exclusively with his own money if he had been aware of the true situation, it would be fairer and more equitable for the beneficiaries only to have a charge over the traced asset for the amount of their money used in the purchase of the asset. They ought only to have a proportionate share where the donee would not have been able to purchase the asset but for the use of the beneficiary's money.[34] Thus, while the process of tracing is an objective one based on transactional links relating the beneficiaries' value input to the traced asset, there is scope where an innocent donee has the traced asset to add a causative dimension.

However, if the donee has actual "Nelsonian" or "naughty" knowledge that he ought not to be treating the gifted property as his own, then, as a constructive trustee, he is subject to the strict tracing rules applying to trustees.

---

[30] *Re Diplock* [1948] Ch. 465 at 554.
[31] [1992] 4 All E.R. 22 at 33, 39, 41, 42, 44, 46.
[32] *Russell-Cooke Trust Co v Prentis* [2003] 2 All E.R. 478, para.55.
[33] *Re Diplock* [1948] Ch. 465.
[34] See *Re Tilley's W.T.* [1967] Ch. 1179, where the judge's decision would have been justified if dealing with an innocent donee and not a trustee-wrongdoer against whom presumptions ought to have been made; see D.J. Hayton, "Equity's Identification Rules" in P. Birks (ed.), *Laundering and Tracing* (Clarendon, Oxford, 1995).

MAKING THIRD PARTIES PERSONALLY LIABLE

Liability for Dishonest Inducement or Assistance

Beneficiaries' equitable interests were not recognised by the common law courts, so no common law remedies in tort were available to them nor would any contractual remedies be available to them since they would not be in a contractual relationship with third parties (or the trustees). What could equity do then if no proprietary remedy was available against a third party (for example because he had never received trust property or had only received it in an agency capacity before passing it on) who had knowingly, and so dishonestly, induced or assisted in a breach of trust or other fiduciary obligation where resort to the primary liability of the trustees was worthless? Where there is such want of probity then equity treats the third party as if constructively he were a trustee, so that he is personally liable to account for losses or profits just like an express trustee.[35] The imposition of constructive trusteeship as a secondary liability of the accessory, is a fictional formula to provide a personal remedy against a third party who never has had, or does not now have, any property to be held on a proprietary constructive trust for the beneficiaries.[36] It is better now to refer simply to the personal liability or accountability of the third party without adding "as constructive trustee".[37] This personal liability will avail the beneficiaries little if the third party is bankrupt.

For the third party's conscience to be affected to justify making him liable for dishonest assistance he must have actual, "Nelsonian" or "naughty" knowledge that he is involved in a breach of trust or other fiduciary obligation.[38] The better view is that it suffices he knows he is involved in something dishonest even if he does not know the precise nature thereof or the identity of the victim.[39] "Knowledge is not confined to actual knowledge, but includes actual knowledge that would have been acquired but for shutting one's eyes to the obvious, or wilfully and recklessly failing to make such inquiries as a reasonable and honest man would make; for in such cases there is a want of probity which justifies imposing"[40] personal liability. The crucial requirement for a defendant's liability

---

[35] *Agip (Africa) Ltd v Jackson* [1990] Ch. 265, [1991] Ch. 547; *Royal Brunei Airlines v Tan* [1995] 2 A.C. 378. All will be jointly and severally liable.

[36] *English v Dedham Vale Properties Ltd* [1978] 1 W.L.R. 93.

[37] *Paragon Finance Ltd v Thakerar* [1999] 1 All E.R. 400 at 409, 414.

[38] *Brinks Ltd v Abu Saleh (No. 3)*, *The Times*, October 23, 1995.

[39] *Agip (Africa) Ltd v Jackson* [1990] Ch.65 at 295; Underhill & Hayton, *Law of Trusts & Trustees* (16th ed) pp.964–965.

[40] *Re Montagu's Settlements* [1987] Ch. 265 at 285.

is that not only did he do something objectively regarded as dishonest by honest people but he subjectively knew that what he was doing would be regarded as dishonest by honest people.[41]

Liability for Dishonest Dealing with Trust Property

Where a third party on his own behalf receives property subject to a trust or similar fiduciary obligation[42] and is not a bona fide purchaser for value without notice (nor protected by paying the purchase price for land to two trustees or a trust corporation[43]) then, once he knows he has received such property, he (like an agent who has knowingly received trust property) must not deal with it inconsistently with the obligations relating to such property.[44] If he does, he will be personally liable to account to the beneficiaries, but "unless he has the requisite degree of knowledge he is not personally liable to account".[45] Liability is fault-based like that for dishonest assistance,[46] so it is immaterial if seeking to make a bank liable whether a bank received payments for its own benefit under a debtor-creditor relationship, as where the account holder has paid money into his account, or received payments as agent for onward transmission to the account-holder or someone else.

In case it might be thought that a person who innocently receives and spends trust money for his own benefit in paying off old debts, whether secured or unsecured, will escape liability, and so be unjustly enriched at the expense of the trust beneficiaries, equity intervenes to prevent this. In the case of a donee innocently discharging a mortgage out of trust money the beneficiaries will be subrogated to the claim of the mortgagee so as to be secured creditors for the amount of trust money used to discharge the mortgage, thereby preventing unjust enrichment of the donee-mortgagor.[47] If the donee, instead, paid off an unsecured debt due to X with £y of trust money then the donee, instead of being personally liable to X for £y, will be personally liable to the beneficiaries to restore £y to their trust fund.[48]

---

[41] *Twinsectra Ltd v Yardley* [2002] 2 A.C. 164, paras 20 and 32.
[42] *Brown v Bennett* [1999] 1 B.C.L.C. 649.
[43] Law of Property Act 1925, s.27.
[44] *Polly Peck International plc v Nadir (No. 2)* [1992] 4 All E.R. 769 at 777; *El Ajou v Dollar Land Holdings plc* [1994] 2 All E.R. 685 at 700.
[45] *Westdeutsche Landesbank v Islington LBC* [1996] A.C. 669 at 707.
[46] Subjective dishonesty will be required as explained in *Twinsectra Ltd v Yardley* [2002] 2 A.C. 164 for dishonest assistance.
[47] *Boscawen v Bajwa* [1996] 1 W.L.R. 328; *McCullough v Marsden* (1919) 45 D.L.R. 645; *Banque Financiere de la Cite v Parc (Battersea) Ltd* [1999] 1 A.C. 221.
[48] *Banque Financiere* (above); *Wenlock v River Dee Co* (1887) Q.B.D. 155.

This liability is a receipt-based restitutionary claim independent of any wrongdoing by the defendant recipient.[49] A person receiving trust money as agent, like a bank receiving money from a person, other than the account-holder, to credit it to the account-holder, has available to it the defence of acting in a ministerial capacity.[50]

More significant is the defence of change of position available to show that the defendant has not been unjustly enriched to the extent that enrichment has been lost by virtue of the change of position.[51] Where a defendant has used trust money to pay off an old debt of £y to X he is normally no worse off than before if, instead of owing X £y, he owes it to the beneficiaries to restore £y to their trust fund. However, if after receipt of trust money or in anticipation of subsequently received trust money,[52] the defendant incurs a debt which he would not otherwise have incurred, the defence of change of position will be available for the amount of that debt.

As Lord Goff states,[53]

"Where an innocent defendant's position has so changed that he will suffer an injustice if called upon to repay in full, the injustice of requiring him so to repay outweighs the injustice of denying the plaintiff restitution. If the plaintiff pays money to the defendant under a mistake of fact,[54] and the defendant then, in good faith, pays the money or part of it to charity, it is unjust to require him to make restitution to the extent that he has so changed his position. ... I do not wish to state the principle any less broadly than this: that the defence is available to a person whose position has so changed that it would be inequitable in all the circumstances to require him to make restitution, or alternatively to make restitution in full. I wish to stress, however, that the mere fact that the defendant has spent the money, in whole or

---

[49] Lord Millett in *Twinsectra Ltd v Yardley* [2002] 2 A.C. 164 at 194 and *Dubai Aluminium Co Ltd v Salaam* [2002] UKHL 48, [2002] 3 W.L.R. 1913 at para 87; Lord Nicholls in *Royal Brunei Airlines v Tan* [1995] 2 A.C. 373 at 382 and in WR Cornish et al (eds) *Restitution: Past, Present and Future* (1998) at p.231; Court of Appeal in *Grupo Torras SA v Al-Sabah (No 5)* [2001] Lloyd's Rep Bank 36 at 62.

[50] See case-law discussion in Underhill & Hayton, *Law of Trusts & Trustees* (16th ed) pp.970-973.

[51] The defendant may be responsible for the change of position (*e.g.* by making a gift to charity or investing in shares in a company that becomes insolvent) or such change may be involuntary, (*e.g.* a burglar steals the relevant property).

[52] *Dextra Bank and Trust Co Ltd v Bank of Jamaica* [2002] 1 All E.R. (Comm) 193, PC.

[53] *Lipkin Gorman v Karpnale* [1991] 2 A.C. 548 at 579.

[54] The unfortunate discrimination against claimants where there was a mistake of law as opposed to a mistake of fact has now ceased: *Kleinwort Benson Ltd v Lincoln CC* [1999] 2 A.C. 349, *Nurdin & Peacock plc v Ramsden* [1999] 1 W.L.R. 1249.

in part, does not in itself render it inequitable that he should be called upon to repay, because the expenditure might in any event have been incurred by him in the ordinary course of things."

To rely on the defence the defendant must change his position in good faith, not having actual Nelsonian or naughty knowledge of the real position,[55] but mere negligence does not deprive him of the defence.[56]

One further defence is available by a quirk of history[57] where an unpaid or underpaid creditor, legatee, or next-of-kin brings a direct personal claim against a donee who innocently, but under a mistake of law or of fact, received a deceased's property from the deceased's personal representatives and then innocently dissipated it. The action cannot be brought until the claimant has first sued the blundering personal representatives and given credit for what he obtains from them.[58] The personal representatives have only themselves to blame for a suit against them because they can fully protect themselves if they advertise for claimants as prescribed by s.27 of the Trustee Act 1925.

NATURE OF BENEFICIARIES' RIGHTS

A beneficiary may be in a very strong position or a very weak position depending on the nature of his rights. Where T holds property on trust for B absolutely, then B has a right to sue T for the income and the transfer of the capital, and B has an equitable interest in the property itself. Where T holds on trust for B for life, remainder to C absolutely, then B has a right to sue T for the income, and otherwise enforce T's duties, and C has a right after B's death to sue T for the capital and otherwise enforce T's duties, while B and C together, if of full capacity, can combine to direct T to do with the trust property as they have agreed. B has an equitable life interest in the property itself while C has a vested equitable interest in remainder in such property.[59] Thus, B and C each have an equitable interest in the trust property and also an equitable chose in action (*i.e.* right of action) against the trustee. They will be left only with this equitable chose in action if the trustee sells the

---

[55]   *Papamichael v National Westminister Bank* [2003] 1 Lloyd's Rep 341, para.209.
[56]   *Niru Battery Manfacturing Co v Milestone Trading Ltd* [2002] 2 All E.R. (Comm) 705, para.125.
[57]   See S.J. Whittaker, "An Historical Perspective to the Special Equitable Action in *Re Diplock*" (1983) 4 J.L.H. 3.
[58]   *Ministry of Health v Simpson* [1951] A.C. 251.
[59]   *Baker v Archer-Shee* [1927] A.C. 844; *Perpetual Trustee Co v C.S.D.* [1977] 2 N.S.W.L.R. 472; *New Zealand Insurance Co Ltd v Probate Duties Commissioners* [1973] U.R.659.

property to a bona fide purchaser for value without notice and dissipates the proceeds.

Beneficiaries under discretionary trusts are obviously in a weaker position. In a rare case they may all be ascertained and of full capacity (for example a discretionary trust of income and capital for X's children where X is dead and there are only four children aged 28, 26, 24 and 22 years) when they can combine under the *Saunders v Vautier* principle to direct the trustees to do with the trust property as they have agreed[60] (for example transfer a quarter of the property to each of them). Obviously, they have an equitable chose in action against the trustees to enforce the trustees' equitable and fiduciary duties, but each beneficiary does not have an assignable interest in the property itself since on his own he has no enforceable right to income or to capital, having no right to compel his co-beneficiaries to act with him to direct the trustees what to do.[61]

Usually, there is a broad fluctuating class of beneficiaries under a discretionary trust, for example (1) a discretionary trust of income and capital for such of X's descendants and their spouses as the trustees may see fit, with the trustees being obliged at the end of the perpetuity period to distribute whatever is left amongst X's descendants then living or, failing them, to such charities as the trustees select; or (2) a discretionary trust of income to provide holidays for employees from time to time of Whizzo Ltd over a specified perpetuity period and then to distribute the capital amongst the settlor's descendants them living or, failing them, to such charities as the trustees may select. A beneficiary of full capacity has an equitable chose in action against the trustees to enforce their equitable and fiduciary duties, so that, for example, they do not benefit persons outside the class of beneficiaries or dissipate the trust property, and so that they consider any claim he may put forward to be benefited by them. Where the beneficiaries are a fluctuating body, so that they cannot all be ascertained and of full capacity and so between them absolutely beneficially entitled, no question can arise of them together having a collective equitable proprietary interest in the trust property itself. Even if it did, one of the discretionary beneficiaries on his own has no equitable interest in the trust property itself as mentioned at the end of the last paragraph.

When creating a discretionary trust a settlor will normally confer on the trustees discretionary fiduciary powers of appointment over income and capital. Objects of such powers are in a weaker position than beneficiaries under discretionary trusts because, in default of exercise of the powers within any specified period or otherwise a

---

[60] *Re Smith* [1928] Ch. 915.
[61] *Gartside v IRC* [1968] A.C. 553; *Sainsbury v IRC* [1970] Ch. 712; *Re Trafford's Settlement* [1985] Ch. 32; *Schmidt v Rosewood Trust Ltd* [2003] UKPC 26, para.40.

reasonable period, the income is lost to the objects and must be distributed between the discretionary beneficiaries. Moreover, objects of a power who are all ascertained and of full capacity cannot collectively positively compel the trustees to exercise the power as they direct him.[62] However, the objects can prevent the beneficiaries if all ascertained and of full capacity from compelling the trustees to divide the trust property between the beneficiaries as directed by the beneficiaries collectively:[63] the *Saunders v Vautier* principle requires the persons collectively claiming to be equitable owner of the trust property to be indefeasibly entitled,[64] and beneficiaries are not so entitled if a power of appointment may be exercised to defeat their interests or expectations.

Thus, if there is a discretionary trust for ABC and D (who are all of full capacity) with a power of appointment in favour of X and Y, ABC and D cannot compel the trustees to distribute the trust fund between themselves, but if ABC and D obtain the consent of X and Y to an agreed distribution of, say, 23 per cent for each of A,B, C and D and 4 per cent for each of X and Y, then the trustees can be compelled so to distribute the trust fund. Because the class of objects of a power is normally a large fluctuating class, so that obtaining the collective consent thereof is impossible, as well as to cope with unforeseeable matters, the trust instrument normally expressly confers on the trustees a power to release[65] any of their fiduciary powers.

Otherwise, beneficiaries under discretionary trusts and objects of fiduciary powers of appointment have much in common, especially if the class thereof is a large fluctuating class. They are both entitled to have their claims considered by the trustees and, in the case of large classes, the trustees can focus upon a smaller class within the class that can reasonably be considered to be the persons primarily intended to be recipients of the settlor's bounty.[66] It seems that members of such small class, if of full age, need to be made specifically aware of the trust, but this is not necessary for those persons who are more remote from the settlor's intended bounty.

However, beneficiaries under discretionary trusts or objects of a fiduciary power all have a right to invoke the inherent jurisdiction of the court to safeguard their interests and to supervise and, if necessary to intervene in, the exercise of the trustees' functions.[67] The court

[62] *Schmidt v Rosewood Trust Ltd* [2002] UKPC 26, para.40.
[63] *ibid*, para.41.
[64] *Re Sharp's S.T* [1973] Ch. 331 at 338.
[65] A beneficiary of a discretionary trust and an object of a power can release their interests themselves if they wish: *Re Gulbenkian's Settlement* (No 2) [1970] Ch. 408.
[66] *Schmidt v Rosewood Trust Ltd* [2003] UKPC 26; [2003] 2 W.L.R. 1442 paras 41-42, *Re Manisty's Settlement* [1974] Ch.17 at 25.
[67] *ibid* paras 51 and 66.

can order the trustees to consider a request from a discretionary beneficiary or object[68]; it can remove trustees and replace them with new trustees; it can order the trustees to disclose trust documents and provide any necessary supporting information[69]; it can authorise representative persons of the classes of beneficiaries and objects to prepare a scheme of distribution or, should the proper basis for distribution appear, itself direct the trustees so to distribute;[70] it can even direct the trustees to exercise a power in a particular way[71] or itself exercise the power in special circumstances.[72]

In safeguarding the interests of beneficiaries and objects the court can not only require wrongdoing trustees to restore to the trust fund assets or value that would have been present in the fund but for the trustees' wrongdoing, it can trace trust property and its traceable product into the hands of a third party. In favour of the claimant beneficiaries or objects or of claimant new trustees, (*e.g.* if the beneficiaries are minors, unborn or otherwise unascertained) it can order the third party to transfer the traced property to the trustees of the trust fund. This proprietary *in rem* remedy ensures that the proper full amount of trust property is then available to benefit the discretionary beneficiaries or objects to the extent, if any, to which the trustees choose in their discretion to benefit a particular beneficiary or object. Thus, the proprietary remedy is necessary so that full effect may be given to the *in personam* equitable chose in action owned by each discretionary beneficiary or object so as to enable him to safeguard his general indefinite expectations as to the trustees' behaviour towards him.

Where the trustee is solvent, reliance on the equitable chose in action against him is all that is needed to protect someone interested under the terms of the trust.[73] If the trustee is insolvent, then reliance will be placed on *in rem* rights against the trust property so that it is not available to the trustee's private creditors. Where the trustee has transferred trust property to a third party, not protected as a bona

---

[68] *Re Manisty's Settlement* [1974] Ch. 17 at 25.

[69] *Schmidt v Rosewood Trust Ltd* [2003] UKPC 26; [2003] 2 W.L.R. 1442.

[70] *McPhail v Doulton* [1971] A.C. 424 at 457; *Mettoy Pension Trustees Ltd v Evans* [1991] 2 All E.R. 513 at *549, Schmidt v Rosewood Trust Ltd* [2003]; UKPC 26 [2003] 2 W.L.R. 1442, paras 42 & 51.

[71] *Klug v Klug* [1918] 2 Ch. 67; *White v Grane* (1854) 18 Beav 571; *Re Lofthouse* (1885) 29 Ch. D.921.

[72] *Mettoy Pension Trustees Ltd v Evans* [1991] 2 All E.R. 513; *Thrells v Lomas* [1993] 1 W.L.R. 456

[73] *Webb v Webb* [1994] Q.B. 696, *Ashurst v Pollard* [2001] Ch. 595. If D holds a French immovable on trust for C but refuses to transfer it into C's name, C's English legal proceedings are not "proceedings which have as their object rights in rem in immovable property" when the French *lex situs* would have exclusive jurisdiction. C is merely enforcing his personal equitable chose in action against D.

fide purchaser without notice or by statutory overreaching provisions, then if the third party is insolvent or the claimant has special reasons for claiming the trust property or its traceable product reliance will be placed on *in rem* rights against the trust property; otherwise, restoration of the lost value to the trust fund will suffice, whether to prevent unjust enrichment of the third party or as compensation for him being permitted to retain ownership of property that would otherwise have to be added to the trust fund.

Actions by beneficiaries, though often being, in a sense, representative actions for restoration of assets or value to the trust fund, can be actions in a beneficiary's private interest so that an order is made in favour of him alone. Thus, where in a commercial arrangement property was held on trust for B absolutely or, in a family trust, property was held on trust for X for life, remainder to Y absolutely, a successful claim by B against T, the trustee, will result in an order to pay all the compensation to B,[74] while a successful claim by X will result in an order for compensation replacing lost income to be paid to X, any compensation for lost capital being added to capital to produce higher income for X, and, on X's death, higher capital for Y.

In these latter instances B and X have an equitable interest in the specific property producing the income as soon as T receives such income, the equitable interest in property having the same location as the property.[75] In contrast, where T holds property on discretionary trusts for class O (including fiduciary powers for class P) it is the location of T, against whom actions need to be brought by discretionary beneficiaries and objects, that is the location of their discretionary interests, irrespective of the location of the trust property.[76] The discretionary trustee, T, will be regarded as owner of the trust property subject to onerous equitable duties enforceable by the discretionary beneficiaries and objects, as in the case of the executor of a deceased's unadministered estate owing equitable duties enforceable by those interested under the will[77] or the trustee of a charitable purpose trust owing equitable duties enforceable by the Attorney General or the Charity Commissioners or an interested person.[78]

---

[74] *Target Holdings Ltd v Redferns* [1996] A.C. 421; *Youyang Pty Ltd v Minter Ellison* [2003] H.C.A. 15.

[75] *Spens v IRC* [1970] 3 All E.R. 295 at 299, *IRC v Berrill* [1982] 1 All E.R. 867 at 880; *New Zealand Insurance Co Ltd v Probate Duties Commissioner* [1973] V.R. 659.

[76] The situs of the debtor or obligated person is the situs of the debt or obligation: Dicey & Morris, *Conflict of Laws* (13th ed) Rule 112.

[77] *Commissioner of Stamp Duties v Livingston* [1965] A.C. 694; *Marshall v Kerr* [1995] 1 A.C. 148.

[78] Charities Act 1993 s.33(1).

CHAPTER EIGHT

The Court

PATERNALISTIC ROLE OF THE CHANCERY JUDGE

At one end of the broad spectrum of the Chancery jurisdiction the judge has to be a stern disciplinarian castigating trustees in hostile proceedings in open court for their breaches of trust. At the other end of the spectrum he is a guide, mentor and friend: privately, in a friendly chambers summons, he may be very liberal and helpful, for example (before English legislation outlawed this) in authorising trustees to pay a bribe in some foreign country where such a payment was in fact necessary to liberate trust property, or to pay for the abortion abroad of a foetus carried by a 17-year-old ward of court in the days when abortion was illegal in England.

If a professional man, like a solicitor or accountant instructed to set up trusts or companies to deal with a client's money, is torn between his duty to his client and his fear that he might be personally liable to another for dishonest assistance in a breach of fiduciary duty if the money was acquired by the client in breach of such a duty, then he can apply to the court for directions to protect himself, for example an order freezing the money until he has notified the possibly defrauded third party and such party has had time itself to consider bringing proceedings.[1]

However, if a solicitor is worried that he may not rank as a bona fide purchaser without notice[2] so far as concerns receipt of his fees for legal work done on behalf of the defendant, he cannot in advance obtain from the court a protective order in case at trial the claimant

---

[1] *Finers v Miro* [1991] 1 W.L.R. 35.
[2] On notice and solicitors see *Carl Zeiss Stiftung v Herbert Smith* [1969] 2 Ch. 276.

succeeds in its claim that the defendant had traceable assets of the claimant, and the solicitors fees were paid out of such assets.[3] The solicitor will need to see if the defendant can arrange matters so that the solicitors fees come from clearly untainted sources.

In a very extreme case where there are ever-recurring difficulties requiring frequent applications to the court and the trustees cannot work together, then the court itself may take over the administration of the trust where an administration action has been brought before it. Almost always, however, it will suffice to bring a specific action under Part 64 of the Civil Procedure Rules for the determination of a particular question arising in administering and executing a trust or for some specific relief needed in the course of administering and executing a trust, for example an order requiring a trustee to furnish and verify accounts, or directing a trustee to do or abstain from doing a particular act, or clarifying the scope of the trustee's power or approving as a proper exercise of trustee's power[4] any sale, purchase, compromise or other transaction proposed by the trustee, or directing any act to be done that the court could order to be done if the trust were being wholly administered and executed under direction of the court, or itself exercise a discretion of the trustee in a particular matter where it finds there is a good reason for the trustee surrendering the discretion to the court. Procedure will begin by issuing a Part 8 claim form simply raising the questions to be decided, except a standard Part 7 claim with a statement of case will be needed where fraud or breach of trust is alleged or the case is otherwise likely to involve some substantial dispute of fact.

The right of trustees or other power-holders or beneficiaries or objects to apply to the court on legal matters arising in the administration and execution of trusts cannot be excluded[5] but questions of fact can be conclusively left for determination by the trustees or by some special third party, with mixed questions of fact and law left to be determined by a nominated expert.[6]

CONTROL OF DISCRETIONS

While trustees have to discharge their duties they only have to

---

[3] *United Mizrahi Bank Ltd v Doherty* [1998] 2 All E.R. 230. Doherty then pleaded guilty and was sentenced to 5 years in the criminal trial.

[4] *e.g. Public Trustee v Cooper* [2001] W.T.L.R. 901; *Bradstock Group Pension Scheme Trustees Ltd v Bradstock Group plc* [2002] W.T.L.R. 1281; *Richard v Mackay* (1991) 11 Trust L.I. 23.

[5] *Re Raven* [1915] 1 Ch. 673; *Re Wynn* [1952] Ch. 271; *Re Coxen* [1948] Ch. 747.

[6] *Dundee General Hospitals v Walker* [1952] 1 All E.R. 896; *Re Tuck's S.T.* [1978] Ch. 49; *Nikko Hotels (UK) Ltd v MEPC* [1991] 2 E.G.L.R. 103 at 108; *Brown v GIO Insurance Ltd* [1998] Lloyd's Rep I.R. 201.

consider the exercise of powers conferred upon them. In a discretionary trust to distribute income between a class of beneficiaries in such amounts as they see fit they must distribute the income, though they have a discretion as to which beneficiaries are benefited and the amounts of the benefits. If the trustees neglect or refuse to exercise their duty to distribute income (for example because it takes five years to determine judicially whether the trust is void or valid) then the court will let them remedy this, though only in favour of such beneficiaries as would have been available to benefit under an exercise of the discretion had it been exercised within a reasonable time.[7] In other cases, whether the discretionary trust be of income or of capital, where the trustees refuse to carry out their duties the court will have the settlor's intentions carried out by directing the trustees on the extent of their duty of inquiring as to beneficiaries and their circumstances, or by directing them to consider the claims of particular beneficiaries, "by appointing new trustees, or by authorising or directing representative persons of the classes of beneficiaries to prepare a scheme for distribution, or even, should the proper basis for distribution appear, by itself directing the trustees so to distribute."[8] Such methods are also available to assist objects of fiduciary powers of appointment.[9]

If a power is not exercised within any specified period or, otherwise, within a reasonable period, it ceases to be exercisable, so a subsequent purported exercise of the power will be an *ultra vires* breach of trust and void.[10] If a trustee acts automatically without appreciating that he has a discretion to act or not, as the case may be, then the apparent exercise of a discretionary power is void, for example if he signs a deed of appointment at the settlor's behest in the belief he had to sign it, without understanding he had a discretion whether or not to exercise the power of appointment conferred on the trustees.[11]

A trustee cannot fold his hands and ignore a fiduciary power such as a power to appoint income or capital to Y's issue. He must from time to time consider whether or not to exercise the power, and the court may direct him to do this and advise him what sort of survey he should make in order to act in a responsible manner and consider the appropriateness of particular courses of action.[12] If he then bona fide decides not to exercise the power, this is his prerogative

[7] *Re Locker's S.T.* [1977] 1 W.L.R. 1323.
[8] *McPhail v Doulton* [1971] A.C. 424 at 457.
[9] *Schmidt v Rosewood Trust Ltd* [2003] UKPC 26; [2003] 2 W.L.R. 1442 at paras 41 and 52. See p.95 above.
[10] *Re Allen-Meyrick's W.T.* [1966] 1 W.L.R. 499.
[11] *Turner v Turner* [1984] Ch. 100.
[12] *Re Hay's S.T.* [1982] 1 W.L.R. 202.

and the court cannot intervene.[13]However, if his attitude is that he is not going to bother to consider exercising any discretion in favour of B because, for example, B married someone against his wishes, then the court may intervene to remove the trustee or even direct a payment pursuant to the power to B in special circumstances where it is one that no trustee could refuse to make unless basing himself upon irrelevant, irrational or improper factors.[14]

Once an equitable power is consciously positively exercised, then the court will not intervene unless the trustee did not confine himself to what is authorised by the power[15] or acted corruptly or acted capriciously, *i.e.* for reasons which are irrational, perverse, or irrelevant to any sensible expectation of the settlor.[16] The court's intervention can restrain the prospective exercise of a power or declare a purported exercise void.[17] Unless removed by the court, the trustee will be free to exercise his discretion afresh, but properly this time.

Exceptionally, ss.14 and 15 of the Trusts of Land and Appointment of Trustees Act 1996 accord an interventionist role to the court. If trustees of land refuse to sell or to exercise their powers of leasing and mortgaging, or of delegating to a life tenant their powers or any requisite consent (for example of X) to such activities cannot be obtained, any person interested or the trustees may apply to the court for the court to make such order as it thinks fit, taking account of the intentions of the settlor, the purposes of the trust, the welfare of resident minors and the interests of any beneficiary's secured creditors.[18] However a beneficiary's trustee in bankruptcy who applies one year after the bankruptcy occurred will almost always succeed in having the bankrupt's home sold so that creditors can be paid.[19]

In pension fund trusts, where beneficiaries have earned their right to be considered for the favourable exercise of a fiduciary or per-

[13] *Edge v Pensions Ombudsman* [2000] Ch. 602.
[14] *Klug v Klug* [1918] 2 Ch. 67.
[15] *Abrahams Will Trust, Re* [1969] 1 Ch. 463, *c.f. Re Hastings-Bass* [1975] Ch. 25 where advancement authorised, so valid. Even a personal power cannot be exercised in favour of those who are not objects of such a power, although it can be exercised spitefully or capriciously: *Re Wright* [1920] 1 Ch. 108 at 118.
[16] *Re Manisty's Settlement* [1974] Ch. 17; *Re Hay's S.T.* [1982] 1 W.L.R. 202; *Edge v Pensions Ombudsman* [2000] Ch.602; *Re Beloved Wilkes Charity* (1851) 3 Mac. & G. 440; *Wilson v Law Debenture Trust Corp.* [1995] 2 All E.R. 337 at 343. Further see pp.147-149 (above).
[17] If the exercise of the equitable power, though invalid, led to legal title being validly transferred by the trustee as legal owner to a beneficiary, B, B will be bound by other beneficiaries' interests, not being a purchaser of a legal estate for money or money's worth.
[18] *Mortgage Corporation v Shaire* [2001] Ch. 743; *Bank of Ireland Homes Mortgages Ltd v Bell* [2001] 2 F.L.R. 809.
[19] Insolvency Act 1986 s 335A, *Re Citro* [1991] Ch 12.

sonal power, the courts are becoming interventionist so that the employer must not exercise its rights in a manner likely seriously to damage the relationship of confidence between employer and employee[20] and so that the court upon the liquidation of an employer-trustee can positively exercise a fiduciary power to distribute pension fund surplus between the beneficiary ex-employees and the employer (and thus the employer's creditors).[21]

AUTHORISING THE UNAUTHORISED

If the beneficiaries are all ascertained and of full capacity and between them absolutely indefeasibly entitled, then they can authorise acts that would otherwise be unauthorised and they can replace the trustees or even terminate the trust contrary to its express terms under the *Saunders v Vautier* principle discussed in Chapter 3.

Otherwise, if in the administration of a trust some disposition or transaction cannot be effected by reason of the absence of a necessary power vested in the trustees, the court may confer upon the trustees, either generally or in any particular instance, the necessary power if it considers such disposition or transaction expedient.[22] This is vital for the protection of the trustees where future unascertained or unborn beneficiaries might otherwise sue for breach of trust in due course, and where the trustees consider it unsafe to rely on personal indemnities given by current consenting beneficiaries of full capacity.

Under the Variation of Trusts Act 1958 the court on behalf of persons who cannot themselves give their approval (for example because unborn, unascertainable or minors) can approve arrangements, consented to by the beneficiaries of full capacity varying or revoking the beneficial interests or enlarging the powers[23] of the trustees. However, the court must be satisfied that the arrangements are for the "benefit" of those on whose behalf it gives approval.[24] Exceptionally, in the case of ascertained persons with contingent discretionary interests under a protective trust, the court can give an approval on behalf of and against the will of such persons, and no

---

[20] *Imperial Group Pension Trust Ltd v Imperial Tobacco Ltd* [1991] 2 All E.R. 597; *National Grid plc v Laws* [1997] Pensions LR 157 at para.51.
[21] *Mettoy Pension Trustees Ltd v Evans* [1991] 2 All E.R. 513 at 459, 562; *Thrells v Lomas* [1993] 1 W.L.R. 456. The independent trustee provisions in Pension Act 1995 ss.22–25 now make court intervention unnecessary.
[22] Trustee Act 1925, s.57.
[23] For enlarging managerial powers it is quicker and cheaper to apply under Trustee Act 1925 s.57: *Anker-Petersen v Anker-Petersen* [2000] W.T.L.R. 581 (dissent of adult beneficiaries can also be overridden).
[24] Even if this is contrary to the wishes of the settlor: *Goulding v James* [1997] 2 All E.R. 239.

benefit to them is required, for example where property is settled on B for life until bankruptcy, and on bankruptcy upon discretionary trust for B, his spouse and children for the rest of B's life, remainder to B's grandchildren, and B, a responsible 50 year old, seeks to convert his protected life interest into an untramelled life interest.

In earlier tax eras the 1958 Act was much used to avoid taxation by rearranging the beneficial interests or authorising export of the trust fund where such rearrangement or export was not possible under the terms of the trust instrument. Nowadays, avoidance of tax is more problematical, but in any event, the flexible sophisticate drafting of trust instruments, conferring very wide powers on the trustees to vary trusts, to release powers, and to transfer assets to foreign trustees to be administered under a foreign law, means there is much less need for recourse to the 1958 Act.

RELIEVING TRUSTEES

Where a trustee is, or may be, liable for an actual or possible past breach of trust, the court (under s.61 of the Trustee Act 1925) may relieve him wholly or partly if he has acted honestly and reasonably,[25] and ought fairly to be excused for the actual or possible breach of trust and for omitting to obtain the directions of the court in the matter in which he committed such breach. This enables the court to excuse not just breaches of trust in the management of the trust property but also payments to the wrong persons. The court expects trustees to seek proper advice and, if matters require it, the directions of the court. The court is very loath, indeed, to relieve a professional paid trustee, but can do so, for example, if the trustee was misled by a skilful forgery of a birth or marriage certificate.

Of course, a trustee will not need to have recourse to the court if the trust instrument exempts him from liability if acting honestly and not personally benefiting from the breach and this is the case; but trustees of an authorised unit trust or a debenture trust cannot exempt themselves from negligence liability nor can pension trustees exempt themselves or their investment manager from negligence liability in the area of investment of trust assets. Moredhover, a person carrying on investment business as trustee may be made liable for damages under the Financial Services and Markets Act 2000 if in breach of his obligations arising by virtue of that Act.

---

[25] Negligent Breaches by a lay person may be reasonably excused in appropriate circumstances: *cf.* lay directors and Companies Act 1985 s.727, *D'Jan of London Ltd, Re* [1994] 1 B.C.L.C. 561 at 564.

IMPOUNDING BENEFICIAL INTERESTS

Where a trustee commits a breach of trust at the instigation or request or with the consent in writing of a beneficiary, the court has a discretion to make such order as seems just for impounding all or any part of the interest of the beneficiary by way of indemnity to the trustee or persons claiming through him.[26] The court in exercising its discretion will take account of the beneficiary's motives and whether he or his family benefited from the breach. The beneficiary may be personally liable beyond the extent of his beneficial interest for dishonest inducement of a breach of trust. It is possible for liability between trustee and beneficiary not to be apportioned but for the beneficiary to be exclusively liable if the trustee be excused from liability under s.61 of the Trustee Act.

---

[26] Trustee Act 1925, s.62.

CHAPTER NINE

Resulting and Constructive Trusts of Homes

THE PROBLEM

Increasingly, courts are having to deal with claims by a female, F, that she has an equitable interest in a house or flat in which she resides but which is owned by a man, M, with whom she has cohabited or whose long-standing mistress she has been while he cohabited with his wife. Occasionally, courts have to deal with similar claims by a man against a woman or by a party to a homosexual or lesbian relationship against the other party.

Where the parties are married the court has a very broad discretionary jurisdiction under the Matrimonial Causes Act 1973 to make such order as it deems appropriate having regard, *inter alia*, to the contributions made by the parties to the welfare of the family, including non-financial contributions made by looking after the home and caring for the family. Such orders are made without first considering the precise property rights of the parties under trust law.[1] Trust law only needs to be invoked to ascertain a precise property share, if any, where one spouse has died or become bankrupt or a mortgagee seeks to exercise his remedies against a spouse whom he believed to be sole beneficial owner.

In such cases and in cases involving unmarried parties resort is made to trust law and s.37 of the Matrimonial Property and Pro-

---

[1] *Fielding v Fielding* [1977] 1 W.L.R. 1146.

ceedings Act 1970[2] in the absence of any contract. Almost invariably, M and F will not have come to any agreement certain enough to be enforced as a contract and will not have intended to enter into legal relations. Even if they had, there is the legal necessity for such a contract, if made before September 27, 1989, to be fully evidenced in writing under s.40 of the Law of Property Act 1925 if it is to be enforceable, unless being enforceable because F's acts amount to part performance of the contract. However, living with and looking after someone are not acts inherently referable to partly performing a contract but are more likely referable to love and affection and wanting to live happily in a tidy home.[3] Since September 27, 1989 all the terms of the contract have to be in writing and the contract, being void, cannot be saved by the doctrine of part performance, though it may be given effect, to some extent, by the imposition of a constructive trust.[4]

In the case of trusts section 53(1)(b) requires a declaration of trust of land to be evidenced in writing signed by M, but section 53(2) exempts the creation and operation of resulting and constructive trusts. An outright or conditional gift by M of an equitable interest in his land will technically operate as a declaration of trust by him.

Where property is being purchased with the assistance of a solicitor or a licensed conveyancer (as is almost invariably the case) then, if it is known that co-purchasers are involved, the lawyer will advise that the property must be purchased in the names of the co-purchasers. This is to enable an overreaching sale to be made in due course by the two co-owners as the two trustees of the land whose receipt is necessary to confer a good title on the new purchaser.[5] The lawyer will further advise that the two co-purchasers should sign a written declaration of trust declaring their precise equitable shares in the property, thereby avoiding future problems because such declaration is conclusive in the absence of being obtained by fraud or undue influence.[6] However, the co-purchasers may not be prepared at the outset to commit themselves to fixed shares, believing that the size of their respective shares should be a fair share in the light of subsequent events (for example how much is contributed to mortgage payments, whether non-payment is due to

[2] If a spouse or fiancée of M substantially contributed to the improvement of M's property the court may award her an appropriate share of the property.
[3] *Re Gonin* [1979] Ch. 16; *Maddison v Alderson* (1883) 8 App.Cas. 467 (part performance still being theoretically available for otherwise unenforceable trusts of land: s.55(d) of the Law of Property Act 1925).
[4] Law of Property (Miscellaneous Provisions) Act 1989, s.2; *Yaxley v Gotts* [2000] Ch. 162.
[5] Law of Property Act 1925, s.27 and s.2.
[6] *Goodman v Gallant* [1986] Fam. 106.

child-bearing or child-rearing). An express declaration of trust of a fair share is void for uncertainty, so there is little point in making any such formal declaration (except as evidence for the subsequent quantification of shares by the court) especially when it can lead M and F to argue over what types of subsequent events should be relevant to ascertaining a fair share.

If M is told that the property must be vested in the joint names of co-purchasers if he is purchasing with someone else, he is likely to hide the existence of F, fearing that vesting the property in their joint names will give F a half interest. In many cases, however, M will already be sole legal beneficial owner of the property into which F moves to live with him, thereafter directly or indirectly contributing to payments of the mortgage taken on by M to enable himself to buy the property. It may be that they then sell up and move to a more expensive house purchased in M's name, with M alone paying the much higher mortgage instalments, which he would not have been able to do while maintaining their normal living standards but for F seeing to payment of the household expenses.

Where the property is vested in M or in M and F but no written signed declaration of trust as to their shares exists, one has to fall back on the law of resulting and constructive trusts. As has been pointed out by Peter Gibson L.J.[7]: "as is notorious, it is not easy to reconcile every judicial utterance in this well-travelled area of the law. A potent source of confusion has been suggestions that it matters not whether the terminology used is that of the constructive trust or that of the resulting trust."

THE RESULTING TRUST

Where M and F purchase a house in the name of M or of M and F there is a presumed common intention that M or M and F will hold the house on a resulting trust for M and F in shares proportionate to their contributions to the purchase price. Each gets what he or she paid for. The date of acquisition of the house is regarded as the relevant date for fixing the size of the parties' interests under a resulting trust, so that reliance has to be placed on a constructive trust if this produces an unsatisfactory result when most houses are being acquired with the assistance of a mortgage so that they are being purchased over a lengthy period. Since the mortgage money, which becomes the property of the purchaser(s) under a debtor-creditor relationship, is forthwith used to pay the vendor all the purchase price, subsequent repayments of the mortgage are not strictly payments of the purchase money but payment towards

---

[7] *Drake v Whipp* [1996] 1 F.L.R. 826.

release of the charge taken on the house as security by the mortgagee. Thus, strictly, mortgage repayments do not amount to payment of the purchase price and so do not give the payer an equitable interest under a resulting trust,[8] although "payment of mortgage instalments will readily justify the inference necessary to the creation of a constructive trust".[9]

As Lord Browne-Wilkinson states[10]: "Under a resulting trust the existence of the trust is established once and for all at the date on which the property is acquired." Thus, if a house costing £100,000 is bought by M paying £60,000 and F paying £40,000, M and F have equitable interests of 60 per cent and 40 per cent. The position is the same if F does not actually pay £40,000 but, as sitting tenant of the house, obtained a 40 per cent discount off the £100,000 market price of the house.[11]

If the £60,000 needed to purchase such house is provided by way of mortgage, then if the house is vested in the names of M and F, both M and F will have to be parties to the mortgage and will be regarded as equally owners of the £60,000 mortgage moneys received by their lawyer on their behalf and paid to the vendor, unless M and F had agreed between themselves that liability to repay the £60,000 to the mortgagee should not be equal.[12] If, for example, M and F had agreed that M should solely be liable to repay the mortgage, then M would be regarded as having 60 per cent of the equitable ownership of the house at the outset.

Similarly, if M and F bought a house for £100,000 in M's name where M and F had equally provided the £10,000 deposit and the mortgage for the £90,000 balance was inevitably in M's name, but F had agreed with M to be equally liable to repay it, M and F would be regarded as 50:50 equitable owners, not as 95:5 equitable owners from the outset. If the mutually agreed undertakings as to respective liabilities for the mortgage repayments are not honoured, then on sale of the property an equitable accounting has to be made, so as to reimburse out of the proceeds of sale the party who paid more than his or her share of the repayments, but setting off, where appropriate, such party's rent-free exclusive occupation of the property after the parties' relationship broke down.[13]

---

[8] *Calverley v Green* (1984) 155 C.L.R. 483.

[9] *Lloyd's Bank Ltd v Rossett* [1991] 1 A.C. 107 at 132, *per* Lord Bridge.

[10] Birmingham University Holdsworth Lecture 1991, "Constructive Trusts and Unjust Enrichment," p. 6; reprinted in (1996) 10 Trust L.I. 98 at 100.

[11] *Springette v Defoe* (1992) 65 P. & CR. 1 (unless F intended to make a gift to M of her discount entitlement).

[12] *Ibid*; *Harwood v Harwood* [1991] 2 F.L.R. 274 at 292; *Huntingford v Hobbs* [1993] 1 F.L.R. 736; *Carlton v Goodman* [2002] 2 F.L.R. 259.

[13] *Huntingford v Hobbs* (above); *Re Pavlou* [1993] 1 W.L.R. 1046.

THE CONSTRUCTIVE TRUST

A constructive trust arises where at any time M and F have (or reasonably appear to F to have) a common intention, express or inferred, that F is to have a specific share in M's house or an uncertain fair share to be ascertained in due course in the light of F's contributions, so inducing F to act to her detriment in the reasonable belief that she has the agreed interest or is thereby acquiring the agreed interest.[14] The detrimental prejudice F suffers makes it fraudulent or unconscionable for M to deny her an interest in the house under an express or inferred declaration of trust arising from his words or conduct, so he cannot plead the lack of written evidence or the uncertainty of the arrangement. F gets what was agreed whereas under resulting trust principles she gets what she paid for.

Thus, in *Re Densham*[15] where F had paid for a ninth of M's house and M went bankrupt, F's one-ninth interest as a purchaser bound M's trustee in bankruptcy and hence M's creditors. The fact that M had gratuitously agreed that F was to have a half share leading her to act to her detriment so that she had a half share under a constructive trust did not help F. Such gratuitous disposition in her favour was set aside under s.42 of the Bankruptcy Act 1914, replaced now by the Insolvency Act 1986, s.339 to 342.

Nowadays, rather than rely on a resulting trust it is usual for F to seek to rely on a constructive trust, for example because she seeks a greater proportionate interest than that which she has paid for, especially where the exigencies of bearing and then rearing young children have restricted the amount of her payments. She may also seek to rely on a constructive trust where she has paid for capital improvements to the house, or where she has gratuitously carried out building works herself,[16] or where she has worked for nothing in a business carried on by M, so enabling M to keep up the mortgage payments.

Ideally, F will show that M and she had an express common intention that she was conditionally or unconditionally to have a specific or fair[17] share in the house. Specious excuses[18] of M to F for not putting the property in their joint names, (*e.g.* she is not old

---

[14] *Grant v Edwards* [1986] Ch. 638; *Passee v Passee* [1988] 1 F.L.R. 263; *Drake v Whipp* [1996] 1 F.L.R. 826 at 830.

[15] [1975] 1 W.L.R. 1519.

[16] Note that a fiancée, as well as a spouse, of M may be awarded a beneficial share of the property appropriate to her substantial improvement to it: Matrimonial Property and Proceedings Act 1970, s 37.

[17] *Stokes v Anderson* [1991] 1 F.L.R. 391; *Gissing v Gissing* [1971] A.C. 886 at 909.

[18] See *Eves v Eves* [1975] 1 WLR 1338 and *Grant v Edwards* [1986] Ch 638 as explained in *Lloyds Bank v Rosset* [1991] 1 AC 107.

enough when 19 years old) are treated as evidence of express intention to have some share of the property. Alternatively, she may show that such intention can be inferred from the circumstances if M, by his words or conduct intended to induce F to act to her detriment in a manner that facilitates the acquisition or improvement of the house, in the reasonable belief that by so acting she will be acquiring a specific or fair interest in the house. Where there is an express common intention and F acts to her detriment, it will be presumed that M's conduct induced F to act to her detriment in reliance thereon and that therefore it is inequitable to allow M to deny F a beneficial interest.[19] As Fox L.J. has remarked[20]: "The Court will not impose a constructive trust unless it is satisfied that the conscience of the estate owner is affected."

Lord Bridge on behalf of the House of Lords in *Lloyds Bank plc v Rosset*[21] has laid down the approach to be adopted by the courts:

"The first and fundamental question which must always be resolved is whether, independently of any inference to be drawn from the conduct of the parties in the course of sharing the house as their home and managing their affairs, there has at any time prior to the acquisition, or exceptionally at some later date, been any agreement, arrangement or understanding reached between them that the property is to be shared beneficially. The finding of an agreement or arrangement to share in this sense can only, I think, be based on evidence of express discussions between the partners, however imperfectly remembered and however imprecise their terms may have been. Once a finding to this effect is made it will only be necessary for the partner asserting a claim to a beneficial interest against the partner entitled to the legal estate to show that he or she has acted to his or her detriment or significantly altered his or her position in reliance on the agreement in order to give rise to a constructive trust or proprietary estoppel.

In sharp contrast with this situation is the very different one where there is no evidence to support a finding of an agreement or arrangement to share, however reasonable it might have been for the parties to reach such an arrangement if they had applied their minds to the question, and where the court must rely entirely on the conduct of the parties both as the basis from which to infer a common intention to share the property beneficially and as the conduct relied on to give rise to a constructive trust. In this situation direct contributions to the purchase price by the partner who is not the legal owner, whether initially or by

[19] *Gissing v Gissing* [1971] A.C. 886 at 906.
[20] *Ashburn Anstalt v Arnold* [1989] Ch. 1 at 25.
[21] [1991] 1 A.C. 107 at 132.

payment of mortgage instalments, will readily justify the inference necessary to the creation of a constructive trust. But, as I read the authorities, it is at least extremely doubtful whether anything less will do."

As Nourse L.J. earlier stated[22]:

"In most of these cases the fundamental, and invariably the most difficult, question is to decide whether there was the necessary common intention, being something which can only be inferred from the conduct of the parties, almost always from the expenditure incurred by them respectively. In this regard the court has to look for expenditure which is referable to the acquisition of the house ... If it is found to have been incurred, such expenditure will perform the twofold function of establishing the common intention and showing that the claimant has acted upon it.

There is another and rarer class of case, of which the present may be one, where, although there has been no writing, the parties have orally declared themselves in such a way as to make their common intention plain. Here the court does not have to look for conduct from which the intention can be inferred, but only for conduct which amounts to an acting upon it by the claimant. And although that conduct can undoubtedly be the incurring of expenditure which is referable to the acquisition of the house, it need not necessarily be so."

In applying the above approach Waite J. in *Hammond v Mitchell*[23] points out:

" ... The court first has to ask itself whether there have at any time prior to acquisition of the disputed property ... been discussions between the parties leading to an agreement, arrangement or understanding reached between them that the property is to be shared beneficially ... If there have been no such discussions ... the investigation of subsequent events has to take the form of an inferential analysis involving a scrutiny of all events potentially capable of throwing evidential light on the question whether ... a presumed intention can be spelt out of the parties' course of dealing. This operation was vividly described by Dixon J. in Canada as, 'The judicial quest for the fugitive of phantom common intention' (*Pettkus v Becker* (1980) 117 DLR (3d) 257) ... The difficulties of applying that formula can be alarming, as this present case has well illustrated. ... The primary emphasis accorded by the law in cases of this kind to express discussions between the parties ... means that the tenderest exchanges of a

---

[22] *Grant v Edwards* [1986] Ch. 638 at 647.
[23] [1991] 1 W.L.R. 1127.

common law courtship may assume an unforseen significance many years later when they are brought under equity's microscope and subjected to an analysis under which many thousands of pounds of value may be liable to turn on fine questions as to whether the relevant words were spoken in earnest or in dalliance and with or without representational intent. This requires that the express discussions to which the court's initial inquiries will be addressed should be pleaded in the greatest detail, both as to language and to circumstance."

In the absence of an express or inferred common intention the court cannot ascribe to or impose upon M and F the common intention they ought to have had as reasonable people if they had directed their minds to the issue. Lord Denning tried to do just that by imposing a new model constructive trust on M whenever justice and good conscience required it,[24] but this was inconsistent with the earlier decision of the House of Lords in *Gissing v Gissing*[25] and so has subsequently been rejected by the Court of Appeal[26] and the House of Lords.[27]

The conduct of the parties has to be considered in the light of the position that "under English law the mere fact that A expends money or labour on B's property does not by itself entitle A to an interest in the property. In the absence of an express agreement or a common intention to be inferred from all the circumstances or any question of estoppel, A will normally have no claim whatever on the property in such circumstances."[28]

The courts have not been prepared to infer a common intention to acquire an interest in the home from keeping house, giving birth to and rearing children[29] or from decorating the home or laying a patio or a lawn[30] or, accounting to dicta of Lord Bridge,[31] from F making regular substantial financial contributions to household expenses, thereby enabling M to make the mortgage payments himself where, otherwise, M could not have paid both the mortgage and his share of the cost of keeping up the standard of living of the joint household. In the latter case, however, there may be some extra evidence to justify a judge to infer that M and F agreed to an arrangement for the pooling of their resources on a 50:50 or other

---

[24] *Hussey v Palmer* [1972] 1 W.L.R. 1286; *Eves v Eves* [1975] 1 W.L.R. 1338.
[25] [1971] A.C. 886.
[26] *Burns v Burns* [1984] Ch. 317; *Grant v Edwards* [1886] Ch. 638.
[27] *Lloyds Bank v Rosset* [1991] 1 A.C. 107.
[28] *Thomas v Fuller-Brown* [1988] 1 F.L.R. 237 at 240.
[29] *Burns v Burns* [1984] Ch. 317; *Layton v Martin* [1986] 2 F.L.R. 227.
[30] *Pettitt v Pettitt* [1970] A.C. 777.
[31] *Lloyds Bank v Rosset* [1991] 1 A.C. 107 at 133 indicating that such conduct of F in *Grant v Edwards* [1986] Ch. 638 "fell far short" of supporting her claim in the absence of an express representation of M she was to have an interest.

basis so as to acquire an interest in the home[32], while the validity of Lord Bridge's dicta has been disputed in *Le Foe v Le Foe*[33] by a deputy judge in the light of dicta in *Gissing v Gissing*[34] and *Burns v Burns*[35]. Of course, regular substantial direct contributions by F to mortgage payments will readily justify the inference of a common intention for F to acquire an interest in the home proportionate to the amount of the purchase price thereby paid off[36] (even though strictly speaking the payments discharge the mortgage *pro tanto* and not the purchase price fully paid at the time of purchase).

Furthermore, where there is a direct contribution at the outset to the purchase price (for example paying part of the deposit and the legal costs) there is scope to increase the size of F's interest under the resulting trust based on a direct relation between the amount of F's contribution and the purchase price. If there is a real common intention[37] that F is to have a half share in the home even if only paying half the 10 per cent deposit, then F will have a half share[38] (in the absence of special circumstances making it unconscionable for her to have such a large share[39]). However, on the springboard of the resulting trust, one can claim that the evidence thereby revealed of an intent for F to have some proprietary interest, amounts to a real common intention that F is to have a proprietary interest (as required by the House of Lords), but that then the court in fixing the size of the proprietary interest "is free to attribute to the parties an intention to share the beneficial interest in some different proportions" from those formed by dealing "with the matter on the strict basis of the trust resulting from the cash contribution to the purchase price".[40]

This was laid down by the Court of Appeal in *Midland Bank v Cooke*[41] where a house in M's name was found not to be held on

---

[32] *Grant v Edwards* [1986] Ch. 638. Cp. *Baumgartner v Baumgartner* (1987) 164 C.L.R. 137.

[33] [2001] 2 F.L.R. 970 endorsed by Law Commission Discussion Paper "Sharing Homes", July 2002.

[34] [1971] A.C. 886 at 907-908.

[35] [1984] Ch. 317 at 319, but it may be, as May LJ points out at pp.344-345, that it is only where F has contributed to the initial deposit that later contributions to household expenses can be taken into account, as now clear from *Midland Bank plc v Cooke* [1995] 4 All E.R. 562, applied in *Le Foe v Le Foe* [2001] 2 F.L.R. 970.

[36] *Burns v Burns* [1984] Ch. 317 at 329, 345; *Ivin v Blake* (1994) 67 P. & C.R. 263 at 273, 276, endorsing *McFarlane v McFarlane* [1972] N.I.L.R. 59 at 74.

[37] *Springette v Defoe* [1992] 2 F.L.R. 388.

[38] *McHardy v Warren* [1994] 2 F.L.R. 338; *Halifax B.S. v Brown* (1995) 27 H.L.R. 511 at 518.

[39] *Grant v Edwards* [1986] Ch. 638 at 657; *Clough v Killey* (1996) 72 P. & C.R.D. 22 at 24.

[40] *Midland Bank v Cooke* [1995] 4 All E.R. 562.

[41] *ibid*. Applied in *Mollo v Mollo* [2000] W.T.L.R. 227 and *Le Foe v Le Foe* [2001] 2 F.L.R. 970.

resulting trust for F as to 6.7 per cent, the proportion that her half share of her parents-in-law's wedding gift (£550) bore to the purchase price (£8,500). The court held M and F were entitled to a 50 per cent interest each "as the proportions the parties must be presumed to have intended for their beneficial ownership", despite the fact that the court found that there was "positive evidence that the parties neither discussed nor intended any agreement as to the proportions of their beneficial interest".

It is a little difficult to reconcile the court's decision that quantification of beneficial interests can be based upon a fictitious invented agreement with the requirement that agreement to share beneficial ownership must be a real, actual or inferred, agreement. However, a subsequent differently constituted Court of Appeal[42] has accepted *Midland Bank v Cooke* as authority for the view that "in constructive trust cases the court can adopt a broad brush approach to determining the parties' respective shares" once direct contributions to the purchase price or subsequent substantial payments (for example for materials for renovating an old dilapidated barn or as regular contributions to mortgage payments) justify the inference of a real common intention to have some proprietary interest in the home.

Of course, if the real common intention is for F to have a fair share then the "broad brush" approach is proper. In *Midland Bank v Cooke* Waite L.J. states[43]:

"The duty of the judge is to undertake a survey of the whole course of dealing between the parties relevant to the ownership and occupation of the property and their sharing of its burdens and advantages. That scrutiny will not confine itself to the limited range of acts of direct contribution of the sort that are needed to found a beneficial interest in the first place. It will take into consideration all conduct which throws light on the question of what shares were intended ... One could hardly have a clearer example of a couple who had agreed to share everything equally: the profits of his business while it prospered and the risk of indebtedness through its failure; the upbringing of their children; the rewards of her own career as a teacher; and, most relevantly, a home into which he had put his savings and to which she was to give over the years the benefit of the maintenance and improvement contribution. When to all that is added the fact (still an important one) that this was a couple who had chosen to introduce into their relationship the additional commitment which marriage involves, the conclusion becomes inescapable that their

[42] *Drake v Whipp* [1996] 1 F.L.R. 826 at 830.
[43] [1995] 4 All E.R. 565 at 574, 576.

presumed intention was to share the beneficial interest in the
property in equal shares".

Here, he seems to be finding that if the parties had thought about it
they would have agreed at the outset to fixed half and half shares,
rather than a floating fair share, but it would seem that such matters
will also be relevant to ascertaining fair shares at the relevant time.[44]

CONSTRUCTIVE TRUSTS AND EQUITABLE ESTOPPEL

The common intention constructive trust is regarded as implementing an intention to make an outright or conditional gift
operating in equity as an informal, valid but unenforceable, express,
institutional trust, which is vindicated by the court's imposition of a
constructive trust (due to the donee's detrimental reliance on the
donor's intention), which retrospectively recognises the earlier
existence of the express trust independently created by the parties,
so that F obtains the promised share from the date of her detrimental reliance.[45] The possible adverse impact of such an earlier
equitable interest, capable of binding third parties who subsequently acquire interests in the property with constructive notice of
the earlier interest or subject to the overriding interest of a person in
actual occupation,[46] requires common intention constructive trust
principles to operate with as much certainty as possible, especially
where the legal action is brought by mortgagees against M, whom
they believed to be the sole beneficial owner, rather than by F
against M. However, mortgagees can easily protect themselves
against being bound by the equitable interests of cohabitees. If they
believe there might possibly be a cohabitee who might have some
claim to a beneficial share of the property, they can insist that the
sole vendor vests the legal title in himself and another. A disposition
by two co-owners of the legal title, who must be trustees, will
overreach the equitable interests of any other co-owners in equity,
such interests being detached from the land and attached to the
proceeds of sale, irrespective of the notice or knowledge of the
disponee who paid his capital money over to the two trustees.[47]

Since overreaching affects equitable interests of co-owners,
whether arising under common intention constructive trusts or

[44] *Stokes v Anderson* [1991] 1 F.L.R. 391 at 400.
[45] *Re Sharpe* [1980] 1 W.L.R. 219 at 225; *Gissing v Gissing* [1971] A.C. 886 at 905,
908; Matrimonial Proceedings and Property Act 1970, s.37; retrospectivity
assumed in *Midland Bank v Dobson* [1986] 1 F.L.R. 171 and *Lloyd's Bank v
Rossett* [1989] Ch. 350.
[46] Land Registration Art 2002 Sch.3.
[47] Law of Property Act 1925 ss.2, 27; *City of London BS v Flegg* [1988] A.C. 54; *State
Bank of India v Sood* [1997] Ch. 276.

equitable proprietary estoppel principles,[48] it should not matter that the latter principles seem to afford more flexible leeway[49] to claimants and the courts. Indeed, Lord Oliver stated that[50] "in essence, the common intention doctrine is an application of proprietary estoppel", while Lord Walker has stated[51] "In the area of a joint enterprise for the acquisition of land the two concepts coincide."

Equitable estoppel principles may be invoked to assist F, where M acted so as reasonably to create expectations in F of acquiring some interest in the house, so inducing F to act to her detriment in the belief she was thereby acquiring an interest in the house.[52] Indeed, claimants like F in some cases may prefer to claim under estoppel principles concerned with expectations engendered in them by M, so that there is no need to bother with M's subjective intention for common intention constructive trust purposes. Moreover, in family property cases the courts are very ready to find that once F acted detrimentally this was in reliance on M's representation, so that the burden falls on M to prove that F did not act in reliance on the representation. In *Wayling v Jones*[53] M and F lived together as homosexuals for 16 years before M died, F being a chef who for uncommercially low wages helped M run M's hotel business. After 10 years M promised to leave F the hotel in his will and did so. Unfortunately, the hotel was sold and a new one bought without M changing his will, so the gift of the hotel failed. The new hotel was sold by the executor and F claimed to be entitled to the proceeds of the sale on estoppel principles. F was asked in cross-examination "If M had not made the promise to you, would you still have stayed?" and replied "Yes", thus appearing to indicate that F had not stayed with M in reliance upon M's promise but stayed with him on low wages out of love, so that no estoppel claim could succeed.

However, the Court of Appeal benevolently held that since M did

---

[48] *Birmingham Midshires Mortgages Services Ltd v Sabherwal* (1999) 80 P. & C.R. 256.

[49] For flexible approach to detrimental reliance see *Grant v Edwards* [1986] Ch. 638 at 656, *Gillett v Holt* [2001] Ch. 210, and for flexible remedies see p.200 post.

[50] *Austin v Keele* [1987] A.L.J.R. 605 at 609, PC.

[51] *Yaxley v Gotts* [2000] Ch. 162 at 176 and *Birmingham Midshires Mortgages Services Ltd v Sabherwal* (1999) 80 P. & C.R. 256 at 263. Also see *Banner Homes Group plc v Luff Developments* [2000] Ch. 372 at 384 endorsement per Chadwick LJ, and *Mollo v Mollo* [2000] W.T.L.R. 227 at 245.

[52] *Grant v Edwards* [1986] Ch. 638 at 657. Estoppel principles are "directed at ascertaining whether, in particular circumstances, it would be unconscionable for a party to be permitted to deny that which, knowingly or unknowingly, he has allowed or encouraged another to assume to his detriment": *Habib Bank Ltd v Habib AG Zurich* [1981] 2 All E.R. 650 at 656; also *Lim Teng Huan v Ang Swee Chuan* [1992] 1 W.L.R. 113 at 117 to same effect.

[53] (1995) 69 P. & C.R. 170; also see *Campbell v Griffin* [2001] W.T.L.R. 981.

make the promise and since F had stated in evidence-in-chief that if M had gone back on his promise he, F, would have left, this was sufficient to prevent M's executor from proving F had not relied on M's promise so F's claim succeeded. As an anomalous concession to human sentiment the court acted not on evidence of what the promisee actually did in reliance on the promise but on speculation as to what the promisee would have done on the hypothesis that M had reneged on his promise. In commercial cases[54] where estoppel principles are pleaded the court acts only upon evidence put before it of what the promisee did in reliance upon the promise.

At the end of the court hearing the court tailors the remedy to fit the wrong and decides what relief is appropriate to satisfy F's estoppel claim,[55] for example ordering the defendant to transfer his house wholly to the claimant, or declaring that he holds the house on constructive trust for himself and the claimant in specified shares, or charging his house as security for payment by him of £X to the claimant, or allowing the claimant to reside in the house till payment of £X to her by the defendant or compelling the defendant to sell his interest to the claimant for £X.

The court will normally order the "minimum equity to do justice". Such order may reverse the claimant's detriment (a "reliance" award) so as to prevent unjust enrichment of the defendant though, in family cases particularly, it may well go further and perfect an imperfect gift (an "expectation" award).[56] Equity is at its most flexible in the remedies available where the claimant successfully invokes proprietary estoppel principles so, in an appropriate case, the courts could declare a remedial constructive trust to take effect as of the date of the court order, so that third parties who earlier acquired any interest in the property will not be prejudiced unless their conscience be affected. As Lord Browne-Wilkinson states[57]: "If the constructive trust is seen to be a remedy imposed by the court ... the constructive trust arises for the first time when the court orders it. The court can make that order retrospective and prospective. But in so doing it can take into account the circumstances existing at the time it makes the order. The trust can be

---

[54] *Meghraj Bank Ltd v Arsiwalla* (CA, unreported, February 10, 1994) discussed with *Wayling v Jones* by E. Cooke (1995) 111 L.Q.R. 389.

[55] *Crabb v Arun D.C.* [1976] Ch. 179; *Williams v Staite* [1979] Ch. 291; *Lim v Ang* [1992] 1 W.L.R. 113; *Burrows & Burrows v Sharp* (1989) 23 HLR 82; *Baker v Baker* [1993] 2 F.L.R. 247; *Voyce v Voyce* (1991) 62 P. & C.R. 240.

[56] *Pascoe v Turner* [1979] 1 W.L.R. 431; *Jackson v Crosby (No. 2)* [1979] 21 S.A. S.R. 280; *Gillett v Holt* [2001] Ch. 210; *Wayling v Jones* (1995) 69 P.& C.R.170.

[57] "Equity in a Fast Changing World" [1996] New Zealand Law Society Triennial Conference Papers, p. 177, dealing with his views in *Westdeutsche Landesbank v Islington LBC* [1996] A.C. 669 at 716; also see p.20 (above).

imposed as against those whom it is just to hold liable and not as against those to whom it would be unfair."

In the absence of developing a remedial constructive trust to prevent unjust enrichment, a claimant's proprietary estoppel interest, as declared by the court in its equitable discretion, is treated as arising when the claimant's first act of detrimental reliance occurred,[58] as in the case of common intention constructive trusts. When, through the application of either estoppel principles or common intention constructive trust principles, the court declares that M holds his house or flat on trust for M and F equally, it seems that the court is retrospectively recognising the existence of an institutional constructive trust.[59]

FUTURE PROSPECTS

In the absence of some initial contribution to the purchase price to give rise to a resulting trust, that can be regarded as a springboard to a greater equitable interest under a constructive trust, or of direct contributions to mortgage instalments to support an inferred common intention constructive trust, there seems only limited scope for the courts to develop estoppel principles to provide some recognition for F's contributions to household expenses, holiday expenses, child-bearing and child-rearing and as handywoman, cook and cleaner.

It had been hoped that the Law Commission would come up with legislative proposals for dealing with cohabitees of the opposite or same sex along lines adopted by Australian States, perhaps allowing more leeway for the weaker partner in disputes involving only the partners as opposed to disputes with third parties like mortgagees or judgment creditors seeking to levy execution against the home. However, the inquiry was broadened to all home-sharers, (*e.g.* sisters, uncle and nephew, grandparent and grandchild, godfather and godchild, brother and sister, elderly person and resident carer,whether related or not) so that the very extensive range of differing circumstances precluded proposing any satisfactory statutory principles, while difficult social and political issues arose as to whether cohabitees of the same sex should be allowed the same rights as married couples or whether persons of the same or opposite sexes could register themselves as "partners" with lesser rights than those who are spouses but greater rights than those who

---

[58] Land Registration Act 2002 s.116; *Voyce v Voyce* (1991) 62 P. & C.R. 290 at 294, 296; *Lloyds Bank v Carrick* [1996] 4 All E.R. 630 at 642; *Lloyd v Dugdale* [2002] W.T.L.R. 863, para. 39 assumption; *Campbell v Griffin* [2001] W.T.L.R. 981 at 994F.

[59] *Yaxley v Gotts* [2000] Ch. 162 dealing with exception for "constructive trusts" in s.2(5) Law of Property (Miscellaneous Provisions) Act 1989.

did not register. These issues are not appropriate for the Law Commission to tackle,[60] so that it has moved on to deal with other topics, leaving it to the courts to cope as best they can with home-sharer's claims to equitable shares in the sharer's house or flat.

Education of home-sharers and potential home-sharers is needed. There is no such thing as "common law marriage" in this day and age.[61] A prospective claimant, F, against M, the legal owner of the house or flat should have M put the property in their joint names or have him sign a piece of paper setting out her share or have him in front of witnesses agree that she has a half or a fair share or, if need be, that he had agreed this with F x years ago before F acted to her detriment.

---

[60] See Discussion Paper "Sharing Homes", July 2002.
[61] *Windeler v Whitehall* [1990] 2 F.L.R. 505.

APPENDIX

Principles of European Trust Law

Article I

MAIN CHARACTERISTICS OF THE TRUST

(1) In a trust, a person called the "trustee" owns assets segregated from his private patrimony and must deal with those assets (the "trust fund") for the benefit of another person called the "beneficiary" or for the furtherance of a purpose.

(2) There can be more than one trustee and more than one beneficiary; a trustee may himself be one of the beneficiaries.

(3) The separate existence of the trust fund entails its immunity from claims by the trustee's spouse, heirs and personal creditors.

(4) In respect of the separate trust fund a beneficiary has personal rights and may also have proprietary rights against the trustee and against third parties to whom any part of the fund has been wrongfully transferred.

Article II

CREATION OF THE TRUST

The general rule is that in order to create a trust a person called the "settlor" in his lifetime or on death must, with the intention of creating a segregated trust fund, transfer assets to the trustee.

However, it may also be possible for a settlor to create a trust by making it clear that he is to be trustee of particular assets of his.

Article III

TRUST FUND

(1) The trust fund consists not only of the original assets and those subsequently added, but also of those assets from time to time representing the original or added assets.

(2) The trust fund is not available to satisfy claims made against the trustee in his personal capacity. Except to the extent that the settlor's creation of the trust contravenes laws protecting his creditors, spouse or heirs, the trust fund is available only for claims made by creditors dealing with the trustee in his capacity as such and, subject thereto, for claims of the beneficiaries or the enforcer, who is an office holder entitled to enforce a trust for purposes.

(3) A trustee of several trusts must keep each trust fund not only segregated from his private patrimony but also from each of the other trust funds, except to the extent that the terms of the trusts otherwise permit.

Article IV

TRUSTS FOR BENEFICIARIES OR FOR ENFORCEABLE PURPOSES

(1) Upon creating a trust, the settlor must designate ascertained or ascertainable persons as beneficiaries to whom the trustee's obligations in respect of the trust fund are owed or will be owed, or must designate purposes in respect of which there is an enforcer.

(2) To the extent that the settlor fails to create rights affecting the whole of the trust fund the trustee will own the assets for the benefit of the settlor or his successors.

(3) Any beneficiary, or any enforcer of a trust for purposes, has a right to information needed to protect his interest and to ensure that the trustee accounts to him.

(4) Subject to the terms of the trust, a beneficiary can make a disposition of his rights.

(5) Any beneficiary, or any enforcer of a trust for purposes, has the right to seek judicial enforcement of the terms of the trust.

Article V

TRUSTEES' DUTIES AND POWERS

(1) The trustee must exercise his rights as owner in accordance with the law and the terms of the trust.

(2) The fundamental duty of a trustee is to adhere to the terms of the trust, to take reasonable care of the trust assets and to act in the best interests of the beneficiaries or, in the case of a trust for purposes, the furtherance of those purposes.

(3) A trustee must keep separate and protect the trust assets, must maintain accurate accounts and must provide the beneficiaries and the enforcer with information requested to protect their interests.

(4) Except to the extent otherwise permitted by the terms of the trust or by law, a trustee must personally perform his functions. He must act honestly and he must avoid all conflicts of interest unless otherwise authorised.

(5) A trustee is accountable for the trust fund, must personally make good any loss occasioned to the trust fund by his breach of trust and must personally augment such fund by the amount of any profits made by him in breach of his duty.

Article VI

REMEDIES AGAINST TRUSTEES FOR BREACH OF TRUST

Remedies that the court can provide against a trustee for breach of trust include an order restraining particular conduct or removing the trustee from his office and replacing him or decreeing payment of compensation for losses or restitution of profits. The court may also have power to declare that particular assets of the trustee have always been part of the trust fund and never became part of his private patrimony or are to be regarded as security for satisfying his liability.

Article VII

LIABILITIES OF THIRD PARTIES

Where a trustee wrongfully transfers part of the trust fund to a transferee who is not protected as a purchaser in good faith or otherwise, the transferee must make good the loss to the trust fund or may be ordered to hold the assets so transferred (or assets representing them) as part of the trust fund separate from his private patrimony or as security for satisfying his liability. This liability may extend to any subsequent transferee who is not protected as a purchaser in good faith or otherwise.

Article VIII

TERMINATION OF A TRUST

(1) Notwithstanding the terms of the trust, where all the beneficiaries are in existence, have been ascertained, and are of full capacity, then, if all such beneficiaries are in agreement, they can require the trustee to terminate the trust and distribute the trust fund between themselves and their nominees as they direct. However, if some material purpose of the settlor remains to be served then the beneficiaries may not be permitted to terminate the trust.

(2) A trust terminates (a) by virtue of all the trust fund having been distributed to beneficiaries or having been used for trust purposes or (b) by virtue of there being no beneficiaries and no person, whether or not then in existence, who can become a beneficiary in accordance with the terms of the trust, or (c) by virtue of a person exercising a power of termination.

(3) At the close of the permitted period for the duration of the trust (subject to the trustee retaining sufficient assets to make reasonable provision for possible liabilities) the trust fund shall be distributed by the trustee as soon as reasonably practicable in accordance with any terms of the trust setting out how the trust fund should then be distributed. However, if there are no such terms then the trust fund shall be owned by the trustee for the benefit of the settlor or his successors.

(4) In the case of a trust for purposes, where such purposes have been fulfilled so far as possible or cannot now be carried out, then the trust fund shall be owned by the trustee for the benefit of the settlor or his successors, unless the terms of the trust are varied or extended.

INDEX

ACCOUNTABILITY,
fundamental right to make trustee
account, 166–172
personal. *See* PERSONAL ACCOUNTABILITY
ACCUMULATION AND MAINTENANCE
TRUST,
figures, 1
nature of, 54–55
ACCUMULATIONS,
rule against, 107–108
ADMINISTRATIVE WORKABILITY,
powers, of, 94–96
requirement of, 93–94
AGENCY,
borderline between trust and, 136–137
civil law states, 8
trust and, 77
ANIMALS,
trust for maintenance of, 59
ANOMALOUS TESTAMENTARY TRUST,
nature of, 59–60
ANTI-TRUST LAW,
nature of, 3
ASSETS,
unincorporated association, of, 1, 64
AUSTRALIA,
role of trusts in, 1
Tuvalu Trust Fund, 2
AUTHORISED UNIT TRUST,
nature of, 66–67

BAILMENT,
civil law states, 8
trust and, 77–78

BANK OF INTERNATIONAL SETTLEMENTS,
creation of, 2
BANKRUPTCY,
security device, trust as, 68–72
statutory trust, creation of, 44
BARE TRUST,
capital gains tax, 50–51
nature of, 50–51
BENEFICIARIES,
accountability of trustees, rights
relating to, 166–172
beneficiary principle,
exceptions to, 103–104
generally, 99–101
rule in *Saunders v Vautier*, impact
of, 93–103
certainty of,
every beneficiary must benefit, 88–89
every beneficiary need not benefit,
89–91
generally, 87–88
is or is not test, application of, 91–92
objects of personal powers, 92–93
trust for purposes benefiting
persons, 93
continuous trustee-beneficiary
relationship, 5
court's power to impound beneficial
interests, 187
enforcement of trust, 4
equitable right to trace,
mixing of trust money with trustee's
own money, 170–171
proprietary remedy, 169–170

207